W9-BFN-638

The Classrooms All Young Children Need

Lessons in Teaching from Vivian Paley

The Classrooms All Young Children Need

PATRICIA M. COOPER

The University of Chicago Press | Chicago and London

PATRICIA M. COOPER is assistant professor of early childhood education and literacy at New York University's Steinhardt School of Education and the author of numerous articles on teaching and learning in early childhood education and *When Stories Come to School: Telling, Writing, and Performing Stories in the Early Childhood Classroom*.

The University of Chicago Press, Chicago 60637
The University of Chicago Press, Ltd., London

Printed in the United States of America

18 17 16 15 14 13 12 11 10 09   1 2 3 4 5
ISBN-13: 978-0-226-11523-8 (cloth)
ISBN-10: 0-226-11523-2 (cloth)

Library of Congress Cataloging-in-Publication Data

Cooper, Patricia M.
The classrooms all young children need : lessons in teaching from Vivian Paley / Patricia M. Cooper.
p. cm.
Includes bibliographical references and index.
ISBN-13: 978-0-226-11523-8 (cloth: alk. paper)
ISBN-10: 0-226-11523-2 (cloth: alk. paper)
1. Early childhood education—Philosophy. 2. Play. 3. Storytelling.
4. Fantasy in children. 5. Paley, Vivian Gussin, 1929– I. Title.
LB1139.23.C66 2009
372.2101—dc22

2009001841

⊗ The paper used in this publication meets the minimum requirements of the American National Standard for Information Sciences—Permanence of Paper for Printed Library Materials, ANSI Z39.48-1992.

In loving memory of my parents,

Ken and Pat Cooper

Contents

Acknowledgments

I was lucky enough to see classrooms as places to study early in my teaching career. For this and for her friendship ever since, I will always be grateful to Gillian Dowley McNamee, who introduced me to classroom research and, specifically, to research on the efficacy of Vivian Paley's approach to storytelling in the classroom. But let it be a lesson to teacher education that I could never have gotten off the ground without Lauranita Dugas, my long ago colleague in Chicago, who gave a young teacher the needed time and space to experiment with curriculum. Later, in a small school I founded in Houston, I had the privilege of working on Paley's application to early childhood education in general with one of the greatest faculty of early childhood educators ever assembled: Molly Bentsen, Connie Floyd, Jennifer Giroux, Carol Heath, Shaundra Simmons, and Mary-o Yeager. In a totally unexpected twist, funding from the Bingham Trust and guidance from Nancy Larson Shapiro helped to create the Teachers' Network for Early Literacy, later renamed the School Literacy and Culture Project, to disseminate Paley's work to a wider audience. What a terrific opportunity that turned out to be. In 1990, codirectors Linda McNeil and Ronald Sass welcomed the project into the Rice University Center for Education. I especially want to thank Linda for her ongoing support of the work, not to mention the innumerable and stimulating hours of shoptalk. Bernie Mathes, Connie Floyd, and Karen Capo followed me as director of the School Literacy and Culture Project. I cannot sufficiently express my gratitude to each of these women for their hard work, wisdom, and counsel. I doubt very much this book would exist without them. I must also thank Sherry Dubin, Sharon Dworaczyk, Pansy Gee, Laurie Hammons, Joan Katrib, Sue King, Debbie Lingrey, Margaret Immel, Judy Rolke, and so many other area teachers and friends of the project, for what they have done to keep the work alive in classrooms and in our hearts. I need to add Martha Hartzell, Zoe Ryder White, and, in particular, Jo Smith to the list as well. Others who deserve thanks for the moral support they have offered over the year I spent writing this book include Maureen Barbieri, Robby Cohen, Rebecca Light, Sara Michael Luna, and Frances Rust.

Like all books, this one took on a life of its own in the final stretch. The hands-on team included Meredith Jacks, an amazing and steadfast research assistant through the spring and summer. Carlisle Rex-Waller was a terrific copyeditor, and Emilie Sandoz a great editorial assistant to the very best editor, Elizabeth Branch Dyson. I thank them all. Closer to home, my daughters, Kyle and Jess, who will tell you they don't remember when Vivian Paley wasn't a fact of life in our house, believed in this book from the very beginning, and boosted my confidence more than they knew. And, like my brothers, sisters, and in-laws, they graciously forgave many an absence from a family event or dropped details of our lives as various deadlines came and went. Kyle also read draft after draft to offer the incredible insight that only someone who read most of Paley's books before she was twelve could do. My sister, Julie, the first person to ever tell me a story, took her librarian's red pencil to every single word of the manuscript before I let it go. She is extraordinary. Finally, the completion of this book came in the nick of time for me to celebrate my thirtieth wedding anniversary with Warren, forever my greatest source of strength.

Prologue

An "*N* of 1"

Speaking at a conference on teacher action research, the renowned author and early childhood educator Vivian Paley recounted the time a professor of education asked her why anyone should listen to what just one school teacher had to say about just one group of children. Paley confided in the audience that she thought the question a bit rude, but she replied politely, "Because it is the only way to find out what one teacher thinks." Whether the professor found this a persuasive answer we don't know from Paley's story, but it was clear from the sighs of recognition that the teachers in the audience did.

I can think of several educational contexts in which the education professor's question about the generalizability of any teacher's thoughts on classroom life would be most warranted. The problems educators are asked to solve are simply too many and too complex for one teacher to have all the answers. Yet in this book I focus on a pedagogical model drawn from the work of one educator—Vivian Paley. I do not pretend to suggest that Paley's story provides a definitive response to all that ails early childhood education today. I do, however, assume that hers is a highly valuable response. The fact is the need for generalizability in education—a cry that has been with us in one form or another since schools began—

does not obviate the need for models, or for giants. From Plato to Dewey to the national board certification movement, the investment in the teacher/sage is a long, valued, and highly instructive tradition in both philosophical and educational thought. This is because an "*n* of 1," or a single sample, is sometimes the only recourse to solving one of the most investigated, but stubbornly recalcitrant problems in school reform: how to find our way home from theory to practice. I leave it to the reader to decide how well I have made the case for Paley in this regard. My assumption, however, is that the expert teacher or the model teacher, as I suggest Paley is, does not leave us at the schoolhouse door, as theory sometimes can, but provides us with road signs *inside* the classroom, which is where we most want to be. We resist the composites and avatars of classroom teachers found in traditional textbooks or on the Web because we don't recognize the route to their success. The teacher's story we hunger for involves "personal, practical knowledge" (Clandinin and Connelly 2000). It is grounded in reality and risk, and provides us with analysis based on true experimentation and experience. It comprises real families and actions in real time, and it welcomes admissions of failure.

Teacher education will always be in desperate need of the expert teacher's story. In a sense, that story functions as the narrative equivalent of Dewey's laboratory for pedagogy, where teachers in training study "practice work." The value of such study, Dewey says, is not measured by its immediacy to the student of teaching. Rather, it is measured by the "intellectual reactions it incites" in the teacher through the chance to study method relative to the "*educational significance* of the subject-matter" (Dewey 1904, 314, emphasis mine). The relationship between method and subject matter is too often neglected in teacher education. The narrative laboratory also allows us to tap into the practitioner's "understandings, practices, dispositions, and tools." These in turn become the seeds for our own pedagogical vision or "images of the possible" (Hammerness et al. 2005, 386). To paraphrase cognitive psychologist Michael Cole (in Paley 1986), the expert teacher proves a better guide to best practice than does the educational theorist, psychologist, philosopher, and, I would add, the economist, because she is uniquely positioned to listen carefully and respectfully to *what the children say and how they think*. All lessons in effective pedagogy begin here.

Our attraction to the exceptional keeper of the classroom keys reflects another dimension of teacher learning that is often overlooked in teacher education. This is our need for inspiration. However quaint an idea, we keep company with the expert teacher because she makes us feel confident of our mission and motivates us to try harder. For this, we are grateful.

Investment in the expert teacher's story is not without risk, of course. If we live by the case studies of great teachers, we die by them, too. This happens whenever we hastily embrace an individual teacher's "philosophy," only to find it either too anomalous or, as Dewey said, too "arbitrary" to be borrowed or applied. It bears reminding that the teacher-as-magician or teacher-as-personality is a seductive force in education, desperate as we are for success and starved for new role models. Ladson-Billings describes her effort to avoid the "cult of personality" in her book on successful teachers of African American children "because it minimizes the tendency to reduce the research findings to individual idiosyncrasies" (1994a, 13). For every story of an individual teacher who has helped to scaffold our understanding of how to teach, the annals of education, including movies and television, offer a dozen other accounts of those who have failed to leave behind any tools for the student of teaching to borrow.

The individual teacher model of pedagogy also suffers from a potential lack of theoretical support. For although there are things to learn from the educational theorist who has never taught, the classroom teacher who possesses practical knowledge only, who lacks a concomitant theory of teaching and learning, can easily derail us. Therefore, the most indispensable rule of thumb in doing teacher education by case study is that the teachers under study must be reliable educational narrators on all fronts. Their work must evince a philosophy of education that not only makes clear why they do what they do but makes sense in a larger, known context. In this view, the "*n* of 1" is not a solo artist, but someone who has used the tools others have found useful to excavate a theoretical pyramid layered with explanations of problems she is trying to solve.

Which brings us to Vivian Paley. Without a hint of irony, Paley describes herself as a schoolteacher who writes books. Whereas pedagogical studies have long struggled to reconcile the competing demands of theory and practice, Paley cannot avoid it. Her vivid and various presentations of classroom life easily bring to mind the work of John Dewey, Lev Vygotksy, Jean Piaget, Jerome Bruner, and Nel Noddings, among others who have mined the early childhood years to uncover the underlying structures and purpose of teaching, learning, and schooling. But a strong theoretical foundation is only the first lesson in teaching that Paley's narrative laboratory offers us. Ultimately, hers is a teacher's story that bears witness to nothing less than the moral underpinnings of effective pedagogy. In the end, listening to what this one teacher of young children has to say is to learn what we cannot learn elsewhere.

Introduction

Why Interpret the Clear?

Whether the topic is play or storytelling, racism or exclusion, Vivian Paley's work has touched a chord with a legion of educational philosophers, psychologists, cultural theorists, and teacher educators. She is beloved by many classroom teachers. Their collective response converges on the critical question that ignites her classroom investigations and guides this analysis of her educational philosophy and pedagogy: What kind of classrooms do young children need? As Paley has repeatedly shown us, the answer must be rooted not only in who young children are, but in who we can help them become.

A reviewer of this book in its earliest phase succinctly captured one of the challenges in writing it. Why interpret the clear when Paley is so wonderfully accessible in her own right? It is a fair warning and exactly the right starting point. My aim is not to restate what Paley has already said about teaching and learning or young children in school. Nor do I mean to present an encomium of Paley's work. Its bounty stands alone for generations of teachers to experience and learn from directly. My purpose in writing this book is to present a synoptic vision of Paley's contribution to early childhood education in the context of what should be her natural home—teacher education.

I contend that while Paley is internationally venerated as an astute observer of young children and early schooling, her philosophy of education and pedagogical methods are underutilized in schools. The loss is felt no more than now, when economic and social pressures are redefining what we want young children to know and do before they move on to first grade. I argue that the underlying theoretical and methodological principles in Paley's work are ripe for harvesting. This is not to suggest that Paley's vision or methods can be standardized or appropriated wholesale. My own field-based efforts in this direction, which I discuss in chapter 3, make clear I am not describing a one-on-one transfer. I also do not deny the body of teachers who have already found their way to applying Paley's ideas in the classroom, particularly her signature practice, the "storytelling curriculum" (Cooper 1993; Gadzikowski 2007; Katch 2001, 2003; Rothman 2006). The reality is, however, that admiration for Paley far outweighs the ability of the teacher education community to make systematic use of her ideas as a whole. The possible reasons for this disconnect are worth considering and shape the contents of this book.

To begin, Paley does not embrace the role of teacher educator or researcher directly. Though clearly operating from a base set of assumptions about teaching and learning, she rarely indulges in theoretical or methodological discussions, which is where teacher education must inevitably end up. Philip Jackson makes note of Paley's unwillingness to step outside her role as "Teacher." Writing in the foreword to *Boys and Girls: Superheroes in the Doll Corner*, he says what Paley knows about teaching is as "fully informative and important" as what she knows about children. But her work on the "theme of teaching and what it is like to be a teacher," he goes on, "is not so clearly drawn" (1984, vi). Paley is no more forthcoming about the theory that supports her teaching. As Ageliki Nicolopoulou writes, Paley consistently demonstrates an "avoidance of explicit engagement with the theoretical issues" in which her work is clearly embedded (1997a, 202). The exception is her repeated citation of Vygotsky's description of the young child in play, revealing a fundamental aspect of her views on the role of play in learning and development.[1] For the most part, however, what wins the day for Paley is not proof of a hypothesis, but the unanticipated evidence against it, not a method of investigation, but an individual child who changes its direction. Obviously conscious of the path she has elected, she tells us, "Such is the way life in the classroom reinterprets the research" (1990, 19). Significantly, despite her refusal to identify professionally as a researcher or teacher educator, Paley is claimed as a member of a number of praxis-dominated research traditions, which reflect one or the other or both roles. These include autoethnography, literary documentary, narrative inquiry, action research, and hermeneutics (see Burdell and Swadener 1999; Carter 1993; Clift and Albert 1998; Cochran-Smith and Lytle 1993; Connelly and Clandinin, 1990; Göncü and Becker 2000; Preskill 1998; Raspberry 1996; Reifel 2007).

Another reason that Paley's pedagogy is celebrated but not frequently employed as a model in teacher education may be that her books and articles almost all focus on a single issue. Examples are racism in *White Teacher* ([1979] 2000), storytelling and story acting in *Wally's Stories: Conversations in the Kindergarten* (1981), gender identity in *Boys and Girls: Superheroes in the Doll Corner* (1984), and exclusion in *You Can't Say You Can't Play* (1992). By default, attempts to disseminate Paley's professional strategies that draw on external research or commentary on her books also focus on individual themes, thus limiting their application (see Bettelheim 1975; Cooper 1993, 2005; Cooper et al. 2007; Delpit 1994; Goodman 2000; Harrist and Bradley 2003; McLane and McNamee 1990; McNamee 1992; Nicolopoulou 1996, 1997a; Nicolopoulou, McDowell, and Brockmeyer 2006; Richner and Nicolopoulou 2001; Sapon-Shevin 1998; Sapon-Shevin et al. 1998). No single study or volume before this has attempted to tie Paley's classrooms together and derive what is needed for teacher education, what Bransford, Darling-Hammond, and LePage call a "vision of professional practice" (2005, 11).

The third reason why teacher education has yet to embrace Paley's pedagogy comprehensively is perhaps the most unexpected. Beneath her warm and elegant writing style is a stance toward critical issues in early childhood education that is more complex and radical than we would like to admit. For example, many see Paley's pedagogy as the prototypical model of teacher-as-guide or facilitator, in keeping with a constructivist philosophy. But while Paley adopts such a position when she deems it appropriate, she often demonstrates a propensity to take a far more active and direct role in young children's learning. She also doesn't hesitate to take the inconvenient side of an argument in early childhood education, such as her uncompromising position on early literacy instruction. Further, Paley is a reformist. Many of her works delve well below the problems of curriculum to confront an even greater issue in young children's experience of school—the pretense of teacher neutrality. She makes clear teaching is *always* a value-laden enterprise that, far too often, can work against young children's best interests. Her work upends many long-held practices in early childhood education that she argues permit racism, sexism, unfairness, and exclusion to go unchecked. In doing so, Paley exposes an uncomfortable truth about early schooling. This is society's ambivalence as to why we invite young children to school at all. *Is it to take them in or weed them out?* Such a charge is rarely associated with early childhood education. But Paley's descriptions of the entwined academic and social hierarchies that crowd the early childhood classroom leave us no choice but to acknowledge it.

Not since Sylvia Ashton-Warner (1963) has a kindergarten teacher been so publicly and unabashedly righteous. Paley is at heart an activist, who urges us to embrace the privilege of teacher as pedagogue and moral authority inside the classroom. Her classroom studies demand to know how far we are willing to go to defend young children against the sometimes pernicious realities of schooling, as a short list of the many pedagogical questions that follow from this perspective suggests:

- How much play is enough in the preschool and kindergarten?
- What is effective early literacy instruction?
- Can we really embrace racial differences in school?
- Can social inclusion be mandated?
- Do boys get short shrift in kindergarten?
- Should schools be preparation for real life?

These questions may be similar to those asked by the educational psychologist, philosopher, and researcher, but Paley takes us one step further. She asks why we have tolerated this ambiguity about what they mean in the everyday lives of young children for so long.

In sum, it's clear that the reasons we are attracted to Paley's teacher's story are the very ones that make it difficult to create a template of her theory and methodology. They also underscore how much she has to offer early childhood education. Thus, while I eschew any formulaic approach to Paley, she offers much to lean on and to borrow from in shaping a pedagogical vision of the classrooms all young children need in the twenty-first century.

Vivian Paley is an intimidating mentor. Her twelve books and numerous articles and chapters complement a teaching career that spans more than thirty years. Over time, she has accumulated an impressive list of firsts. She is the first classroom teacher to win a MacArthur Fellowship, the American Book Award for Lifetime Achievement, and the John Dewey Society's Outstanding Achievement Award. She is the first pre–first grade teacher to win the National Council of Teachers of English's Language Arts Educator of the Year. There are other awards too numerous to mention.

The task I set for myself in writing this book has had other challenges as well. From a scholarly perspective, the sheer range of Paley's classroom investigations present a true dilemma regarding the best use of supporting literature on any given topic. Since a full-scale review would surely overwhelm the book's usefulness as a companion to Paley's work, I opted for a judicious selection of what best aids our understanding in the context of the specific questions being raised. I apologize in advance for any scholarship I have not included here that would also fit this bill. An even greater challenge in writing this book was to create a unified framework that could do two things at once. From a critical perspective, it needed to efficiently illuminate Paley's seminal concepts and practices, their place in the evolution of her thinking, and their theoretical underpinnings relative to scholarship. At the same time, it needed to reveal a methodological approach for use in teacher education. Fortunately, analysis reveals two overlapping but still distinct strands in her practice that lend themselves to the task quite well. One is overtly curricular, which I call Paley's "pedagogy of meaning."[2] The other is predominantly relational, which I call her "pedagogy of fairness." I define a pedagogy of meaning as teaching to help young children explore those things, including ideas, they find meaningful in the world. This includes the meaning they have already discovered and treasure, as well as the meanings that are bubbling up for them in response to new information or experience. The teacher's role is to provide both the curriculum and support, direct and indirect, in which the children's explorations can thrive. The two critical tools are play and story. I define Paley's "pedagogy of fairness," simply, as the prohibition of exclusion on every level. Together these twin pedagogies constitute an eminently useful and morally well-lit path from theory to practice in early childhood teacher education.

I also show that Paley's pedagogy did not emerge fully blown at the start of her teaching career. Fueled by reflection and experimentation, her decisions shifted and became more nuanced with time, affirming Dewey's belief that the best teachers are "adequately moved by their own independent intelligence" (1904, 321). This is a most valuable story for teacher education. Too frequently we give but scant coverage of what individual professional growth looks like over the long haul. The sheer force of Paley's teaching and writing career gives it to us fully dressed. The fact that I write in an educational era virtually bankrupt of the courage to value such self-study further underscores the need for an analysis of it.

Part 1 focuses on Paley's pedagogy of meaning and highlights her views on the role of fantasy play, storytelling, and story acting in early childhood education. Though the term "early childhood education" has been broadened of late to include the first, second, and even third grades, I use it in this book in the more traditional sense of preschool and kindergarten. Chapter 1 sets the parameters of the discussion. I begin by examining the phenomenon of how early childhood education has abandoned its historical emphasis on play in favor of early literacy education. I then explore the theoretical underpinnings of Paley's philosophy of education relevant to play, story, and early literacy, giving attention to Vygotsky's theory of the role of play in development and Dewey's view of play as meaningful activity. Finally, I consider the hidden effect this change has wrought on the professional development of teachers, especially new and less experienced ones.

Chapters 2 and 3 examine play and story as the pillars of Paley's pedagogy of meaning. In chapter 2, I consider first Paley's discovery of the deeper, psychological significance of children's fantasy play. Next, I turn to the general functions of play in young children's development as depicted in Paley's classroom observations. I then review the link between fantasy play and early literacy development.

Chapter 3 explores Paley's signature "storytelling curriculum" from a variety of angles. I delineate its essential components and reflect on its similarities and differences to fantasy play. I then describe what the storytelling curriculum has meant to my own identity as a teacher of young children, as well as to my work with a teacher who has only recently become a teacher of storytelling. I detail the power of the storytelling curriculum to early literacy development, including its usefulness in teaching young children to "written language" (Vygotsky 1978). I contrast the storytelling curriculum in this regard with the writing workshop approach.

Paley's pedagogy of fairness comprises part 2, throughout which I address her vision of psychologically safe classrooms, in which children are not divided by the insidious categories of race, difference, gender, or talent. Chapter 4 introduces the concept of fairness as a legitimate pedagogical concern. Its focus is not the curricular, but the relational aspects of pedagogy, the framework for the unscheduled but inevitable human interactions in all classrooms. For this reason, fair teaching becomes a synonym for teaching to include. I introduce three issues that underscore the need for a pedagogy of fairness: the impact of separation from home (and departure from toddlerhood) on young children's adjustment to preschool and kindergarten; the insidious prevalence of bias toward some children by teachers and other children; and the purpose and potential of early schooling in a democratic society. I review the theoretical support for a pedagogy of fairness and consider the "paradoxical" nature of democratic goals in school (Covaleskie 2003). I then apply the standards for teaching fairly to a page from my own teacher's story to find how my self-satisfaction as a "good" teacher led me to fail as a fair one.

Chapters 5 and 6 set forth what a pedagogy of fairness looks like in Paley's practice. In chapter 5, I approach her journey as a white teacher of children of color, of black children in particular, through the three books that focus on the subject. *White Teacher* ([1979] 2000) centers on self-examination. I examine the significance of *White Teacher* in Paley's personal development, as well as in the white teacher studies movement. I also explore its limitations in light of her later work, which is often ignored in the multicultural education literature. *Kwanzaa and Me: A Teacher's Story* (1995), Paley's second investigation into race in the classroom, cedes center stage to community members. In her third work, *The Girl with the Brown Crayon* (1997), Paley lets five-year-old Reeny tell the story. Taken together, the three books reveal Paley's evolution as a fair teacher of children of color in the context of the many complex issues that accompany her efforts to recognize race and ethnic differences in the classroom.[3]

In chapter 6, I turn from race to gender, developmental difference, and popularity as sources of exclusion in the preschool and kindergarten, which Paley exposes in *Boys and Girls: Superheroes in the Doll Corner* (1984), *The Boy Who Would Be a Helicopter: The Uses of Storytelling in the Classroom* (1990), and *You Can't Say You Can't Play* (1992). Each of these works contributes to our understanding that Paley's pedagogy of fairness works as a safeguard for her young charges against the unexpected, and often ignored, sources of exclusion in the early childhood classroom.

While I bring to this project my collective experience as a researcher, college professor, teacher educator, school director, classroom teacher, and parent, I write this book as a student of teaching. The "we" I refer to throughout includes all who identify with this role. This book aims to start a conversation about "doing Paley" in the context of "doing teacher education." If there is a place in teacher education to learn from great teachers, this is my attempt to delve more deeply into Paley's role in it. Since Paley's vision is the soul of this effort, I naturally do not hesitate to draw on it as necessary to make my case.

That said, I must add a final note on the source of this book. I have spent more than twenty years in disseminating Paley's work around the country through my writing, through my founding of and extensive work with the School Literacy and Culture Project at the Rice University Center for Education, and as a teacher educator at Hofstra University and New York University. In that time, I have gotten to know Vivian Paley as a friend and mentor. She has been aware of this project since its inception. In the interest of maintaining both purpose and integrity, however, I chose not to seek her input on its content in any way. All interpretation, claims, and conclusions, whether valid or faulty, are therefore mine and mine alone.

PART I

Curricular Matters: A Pedagogy of Meaning

1

Early Literacy, Play, and a Teaching Philosophy

Once teachers discover certain truths, they can no longer teach in another way.

VIVIAN PALEY, *A Child's Work: The Importance of Fantasy Play*

This chapter is intended to provide a context for assessing the significance of Vivian Paley's play-based approach to the early childhood curriculum by examining, first, current opposition to it. How have we arrived at the point where play is disappearing in early childhood classrooms and best practices in early literacy instruction are in great dispute? Following upon this question, I consider the relationship between what is commonly referred to as the "academicization" of preschool and kindergarten and larger goals like closing the achievement gap. I then review the theoretical influences, including Dewey and Vygotsky, on Paley's play-based pedagogy. I conclude by stepping back and taking a longer view of what the press for less play, including less recess, in preschool and kindergarten means for young teachers whose experience may not offer an alternative view. What is lost for early literacy instruction when teachers' opportunities to examine young children's thinking and learning across dimensions are reduced?

✫

The history of early childhood education in America is a patchwork quilt of learning theory and social movements, of privilege and poverty. As in any quilt, each small block of fabric is distinctive, but all are connected in some way that contributes to the whole. Time rearranges the pattern of the blocks often. Montessori schools and Head Start programs, for example, currently occupy very different places on the quilt. Yet both began as an effort to educate poor children and provide an antidote to social ills (Beatty 1998).[1]

If we examine the section of the quilt depicting preschool and kindergarten education in the new millennium, it seems largely monochromatic. One issue—early literacy instruction—dominates the conversation for poor and middle-class children alike. This is not to say there is consensus among the stakeholders as to the best way to go about teaching beginning reading and writing; there is not. Heated debate swirls around several issues: the appropriateness of formal instruction, the best method to teach literacy subskills like phonemic awareness and phonics, and the role of language and play-based activities in early literacy development. Driving the debate are questions that touch the lives of teachers and young children in very real ways. How do young children learn before so-called formal schooling? Do poor children need a different curriculum than middle-class children? What is lost when time for play is reduced? What is the purpose of early schooling in general?

The issue of beginning reading and writing instruction could not be any more relevant to my analysis of Paley's contribution to early childhood teacher education. Her classroom studies in fantasy play, storytelling, and story acting are inherently directed to literacy learning and constitute a major aspect of her pedagogy of meaning. This is good news for anyone interested in the potential of early childhood education to influence children's long-term school literacy success. But it is not to imply that Paley's approach is in concert with recent trends in early literacy education. Deeply concerned about the diminishing opportunities for both fantasy play and language practice, she rejects outright the idea of all but the most minimal direct instruction in skills before first grade. Her instructional priorities revolve around play and story, not the formal teaching of reading and writing. She makes this argument explicitly in *A Child's Work: The Importance of Fantasy Play*: "There was a time when play was king and early childhood was its domain. Fantasy was practiced leisurely and openly in a language unique to the kindergarten" (2004, 4). In Paley's view, fantasy and language simultaneously provide the source for and boost to young children's "literary strivings," a point I will return to when I examine the specifics of Paley's literacy-related practices in chapters 2 and 3.

EARLY CHILDHOOD EDUCATION OR EARLY LITERACY EDUCATION?

Much has been written in recent years about the academicization of the early childhood classroom. The term describes the pushdown of academic content from the upper grades. Practically speaking, it means a concomitant pushout of play-based education, the time-honored staple of the early childhood curriculum. Of course, in the broader arena, all learning is in some way academic, including play. In this discussion, however, academics is used in the sense of formal learning that decontextualizes knowledge and presents it as a commodity to be acquired in organized, sequential units. While early math education gets some attention, arguably the majority of children's time on academics is going to early literacy, beginning with phonemic awareness and moving on through comprehension strategies. As Paley notes, this process historically began in the Western world around six or seven years of age, usually in first grade (Paley 2004; also see Tracey and Morrow 2006). The evidence that literacy learning is now endemic to kindergarten and preschools is overwhelming. Most startling, however, is the idea that an early childhood curriculum devoted largely to literacy subskills is *the same as* high-quality early childhood education. This requires us by default to also accept the consequential reduction in time for, and in some cases elimination of, play and other foundational early childhood activities.[2]

Critics of the trend to reduce play time in the early childhood curriculum in favor of academic skills have become increasingly vocal. Christie and Roskos sum up the situation sharply:

> Play is being shunted aside in early childhood programs in favor of more direct forms of instruction that address the new "pre-K basics" of language, early literacy, and numeracy skills. Although play was

> once seen as a key promoter of child development, administrators, policy makers, and some teachers increasingly regard play as a waste of instructional time with no clear benefits for high-priority cognitive outcomes, such as prereading skills. (2006, 57)

Zigler and Bishop-Josef write that play is under "attack" and speak of its status as a "four-letter word" (2006, 15). They note that even recess, once an unquestioned right of all schoolchildren, has been co-opted for academic ends. They write of a new public elementary school in Atlanta that was built without a playground. They also cite an article in the *New Haven Register*, which reported that opponents of a bill before the Connecticut legislature requiring schools to schedule a twenty-minute recess each day objected to the time it would take away from academic instruction. Pellegrini has written extensively on the merits of recess in early childhood education (see Pellegrini 2005; Pellegrini and Holmes 2006). His review of the research with Davis (1993) points to significant cognitive benefits related to free-ranging, child-led play time with peers on the playground.

In its most direct application, the benefits of play, inside and outside the classroom, to early literacy are felt in the opportunities it offers young children to practice language and to engage in language extension activities with peers and teachers. Dickinson examines the reciprocal relationship between early literacy development and guided, but open-ended, oral language development in the preschool and kindergarten classroom in *Beginning Literacy with Language: Young Children Learning at Home and School* (2001b). As I show in chapters 2 and 3, this view is a cornerstone of Paley's approach, from her emphasis on morning free play to her storytelling curriculum.

It is important to recognize that a long list of heavy hitters in early childhood education, with ties to policy and the standards movement, are boosters of an academic focus in preschool and kindergarten. Among them is Grover Whitehurst, current director of the Institute of Education Sciences. His article "Young Einsteins: Much Too Late" (2001) advocates for "academically oriented" and "content-centered" preschools where "less time is devoted to free play." Contrasting two prekindergarten classroom experiences, he endorses one in which all the children are following the teacher's directions in creating a one-size-fits-all book for Halloween, and disparages one in which children are engaged in a play dough activity. The first, Whitehurst explains, teaches needed literacy subskills, while the second is merely fun. We are meant conclude, it seems, that literacy development no longer requires the physical stamina, small motor control, or imagination traditionally associated with the inclusion of play dough activities (or finger painting, cutting and pasting, shape tracing, and so on) in the curriculum.

The policy face of the push for skills-based early literacy instruction in prekindergarten and kindergarten in the first decade of the twenty-first century is the Reading First Initiative of the 2001 No Child Left Behind Act (NCLB). The components of Reading First were propelled by a report in 2000 by the National Reading Panel and are described in the panel's 2003 publication *Put Reading First: The Research Building Blocks for Teaching Children to Read*. The document calls for formal instruction in five specific subskills of reading: phonemic awareness, phonics, vocabulary, fluency, and comprehension in the K-2 classroom. Controversy has surrounded the National Reading Panel's recommendations since NCLB went into effect. Critics question everything from its mission to the validity of its research base (Coles 2000, 2003). Proponents point to the qualifications of the panelists. Regardless of where one stands, the impact of the National Reading Panel on kindergarten, and its trickle-down effect on preschool has been undeniable. Evidence can be found in the widespread replacement of traditional early childhood curricula, such as open-ended reading aloud to children, singing, dramatic and block corner play, and, as mentioned, art and recess, with direct instruction in content areas, especially literacy.

Whatever fault we might find, neither the National Reading Panel nor NCLB can be blamed for the creep toward the academicization of early childhood education. The push for earlier and earlier direct instruction in literacy subskills began long before either arrived on the scene. Paley (2004) herself notes that she wrestled with the back-to-basics movement in the late 1970s, which followed on the heels of Jeanne Chall's prominent study of effective early reading instruction, described in her book *Learning to Read: The Great Debate* (1970). Chall's findings were widely interpreted to favor a synthetic phonics-based approach to beginning reading instruction. They were also instrumental in dismantling the forty-year hold on reading instruction of basal readers that relied on pictures and the repetition of whole and sight words, such as Scott Foresman's Dick and Jane series.

Though back-to-basics was largely concerned with skills instruction in the first and second grades, it created a spin-off problem for kindergarten in the form of an increased emphasis on teaching the alphabet and beginning phonics skills. I describe in chapter 3 what happened when I ran into this phenomenon as a young teacher. The impact of the movement, however, was unexpectedly blunted when not long afterward the National Association for the Education of Young Children (NAEYC) introduced the instantly popular concept of "developmentally appropriate practices" in a publication of the same name (Bredekamp and Copple 1986).

Developmentally Appropriate Practices in Early Childhood Programs (*DAP*) promoted a developmentalist view of early learning, through its focus on early childhood education as a time for laying the social and intellectual foundations of school success through play and other so-called natural interests of the young child, like music and art. Dickinson notes that the original *DAP*, among other pro-play statements, warned against "recent trends towards formal instruction" in early childhood classrooms, including a focus on "isolated skill development such as recognizing single letters, reciting the alphabet" (2002, 28). As it turned out, however, the victory of developmentally appropriate practices over a skills approach was to be relatively short-lived. Paley writes that by the 1990s "large chunks of the neighboring first-grade territory shook loose and began to roll into the garden of children, depositing numbers and letters everywhere" (2004, 31). The revised version of *DAP* (Bredekamp and Copple 1997) indicated a significant retreat from its earlier endorsement of an informal, embedded approach to early literacy. Dickinson documents this unexpected shift in perspective in his analysis of the two versions of *DAP* and *Learning to Read and Write: Developmentally Appropriate Practices for Young Children* (Neuman, Copple, and Bredekamp [1998] 2005), a joint position statement by the NAEYC and the International Reading Association (IRA). "Gone are the alarmist concerns about academic pressures, replaced by discussion of increases in the diversity of populations served, with reference to

Head Start and welfare reform efforts" (Dickinson 2002, 27). Both the 1997 *DAP* and *Learning to Read and Write* stress the need to systematically teach the alphabetic principle, letter-sound relationships, and other skills before first grade, specifying standards for achievement at each age level.

Given the weight that the NAEYC and IRA enjoy in early childhood teacher education, the significance of this shift cannot be overstated. Nor can we ignore the implications of positioning poor children as chronically in need of more academic content than their middle-class peers. Despite opposition (e. g., Neuman and Roskos 2005), both trends are well on their way to crystallizing as recommended practice in the field. This was evident in my experience at the NAEYC's 2007 annual meeting in Chicago. As I waited for a conference session to begin on revising *DAP* a third time, I overheard many participants discussing their eagerness for relief from content-based curriculum and formal instruction, particularly around early literacy development. I caught murmurings of hope that the panel of speakers, all respected leaders in the field, would surely acknowledge that things had gone too far. When the session opened, however, the room reverberated with shock, as former Erikson Institute president and early childhood advocate Barbara Bowman and *DAP* author and researcher Sue Bredekamp rolled out the key components of the new *DAP*. To the surprise of what appeared to be the majority of the crowd, Bowman and Bredekamp called for more, not less, emphasis on formal instruction in language, literacy, and math in the early childhood curriculum. They urged the audience to take stock of two realities. The first was the need to prepare all young children for the higher expectations of literacy achievement in the older grades. The second was the lack of literacy and language background among poor children and children of color. The clear implication was that there was no time to waste on other, less goal-directed curricula, even play. The question and answer period left a strong impression that the vast majority of the audience was bewildered, if not angered, by the presentation. At the same time, it is probably safe to say that most members of the audience left with the impression that whatever decisions they made regarding developmentally appropriate practice, their plans for early literacy education needed to be explicitly defined.[3]

PALEY, SUBSKILLS, AND THE GAP

David Kirp's *The Sandbox Investment: The Preschool Movement and Kids-First Politics* (2007) is a review of the campaign for preschool education across partisan lines to offset such national problems as the achievement gap, crime, and unemployment. Kirp begins by making a distinction between early childhood education for the privileged and that for the masses, opening the first chapter with a description of Paley's territory: "The preschool at the University of Chicago's Lab School, a Gothic pile located across the street from the university, is a hothouse for the imagination, a place where children engage with their teachers to construct a universe of knowledge." He reminds the reader of the Lab School's founding by progressivist John Dewey and Dewey's belief that the best learning begets more learning. Kirp also notes that Paley, whom he describes as "revered" for her books on fantasy play, taught at the school for more than three decades. But while Kirp acknowledges that the Lab School's imagination-based early childhood curriculum is "as good as prekindergarten gets," he also suggests it may be custom-tailored for the "chattering classes," the offspring of professors in a university community where "thinking is as instinctive as breathing" (15). His inference is clear. Whatever the value of the Lab School or Paley's focus on imaginative play, it is not available to—or necessarily desirable for—average children, let alone the poor children implicated in the DAP revision and other policy changes. As an alternative, Kirp describes what goes on in the publicly funded Chicago Child-Parent Centers, which have opted for less play and more instructional time spent on language, reading, "words and more words," in their effort to head off the achievement gap.

To be clear, Kirp, a public policy analyst, does not endorse "skill-and-drill" instruction (266). He favors "guided discovery" or "routinized learning" (as in part of a regular routine, not to be confused with a rote approach) to teach needed skills indirectly. Referring to a conversation he had with Paley, he suggests that her desire to delay formal instruction until age six or seven is simply nostalgia for a bygone era: "There can be no return to a more innocent world in which nursery school celebrated play and reading was something that youngsters were formally introduced to when they were six years old. *Nor should there be.* There are creative, intellectually, challenging ways to teach young children how to decipher their letters and numbers, as well as how to use them—ways to develop cognitive skills at an early age without making a child gnaw at his nails" (47, emphasis mine).

By way of example of a compromise between the pro- and anti-skills forces in preschool education, Kirp describes a scene in which a teacher asks young children to vote for the book they would like her to read. The children put checkmarks beside their choice on a list and then determine the winner by counting the votes in unison with the teacher. Kirp applauds this as teaching arithmetic in the context of "ordinary life," which in fact it is. The problem comes in his contrast of this approach with Paley's preferences and teaching methods. The task he describes is highly compatible with Paley's well-documented style of getting input from the children on any number of classroom choices, for example, having them count quarters for grocery shopping (1981, 182). Further, Kirp misreads Paley as being opposed to all formal teaching of "letters and how to use them" just because her preschoolers are not yet six or seven years old. Paley does not deny that she teaches letters and other "school work" (1981, 1984). Indeed, she is aware that, as Vygotsky (1978) notes, some young children possess a level of knowledge that makes the formal teaching of writing a good thing in the early years. Paley's objection, as Kirp himself informs us (2007, 47), is not to academic content per se in the preschool and kindergarten, but rather to its context and the pressure to perform that accompanies highly unreasonable expectations of academic mastery being placed on children as young as three. We should also note that ideas similar to Kirp's "guided discovery" and "routinization" were mainstreamed in early childhood education even before the original *DAP*. Early childhood teachers have long embedded arithmetic lessons in ordinary life, as well as literacy (as Kirp's example also demonstrates). Kirp is therefore right to call for a multilayered view of curriculum in the preschool and kindergarten years. The only issue is the level of the teacher's autonomy in determining when, what, how, and to whom she teaches.

A major influence in the pushdown of academics into early childhood education for literacy ends has been the late-twentieth-century research on early brain development (Fuller 2007; Kirp and Wolf

2007). We now have scientific evidence that the young brain is not only disposed to incredibly rapid growth, but also highly responsive to environmental factors of all types. This research, often couched in some type of it "use it, or lose it" euphemism, is frequently cited in arguments for increased spending and resources on early schooling. Adding to the sense of urgency is a similar view on oral language learning. Hart and Risley's widely disseminated and influential 2003 study refers to the "early catastrophe" in language for poor children (in addition, see their 1995 work on meaningful differences among young children). The authors write that middle-class children "have heard 30 million more words than underprivileged children" by their third birthdays. They echo Snow and Dickinson's 1991 findings on how middle-class children are more familiar with and adept at the use of decontextualized language, an aspect of language use now seen as critical to later schooling. The specter of an insurmountable literacy and achievement gap raised by this research looms large over early childhood teacher education. We hear this in Leslie Mandel Morrow's ominous statement in 2003, when she was president of the IRA: "By three, their fate is sealed."

Ironically, as Fuller and Kirp and Wolf, among others, point out, scientists do not support a deterministic reading of the brain research. Whatever development is possible in the early childhood years does not appear to exclude development after this period. And the research in early language acquisition has not curtailed interest in using programs like Head Start and universal prekindergarten to minimize the distance between poor and middle-class children's language development. More important in a discussion of Paley's work is the lack of evidence regarding the efficacy of direct instruction in literacy subskills in countering the language experience gap. At the very least, we must recognize the Sisyphean nature of attempts to give poor children the same language skills as middle-class ones without the play and conversation opportunities that characterize middle-class family life.

A problem for those who favor an emphasis on oral language development through play and practice as the true gateway to early literacy is that the power to decide how to best teach early literacy is unevenly distributed among the stakeholders. We know that those children most in need of language development support in school are enrolled in programs and schools whose teachers are least able to fend off a reduction in or elimination of free-ranging language activities. Too many of these teachers are forced to comply with the kind of efforts that would, to quote President Bush, turn Head Start into a "reading machine," or they must follow scripted curricula that emphasize language in isolated contexts. For example, according to an evaluation of kindergarten and first-grade reading in the Montgomery County Public Schools, "Children who are impoverished, cultural minorities, and learning English as a second language are at a greater risk of academic failure than those students who do not have these risk factors" (Nielsen and Cooper-Martin 2002, 89). In response to this problem, the authors state, "[t]he Montgomery County Public Schools (MCPS) has pledged to narrow this gap in student achievement by providing effective instructional programs delivered by highly trained and dedicated staff within a supportive learning community, both inside and around our schools" (3).

The instructional program described in the evaluation delivered heavy doses of early literacy subskills. The county also converted the half-day programs in the lowest-performing schools to full-day ones in order to give the children more instructional time. By 2007, the MCPS reported nearly a 90 percent success rate in children leaving kindergarten with beginning reading skills. In a *Washington Post* article called "More Work, Less Play in Kindergarten" (de Vise 2007), the superintendent is quoted as saying that the old play-based kindergarten was "shooting too low."

The obvious response is, Too low for what? What justifies giving young children in poverty "more work, and less play" in kindergarten? A nearly 90 percent success rate in skills achievement would seem phenomenal. Yet research is accumulating that the effects are by no means sustained over time. As early as 1991, Rescorla reported that children in early childhood programs that deemphasize play were no further ahead academically by the end of first grade than those in play-based ones. They also scored lower on measures of motivation to learn, which obviously portends poorly for future learning. In a large study of 812 children, Howes and Byler (as cited in Singer, Golinkoff, and Hirsh-Pasek 2006) found that young children, including poor children, in a developmentally based early childhood program achieved higher in mathematics, literacy, and receptive language by second grade. More recently, findings from the Reading First Impact Study have not shown the desired effect on comprehension, the endgame of reading instruction (Manzo 2008).[4] Though both critics and proponents of Reading First question some aspects of the study's design, it seems clear that it is difficult at best to measure the relationship between young children's comprehension learning and the five elements of reading instruction required by the Reading First Initiative (phonics, phonemic awareness, fluency, vocabulary, and comprehension). Beyond the immediate goal of teaching comprehension is the question of how we define intelligence. On this subject, Kirp acknowledges a problem. Writing on the universal prekindergarten movement, he agrees that four-year-olds won't benefit from teachers who "substitute skill-and-drill for thinking" (2007, 266). But teachers cannot teach thinking in five easy steps. As Kirp suggests, the balance of early childhood instruction must be tipped in favor of activities that are inherently interesting to young children. There can be no doubt that young children find the outdoor, imaginative, and story-based play of Paley inherently interesting. That said, it is also fair to ask whether the methods she advocates for are theoretically sound. What is the justification for their retention in the modern early childhood curriculum?

THE THEORETICAL ROOTS OF PALEY'S PLAY AND EARLY LITERACY PEDAGOGY

Though Paley is not explicit about the theoretical foundations of her beliefs regarding how young children develop and learn, analysis suggests the overlapping influences of Locke, Rousseau, Dewey, and Vygotsky on her thinking. I briefly review the significant features of each that enhance understanding of Paley as a teacher and observer of young children in school.

Briefly, Locke's theory of education is commonly summarized by his famous metaphor of the child as an empty vessel. Less cited, but equally relevant, is his idea of the child as a traveler newly arrived in a strange country. In other words, Locke sees teaching as a didactic enterprise and schools as places of enculturation. Modern behaviorism theory is rooted in Locke's work. In fact, the call for literacy subskills instruction reflects a behaviorist approach (Tracey and Morrow 2006). Paley's identification with Locke, however, is found in the more traditional sense of classroom management. She is very clear that children are expected to follow such teacher directives as no running in hallways, no hitting, and so on. More important, she also embraces her role as the model for certain social values, as I discuss further in part 2. Rousseau offers an alternative view of children's learning. Known as the father of developmental stage theory, Rousseau stresses the innate and unfolding interests of children to which all teaching should be addressed. Paley sides with Rousseau and other developmentalists in her respect for children's innate interests, as is clearly exemplified by her intense focus on what young children do and say. This "romantic" perspective is closely associated with both Freidrich Fröbel's child-centered kindergarten movement and the educational theory of constructivism later linked with Dewey and Piaget.

Dewey writes that children are motivated "to inquire" about a given subject through personal or natural interest ([1900] 1990). As a consequence, school life must be organized around likely interests in a way that promotes growth and development, the twin pillars of learning, across subject areas. To Dewey, true education is always "progressive," that is, activities look forward to where children can intellectually go next.[5] In a departure from a strict constructivist perspective, he also calls for the teacher to have an active response to the children's inquiries. At the risk of oversimplifying this complex argument, I would say that Dewey's philosophy revolves around the teacher, who is fully armed with subject-matter knowledge and classroom management skills. Through "the mutual interaction of different minds" (325) or the "social factors" that inevitably shape experience, the teacher engages the children's natural interests. Children are presumed uninterested in learning anything they cannot tie back to some native experience.

In the past three decades or more, sociocultural learning theory has emerged as a third and significant factor in American educational practice. The work of the Russian psychologist Lev S. Vygotsky is closely associated with this. Vygotsky combines both enculturation and developmental theories to focus on "social situatedness" of mind (Wertsch 1991). Vygotsky writes, "Human learning presupposes a specific social nature and a process by which children grow into the intellectual life of those around them" (1978, 88; see also Vygotsky 1962). Not even the concept of mind can be understood a priori in sociocultural learning theory, as it is always reinventing itself through mind-on-mind interaction (Berk 1994; Wertsch 1991). According to Vygotsky, young children's learning in the years before formal schooling (around age seven) is shaped by their language experiences, imaginative play, and the mediation of thinking with significant others. He says their capacity or potential for learning is situated at once and always between two poles, what they have learned to date and what they could learn with assistance. Vygotsky calls the space between these poles children's "zone of proximal development." All learning, including early literacy, is mediated in the zone of proximal development through "scaffolding" by significant adults, such as a teacher (Bruner 1986). Nicolopoulou's 2002 research on scaffolding in storytelling situations suggests significant peers may influence this process, too. A critical aspect of Vygotsky's thinking is that, whereas both Locke and Rousseau see development as *leading to* learning, he views learning as *preceding* development. This naturally changes the weight given to experience, tutelage, and training in development, as well as to the specific institutional, cultural, and historical influences that make up the child's world (see also Cobb and Yackel 1996; Dahlberg, Moss, and Pence 2007; Daniels, Cole, and Wertsch 2007; Forman, Minick, and Stone 1996; Irvine 1990; Moll 2005; Wertsch 2005).

Paley's views of early literacy learning intermingles stage theory, Dewey's work on education as always forward moving, and a sociocultural view of young children's interests in literacy activities. But at the core of her thinking on early literacy development are the requirements of fantasy play, including oral language and narrative development, as well as the young child's need for community. Pellegrini and Boyd write that dedicated research on play is a "broad and sometimes ambiguous construct" (1993, 118). Methodological problems, from control groups to cultural differences, are not uncommon. Much is given over to the theoretical. Johnson,

Christie, and Wardle organize modern theories of play into three general categories: psychodynamic, social learning, and cognitive, which in turn describe emotional, social, and intellectual development. Postmodern approaches locate play and development in the wider context of learning, as explained by sociocultural, critical, and chaos theories (Johnson, Christie, and Wardle 2005, 37). Each theory in its own way attempts to explain why young children do what they do (or don't do) in play. My goal here is not to resolve the issues in play research, but to provide a more formal context from which to appreciate Paley's stance on play as the cornerstone of early literacy instruction in the preschool and kindergarten classroom.

Dewey's influence on Paley is most felt in her work on fairness, which I discuss in chapter 4. However, his characterization of play lights Paley's path in several other ways as well. For Dewey, the definition of young children at play is not limited to what children do, but to their "mental attitude" ([1900] 1990, 118). In this, he foreshadows Paley's belief in the young child's ability to invent, in a playful way, possibilities in life. Also, his dissatisfaction with so-called representational activities and materials for play (such as those advocated by Montessori) is compatible with Paley's belief that children impose their imagination on naturally occurring activities in the world and inject them with personal meaning. And, while Dewey never considers the link between play and early literacy directly, he refers to the "story-form" as the link to more formal learning, just as Paley does throughout her work.

On the whole, Dewey's views on play are not dissimilar to Vygotsky's, though it is Vygotsky to whom Paley turns directly in her assessment of young children at play. We see Vygotsky's theory of play's role in development (1978) at work most visibly in Paley's language-based methods and emphasis on imaginative play and story.[6] His idea that play creates its own zone of proximal development in which the child can explore new hypotheses about the world is seen in Paley's detailed observations of children at play and their response to teacher intervention. In *Boys and Girls: Superheroes in the Doll Corner*, for example, she suspects the "Three Little Pigs" play in the block corner and the doll corner is stirring the children's anxieties about separation. She helps them wrestle with various disturbing details through a directed class discussion:

PALEY: I wonder why the three pigs decide to build separate houses.
CLARICE: They didn't have enough room and they needed a small house because they were all small. . . .
PALEY: Did [the mother] know that a wolf lived in the woods? . . . Is there a father? (1984, 47)

At the end of the discussion, Paley asks the children outright whether they prefer the safer ending, where all the pigs are saved, or the scarier version when the wolf eats the pigs. Later that day, she directs the children in the dramatization of the story, which demonstrates her support for their explorations and allows her further insights into the meaning of their play. Curious that eight boys want to play the wolf despite their earlier identification with the frightened pigs, she asks them to explain their choice. They tell her that the wolf is stronger. They have found a way around their fears of being eaten, she concludes.

Paley's stories of children at play are full of moments where the rules are made, tested, broken, or repaired. One has the sense that the children are on guard to keep play from being nothing but emotional mayhem. This maps onto a distinguishing feature of Vygotsky's play theory, its rule-bound nature, where wandering feelings are held in check according to preestablished behavioral and cultural norms. Observance of the expected is definitional. Vygotsky offers the example of a child playing house. "The child imagines himself to be the mother and the doll the child, so he must obey the rules of maternal behavior" (1978, 94). This transfer of behavior is simple enough, but as the children become more adept at fantasy play, they actually test out more theoretical norms, especially in relation to other children (Cooper 1993; Nicolopoulou 1993). We see this often in Paley's classroom stories. For example, when three-year-old Frederick attempts to take the cash register away from Mollie in the doll corner, she protests and another child calls him a robber. Surprised but pleased by the new role, he agrees. He is reminded by another child, however, that robbers are not allowed in the doll corner. He must choose between his delight in being a robber and his desire to stay near Mollie. Samantha, apparently sensing Frederick's dilemma, comes to the rescue and offers him yet another role. "He can be the father," she says. "Put on this vest, Frederick." He does and he stays (Paley 1986, 3).

In *Bad Guys Don't Have Birthdays: Fantasy Play at Four*, Paley writes, "No character is more rule-governed than the bad guy. In this class he cannot have a birthday or a name or share the stage with a baby" (1988, 19). She notes that while an adult would not limit so-called bad guys in this particular way, young children, even the would-be robber Frederick, are always willing to limit their powers. This is a most necessary accomplishment of early childhood if young children are to emerge in control of enough of their fears to leave home for big school and the world at large.

> "Look, Frederick," Christopher breathes heavily. "Rich gold and lots of real money. Pretend this is the hideout . . ."
>
> "Robbers!" Fredrick shouts. "Hide the drinks."
>
> "You don't have to," Barney reminds him. "Good guys don't hide drinks. Nobody can steal from good guys." (1988, 30)

Vygotskian scholars Bodrova and Leong note that the roles and rules of imaginative play aid another developmental task of early childhood, self-regulation.

Self-regulation is the capacity to both *stop* what one wants to do and *do* what one doesn't (2008, 56, emphasis theirs). The implications for overall development are obvious, but it must be said that the relationship between play and self-regulation with regard to developing empathy cannot be underestimated. Consider the following example from Paley's *The Boy Who Would Be a Helicopter: The Uses of Storytelling in the Classroom* (1990). Jason, whose undisciplined behavior alternately frustrates and confuses other children, is walking through a "marsh" some boys have built from blocks. "That's dangerous, don't walk over there," Alex orders Jason. But Jason causes the blocks to fall nonetheless. "No, Jason!" Alex screams and pulls his arm. When Jason starts to cry, Paley says Alex's voice becomes gentle, but he stays within the fantasy. "Please don't go by the marsh way again," he tells Jason, "or we'll have to explode you." Samantha, however, knows the rules of fantasy play better than Alex and doesn't let even this mild threat linger.

"Oh, yeah," Samantha sticks out her tongue. "Well you can't explode someone that they're not even playing with you that they're playing something different."

"So what, Samantha. We'll blast *you* to pieces."

"So, I'll be a poo-poo bug," is her retort. (75)

Paley says Samantha is reminding Alex that children control the fantasy; they are not controlled by it. Berk, Mann, and Ogan (2006) write that although more empirical research on self-regulation and make-believe is called for, studies to date firmly link fantasy play to a host of positive outcomes related to school success.

A critical feature of Vygotsky's play theory that has become a mantra for Paley involves the psychological nature rather than the intellectual function of imaginative play. This is the idea of the young child "out playing" his actual self. It arises, Vygotsky writes, at the end of the toddler years in the child's attempts to manage the "unrealizable tendencies and desires [that] emerge" by pretending he is more capable or in control than he realistically can be. "In play, a child always behaves beyond his average age, above his daily behavior; in play it is as though he were a head taller than himself" (1978, 93, 102). While fantasy play requires that the child be able to "act independently of what he sees" (93), Vygotsky says it is not to be understood as symbolic in the sense of arbitrary signs. Meaning always dominates in fantasy play (while a stick can be a horse, it cannot be a ball). Also, meaning accounts for the "emotional tone" (94) of play since it is the source of the motivational and circumstantial features of play. Vygotsky argues that "if we ignore the child's needs, and the incentives which are effective in getting him to act, we will never be able to understand his advance from one developmental stage to the next" (92). Motivation and circumstance also figure centrally in Paley's attention to the content of fantasy play.

Research supporting a Vygotskian approach to play in early childhood education is strong (Berk 1994; Berk and Winsler 1995; Bodrova and Leong 1996; Dixon-Krauss 1996). As Vygotsky points out, the "play-development" relationship is superior to the "instruction-development" relationship by virtue of the greater range of possibilities it covers in children's thinking (1978, 102). Vygotsky concludes that the characteristics of imaginative play in early childhood make it a leading factor in development. It looks forward to higher-level critical thinking: "[C]reating an imaginary situation can be regarded as a means of developing abstract thought" (103). There can hardly be a greater endorsement of play's role in development in general or early literacy education specifically.

THE PLAY EXPERIENCE TEACHERS OF YOUNG CHILDREN NEED

Dewey (1934) tells us that effective pedagogy in all areas requires teachers to continually engage in child study and refinement of their subject-matter knowledge. One question that has gone begging in the debate over early literacy instruction is what new teachers can learn from young children's play that is relevant to effective early literacy instruction. This is a vitally important aspect of Paley's teacher's story, which I describe in the next chapter. But here I'd like to consider the problem from a more clinical perspective, using the example of recess from my own teaching history. As a preschool and kindergarten teacher in Chicago, I clocked a minimum of two forty-minute periods every day on the school's playground. Since the children were more or less free to play as they wished, this gave me ample opportunity to observe their bodies in motion and space, not to mention in all types of weather. In time I learned to gauge not only their physical stamina and coordination as they roved about the playground, but their moods and confidence levels as well. Helping them climb to the top of the climbing structure and down the fireman's pole over and over again gave me insight into what they saw as challenges and when they needed new ones. Their urge to touch and poke and pry anything within an arm's length became as familiar to me as their proficiency with small sticks. I heard them experimenting with bellowing and whispering as they called to each other through the playground fence. The fragility and strength of their friendships were constantly on display as I watched them grab each other's hands to form a snake or sit alone under the slide. I consulted with other teachers about what I was seeing.

Of course, it wasn't long before I put my trove of information to practical use inside the classroom. Without question, my attempts at early literacy instruction improved. I got better at predicting how much time the children could spend working at tables, looking at books, sitting in the circle, and when they needed a break. I also knew to watch their eye movements when they were tracking print and when and how to help them utilize pencils and markers. An added bonus from my time on the playground was the unwavering respect I developed for young children's need to be physically active indoors and out. In this I am not invoking the progressivist principle of learning by doing. I mean the biological necessity of using one's own limbs and senses to stimulate and self-regulate learning. The children's interest in vocal play outdoors led me in the classroom to favor literacy leading activities like singing and song-driven movement games. Although, however much the children loved them, I won't plead the musical virtues of "Mairzy Doats," "Do Your Ears Hang Low?" or "Farmer in the Dell," as research suggests (Dickinson 2001a), song helped them expand their vocabularies and gave them added practice in rhyme and phonemic awareness.

There were lots of other lessons I learned as a young teacher from observing young children on the playground that transferred into the classroom and made me better at early literacy instruction. But none was as important to my development as the initial one—the children's need for me to be a teacher of play first.

2

Fantasy Play and Young Children's Search for Meaning

> I measured my resistance against the children's eagerness and wondered what I was missing.
>
> **VIVIAN PALEY**, *The Boy Who Would Be a Helicopter: The Uses of Storytelling in the Classroom*

Paley's observations on young children at play have proven an incredible resource for teachers, indeed for anyone interested in looking at development from the child's point of view (including Cooper 1993, 2005; Cooper et al. 2007; Katch 2001, 2003; McLane and McNamee 1990; McNamee 1992; Nicolopoulou 1997b; Nicolopoulou and Richner 2004; Nicolopoulou, Scales, and Weintraub 1994; Rothman 2006). This chapter focuses on Paley's pedagogy of meaning. I begin with an in-depth look at a guiding principle of Paley's teaching for meaning through children's play. I refer to her belief that what goes on *inside* of sociodramatic play—its "subject matter" (Dewey [1900] 1990, 125)—is what must guide the teacher's response. For Paley, it is a belief that is as critical to the children's experience of play as the issue of making space for it in the curriculum in the first place. This was not always the case, however. Paley admits she didn't always recognize the inside story of fantasy play. Her accidental discovery offers teacher education a highly valuable example of how the best teachers are those who are never too experienced to be surprised or humbled.

Following this discussion, I turn to the link Paley makes between play and academic readiness, including literacy. In the chapter's last section, I discuss the specific lessons to be gleaned from Paley concerning a pedagogy of meaning through fantasy play. I call on an array of Paley's books in this discussion, though I focus on *Mollie Is Three: Growing Up in School* (1986) and *Bad Guys Don't Have Birthdays: Fantasy Play at Four* (1988).

❖

The literary fantasy is a beloved fixture on the elementary school reading list. From *The Wonderful Wizard of Oz* to *The Golden Compass*, fantasy readers travel through cyclones and wardrobes, down rabbit holes, and into parallel universes to find the answer to the one question they cannot answer in real time: What must we know to grow up whole and well? The enormous popularity of the Harry Potter series, the *Lord of the Rings* trilogy, and even the Star Wars films suggests it is a question we may never outgrow. It doesn't originate in middle childhood, of course. As any preschool and kindergarten teacher knows, interest in literary fantasy is the direct descendant of the fantasy, imaginative, make-believe, pretend, or story-based play of early childhood. (In this chapter, all modifiers of play listed in the previous sentence are used interchangeably.) Theoretically, fantasy play emerges somewhere between the symbolic explorations of toddlerhood and peaks before the mastery of games with rules in middle childhood.[1] It is not the only kind of play in early childhood, of course. Physical play thrives there as well, as does playing with objects. Games with rules are beckoning in the first versions of cards, Simon Says, and so on. Yet imaginative play reigns as the highest level of development in early childhood (Vygotsky 1978, 92).

Vivian Paley describes fantasy play as the young child's "curriculum in its natural form" (2004, 3). It leads to literacy, but it serves other academic, social, and cognitive goals as well. Formal definitions of play speak to its elements. Mitchell characterizes it as "a mental activity involving imagination that is intentionally projected onto something" (2002, 4) Fein's review of the research identifies decontextualized behavior, relation to self and others, and the use of substitute objects as the common "components of pretense." These elements merge in full-blown sociodramatic play through role enactment and communication among the players (1981, 1098). In Paley's stories of classroom life, however, the "decontextualized" becomes "let's make believe." The "relation to self and others" becomes "who do you want to be," and the "use of substitute objects" becomes whatever prop is needed to enhance the fantasy in the children's minds. Fantasy play takes place in designated locations, like the doll corner and the block corner, and just about anywhere young children gather.

Fantasy play makes its appearance in two distinct ways in Paley's classroom studies. The first is what we think of as unstructured play. Historically, it reigned in the preschool and kindergarten morning during free play, which typically lasted from forty-five minutes to an hour.[2] The second is fantasy play's more formal appearance in storytelling and story acting. Paley writes that fantasy play, or "story playing"—she describes it as "story in action"—is half the "curriculum of any class in which I am the teacher." The other half is "storytelling," which she describes as fantasy play's alter ego, or "play put into narrative form" (1990, 4). For the sake of clarification, Paley (and others) often uses the term "storytelling" as shorthand for both the telling and the acting of stories. In my own writing and work in teacher education, I refer to the combination as the "storytelling curriculum." I also interchange the word "dictation" with storytelling and "dramatization" with story acting (Cooper 1993, 2005; Cooper et al. 2007).

Both fantasy play and storytelling share such fundamentals as imaginative language and pretend situations, and both figure prominently in Paley's pedagogy of meaning. As I have defined it, a pedagogy of meaning involves teaching to help young children explore those things in the world, including ideas, that they find meaningful. Theoretically, children's motivation to construct knowledge and learn from others is directly tied to personal interest and the support they receive from the learning environment, including the teacher (Dewey [1900] 1990, 1913; Vygotsky 1978). From a practical perspective, a pedagogy of meaning requires teachers to implement a curriculum that stokes young children's immediate interests and yet stimulates their attraction to new ideas and ways of thinking about the world. A pedagogy of meaning thus (a) creates opportunity, (b) affirms significance, and (c) helps generate new lines of thought. The last goal gets its start in the burgeoning ideas and feelings that stir beneath every young child's consciousness. In all, a pedagogy of meaning builds on Dewey's theory of "interest and effort" in education and Vygotsky's "zone of proximal development." Its promise for teaching is that it keeps the child moving in a forward direction. Otherwise, we are merely confirming yesterday's news.

Although I want to emphasize that a pedagogy of meaning supports learning and development across the curriculum, its value is most visible when applied to young children's fantasy play. Paley writes that children turn to fantasy play to explore "nothing less than Truth and Life" (1990, 17). For this reason, their play is where she goes to address the questions, hopes, and fears that arise in their journeys. Along the way, she leaves no developmental stone, from the psychological to the cognitive, unturned.

INSIDE MAKE-BELIEVE PLAY

Young children's fantasy play doesn't arrive all at once in the early childhood classroom. Just as the toddler teacher awaits the monsters, tigers, lost babies, and firemen who will have taken up residency in her classroom by year's end, the preschool teacher prepares for their formation as a dramatic troupe. Paley's descriptions of young children bringing their inner lives to the classroom stage have proved groundbreaking. She writes of three-year-olds in "search of characters" and four- and five-year-olds in "search of plots" (1986). But fantasy play's apotheosis, she says, is reserved for the kindergarten teacher. "By kindergarten, children have the added patience, experience, and vocabulary with which to carry the plot and the characters to places they have never been before, and to apply what they know to their social relationships" (2004, 23). It turns out, however, that just acknowledging the children's classroom dramas is not enough.

The first challenge in teaching for meaning through play, as Paley demonstrates, is to know what story the children are telling *behind* the story they actually stage or share. Paley sees children's narratives as their attempts to control their ever present and evolving developmental concerns. Nicolopoulou (1997a) refers to this as Paley's "interpretive" approach to children's fantasy play. Leaning on Bruner's view of narrative as a symbolic representation of the felt experience (1986, 1991), Nicolopoulou distinguishes this from a structural or linguistics approach to analyzing story content: "Paley's work demonstrates convincingly the value of an interpretive approach to children's narrative activity that treats it as a vehicle of their symbolic imagination and is guided by an informed appreciation of the interaction among its cognitive, emotional, and sociocultural dimensions" (1997a, 203). But whereas Nicolopoulou and many in the field align Paley's interpretation of fantasy play's meaning across development with her emergence as a researcher, Paley herself credits it with her progress as a "Teacher" (1997). Thinking back on a course she took in college, Paley recalls that she was taught that young children use their imaginations to get around the obstacles that stand in the way of their goals (2004, 2), a commonly accepted concept of early childhood development that's found in any entry-level child development course. Unfortunately, Paley says, she didn't fully grasp the significance of the imagination half of this equation for a long time, and for a large chunk of her career, she viewed children's fantasy play only through the checklist of assessments she routinely filled out. "This child knows how to play, I would note," Paley tells us. "[H]e is able to include other children and thus be a friend" (2004, 17). Duly recording the fact of pretend play, however, gave Paley no insight as to what was actually being enacted in play. "I would pass over the story the child had imagined and the questions of identity being posed," she goes on (17). Many teachers can identify with Paley's efficient record keeping.

Two seemingly unspectacular developments made Paley realize that she had been assessing the wrong thing in children's play. Help came first in the form of the tape recorder. A professional development experience led her to question whether teachers interacted with children differently according to their preconceived expectations of the children's intelligence. She began to tape her conversations with the children in the morning's circle time, the hallowed gathering to talk that occurs each day in the preschool and kindergarten.[3] She needed to know where she stood (1988, 8). What Paley didn't anticipate, and what she only discovered serendipitously one day after leaving the tape recorder on during free play, was that the children, all the children, were leading double lives in their classrooms. She writes in *Bad Guys Don't Have Birthdays*, "A relentless connection-making was going on, the children inventing and explaining their rules and traditions every time they talked and played. 'Let's pretend' was a Socratic dialogue, and the need to make friends, assuage jealousy, and gain the sense of one's own destiny provided the reasons for agreement on goals and procedures. An astonishing marketplace of ideas flourished in the kindergarten classroom, and I was just beginning to sample its wares" (1988, 12).

Clearly, the developmental checklist had been leading Paley in the wrong direction. Determining that a child "knows how to play" suggests knowing *how* is more important than knowing *what*. Paley notes that by "passing over" the content of young children's play—that is, the story they were telling in the language of pretend—by failing to ask herself what the story might mean, she had "confused the extraordinary with the mundane" (2004, 17). Up until this point, she had missed the fact that young children's fantasy play always holds a deeper, psychological meaning. She was "in the wrong forest," she writes (1990, 5). It is a generous admission on Paley's part, and an exceedingly instructive one for teacher education. Too often we speak of professional growth as a matter of course, not admitting that many very good teachers, as I'm sure Paley was then, will never be truly great teachers unless they habitually investigate not just new ideas, but old ones as well.

Paley's teaching life was forever changed by another play-related event when she stumbled upon the benefits of the more formalized fantasy play in storytelling and story acting, in which play motifs survive and are transformed. First introduced in *Wally's Stories: Conversations in the Kindergarten* (1981), Paley immediately saw the kinship of storytelling (dictation) and story acting (dramatization) with imaginative play and thus the appeal and usefulness of both to the children. I examine storytelling and story acting, including their relevance to early literacy development, in detail in chapter 3. The important point here is that Paley shifted her attention to fantasy and play in a way that profoundly changed her teaching.

Interpreting children's play at the classroom level is a matter of attending to the details in the context of what you know about child development, the particular child, and, just as important, the group. Fantasy play paints with both broad and narrow strokes depending on the merger of all these factors. Of one preschool class, Paley wrote, "If play is the book, then the chapters turned to most often in this class deal with the birthdays, bad guys, and babies. These three leitmotifs are pivotal to the daily drama and perhaps to intimations of reality itself" (1988, 21). And the list will grow longer as superheroes arrive to save the day. By kindergarten, she shows us, magic and fairness are making steady appearances. Further, the hierarchy of power in early childhood is an ever- evolving theme, subject to the vagaries of group life, but there are constant characters who show up along the way. In kindergarten, Paley discovers, the tooth fairy debuts and wields great strength, but almost all children conclude that she is not as powerful as Santa Claus, who in turn is not as powerful as God (1981, 86). The teacher, of course, would not have seen the three in ascending order—and that is exactly Paley's point. She didn't either, until she listened.

Paley identifies friendship as a dominant theme of early schooling that is deeply felt throughout preschool and kindergarten fantasy play. Ladd and Coleman (1993) suggest the interpersonal communication (as distinct from language development) required to sustain fantasy play helps young children practice what it takes to be friends in real life. Göncü (1993) finds the overall the requirements of play—the initial agreement to participate, the creation of a scene and objective, and the continuing negotiation between players that is necessary for it to proceed—to be a significant accomplishment of early childhood. Paley offers many examples that reveal friendship's push-me / pull-you terrain. In *Bad Guys Don't Have Birthdays*, Margaret, for instance, is jealous to discover Mollie playing Rainbow Brite with Barney when she arrives at school. The two ignore Margaret's attempts to enter their play. But when they pretend a bad guy has arrived on the scene, Margaret immediately interjects to tell them she has blown him up with her blasting powder. "Did you kill him?" Barney wants to know. Margaret says she did, and declares herself "the blasting powder guy." Barney then gives her a role in the play. Margaret, however, first checks to see if she has succeeded in winning Mollie over as well. "Are you my friend, Mollie?" she asks (1988, 83). Mollie says she is.

Paley names fear as another grand theme in make-believe, though it is not always as unwelcome as adults might assume. Echoing Vygotsky's theory of playing ahead of capacity, she writes, "[T]he fantasy play is filled with warnings, and the children continually find new ways to describe the risks in life" (1988, 77). Child psychologist Susan Linn states that young children use pretend play "as a conduit for honest feelings" that scare them (2006, 139). The distinction between feelings and ideas is a critical one when interpreting fear in the fantasy play of young children, who don't always name what they feel and act out. The teacher must read between the lines. For example, it turns out that aggression is masking Barney's fear of losing his mother's love when he tells the girls in the doll corner not to worry about the bad guy in the well because he has killed him. Curious, Paley questions who the bad guy is. Barney tells her he is the big brother from *Tikki Tikki Tembo* (one of two young brothers who fall into a well accidentally). Paley, stumped, asks for an explanation, "The little boy? How can he be a bad guy?" And Barney answers, "Because the mother is more sadder when *he* falls in, don't you remember?" (1988, 81).

The subject of babies also tests the teacher's interpretation skills. After all, a baby is never *just* a baby in the fantasy play of three- or five- or six-year-olds. Paley calls it an "uncertain symbol." In some play, she finds, the baby "has to be dead." In others, he is in danger of being hurt by He-Man, unless, of course, he is *baby* He-Man. There have to be new babies, as well, or "you can't be older" (1988, 108). The differences among the babies waiting to be born or rescued or replaced are the differences among the players, including their developing sense of experimentation and exploration. Paley cautions teachers not to read disturbance into fantasy play that is not there.

In my view, interpreting young children's fantasy play has much in common with how an older doctor once described the doctor-patient relationship to Robert Coles, then a psychiatrist-in-training. I've substituted "children" for "patients" in Coles's quoting of his mentor:

> The children who come to see us bring us their stories. *They hope they tell them well enough so that we understand the truth of their lives.* They hope we know how to interpret their stories correctly.

We have to remember that what we hear is their story. (1989, x, emphasis mine)

Granted, the art of interpretation does not come automatically to all teachers, as it did not initially for Paley. However, it must come eventually or teachers will be unable to help children create accounts of their world that make more sense today than they did yesterday or could tomorrow.

Allow me to point out that the researcher may view the discovery of fantasy play's content as an opportunity. A visitor to the classroom may find it endearing. In neither case, however, is it necessarily significant to the researcher's or visitor's identity. As Paley reminds us over and over again, however, it is the early childhood teacher's passkey to her teaching soul. It also exemplifies a pedagogy of meaning because it, simply and elegantly, gives the teacher something to talk about and ponder over with the children. Paley explains the experience in this way: "It is in the development of their themes and characters and plots that children explain their thinking and enable us to wonder who we might become as their teachers" (2004, 8). Paley helps us see that every time we're asked to slip a nightgown over a little one's dress (or jeans), to create Ninja Turtle costumes out of paper, or that we overhear that Batman is coming but Superman is being punished, we must reinvent ourselves as a teacher of that particular fantasy.

PALEY: PLAY ADVOCATE AND TEACHER OF EARLY LITERACY

Typically, whenever I teach one of Paley's books in my education classes, I am asked how Paley gets away with a curriculum limited to free play and storytelling. I tell them she doesn't because it isn't true, and then I take them back through the narrative. My students are always surprised to be shown that they have somehow glossed over the carved pumpkins, grocery store budgets, rug measuring, Chinese New Year parades, play-dough tables, and so on, that line Paley's stories of classroom life. In those rare classes when my students don't ask about Paley's seemingly restricted curriculum, I ask for them. I explain I want them to understand that for all the virtues of making fantasy play the engine of the kindergarten and the preschool, it would be irresponsible of Paley or anyone not to make sufficient room in the schedule for beginning math, science, music, social studies, and even some literacy subskills activities as well. I will admit, however, that my motive in calling my students' attention to this is less than pure. My goal is to get the issue on the table so we can discuss imaginative play's unique role in the early childhood classroom. I assume Paley gets asked the same question even more often. In *The Girl with the Brown Crayon*, she appears to anticipate the reader's concern: "In the telling of this literary tale, it may seem that other significant details of school are obscured. . . . Stories do proceed as if nothing else is going on" (1997, viii).

In chapter 1, I discussed the fallout of an academically top-heavy curricula on young teachers' experience and knowledge base. Paley looks at it from the children's perspective to ask what happens to their developing identity as learners when they cannot comply with the increased academic expectations in preschool and kindergarten. "This conundrum does not exist in the abstract. Expectations for incoming first graders are quite precise, and the tension begins even before the [first-grade teacher] and student meet. The potential for surprise is largely gone. We no longer wonder 'Who are you?' but instead decide quickly 'What can we do to fix you?'" (2004, 47). In essence, Paley is arguing that the pushdown of academics represents a deficit view of young children's potential. It is wrong, and it leads to bad and unfair pedagogy. Ironically, it does not have to be this way. A different reading of the very same factors that led to the academicization of early childhood instruction can lead us in a direction that throws our weight behind play-based education. Graue (1995) points out that the definition of readiness for so-called formal learning depends on what question is being asked. Is readiness a matter of development or of instruction? Does readiness depend on prerequisites, prior knowledge, or experience?

In dispute here is the issue of what is really expendable in the best preparation of young readers and writers. As Pellegrini and Galda (2000) suggest, if literacy is defined as a *developmental process*, then fantasy play becomes the core of the early childhood curriculum. If literacy is defined as a *collection of skills*, then fantasy play becomes a luxury. At the center is the issue of language development, including vocabulary, and the narrativization of language. Disparities between the language experiences of children from lower-income homes and their middle- and upper-class peers related to these factors are well documented (Dickinson and Tabors 2001; Hart and Risley 1995, 2003). One way to address these disparities is to create early childhood education that mimics or borrows from rather than decontextualizes the real language and literacy experiences of children from middle-class homes (Cazden 1992; Clay 1991; Dickinson 2001b; Sulzby 1986; Tabors, Roach, and Snow 2003). Fantasy play offers us many opportunities for authentic interaction and easily lends itself to extension activities that stimulate deep and authentic immersion in language and print (Morrow 1990). This begins with what Dickinson and Tabors (2001) call "extended discourse," that is, the use of language that goes beyond immediate demands. Wolf calls for language learning that helps young children move from "here-and-now" language to "there-and-then," thus fostering the skills required to make narrative. According to Wolf, the passport to reading and writing begins in narrativization, that is, "the affective work of realizing what we feel, the cognitive work of making sense, the social work of sharing experience, and the cultural work of taking up tools and forms we inherit for composing personal, familial, or community histories" (1993, 44). She highlights Paley's classroom studies as exemplars of how learning to narrate experience through fantasy play (and the storytelling curriculum ahead) embody three processes: becoming a narrator, becoming an author, and making texts. The first involves developing the language of narration, as assisted by both caregivers and teachers. The second means going beyond reporting on experience to creating it, which includes evaluation. And the third refers to a systematic accounting of experience, written or not.

Advocates of a language rich, play-based approach to early literacy instruction are concerned with the ways in which young children are characterized as inadequately prepared for literacy learning before they've had the full advantage of early schooling. Paley writes, "Since the earlier we begin academics, the more problems are revealed, were the problems there waiting to be discovered or does the premature introduction of lessons cause the problems?" (2004, 47). It is a daring question because it doesn't just neutralize Whitehurst's tabletop academics in the preschool, it boldly warns of negative expectations and effects. Pedagogically speaking, teachers cannot scaffold the foundations of literacy, language, and narrative by requiring children to perform on decontextualized subskill tasks. Self-regulation, so central to success in the tasks of learning (from patience to contemplation) is not furthered when—as I have witnessed myself—young children are prematurely required to sit, take directions, and constrain their bodies and ideas for twenty, thirty, and even forty-five minutes at a time, many times over the course of the school day. Nor is comprehension enhanced when twenty, thirty, or forty-five minutes go by in which there is no opportunity for a truly free exchange of ideas. None of these complaints is meant to suggest that young children should never be asked to sit and attend in the preschool or kindergarten. But multiply this demand several times a day and the problem grows insidiously. All told, to take up Paley's charge, an early childhood program top heavy with literacy skills–based instruction is not a defense against future academic problems, it is a petri dish of problems waiting to develop. It is also an indignity that will do little to close the achievement gap because it fails to lay the groundwork for the higher-level skills, including analysis, synthesis, and evaluation, to borrow from Bloom, needed to advance in literacy.

As we've seen, Paley's play-based counternarrative to the formalized early literacy curriculum and general academicization of the preschool and kindergarten is rooted in Vygotsky's theory of play. Her collective work stands as a cornucopia of examples of this theory in action. *A Child's Work: The Importance of Fantasy Play*, however, diverges from her usual format of classroom stories and offers a formal rebuttal: "Fantasy play is the glue that binds together all other pursuits, including the early teaching of reading and writing skills," she writes and, given the times, she is "compelled to put it on display" (2004, 8). Susi Long, in her review of *A Child's Work*, takes note of Paley's unusual change of focus. "An important difference between this book and her other books is that, in this text, Paley directly addresses today's politically-driven policies that too often result in the elimination of time for play in schools" (2005, 313). In this sense, *A Child's Work* is Paley's call to arms. Her assessment of modern early childhood classrooms in which "alphabet-as-art" covers the wall space once reserved for drawings and paintings is no mere lament. It is a cautionary tale about what there is to lose in pushing out play for skills-based reading instruction: "[O]ne cannot tamper indefinitely with a magical kingdom" (2004, 31).

In many ways, Paley is an unexpected soldier in the campaign against the academicization of the early childhood literacy curriculum because she might have ignored it. Her work will always be attractive to some subset of the early childhood community, and she was never in any danger from her school's administration of being forced to succumb to the new world order. Her immunity, however, makes her protest all the more invaluable because (as Kirp suggests) her standards are so high. She is not demanding a fantasy play–based early childhood education for the privileged children in her university neighborhood, but for *all* children. Her message is that if early childhood education is to have any impact on closing the achievement gap, it must hold fast to the fundamental achievement of early literacy. This is not isolated alphabet knowledge or even decoding, but the use of oral and written language and narrative to know and to be known. Such a view does not eliminate all teaching of letters, sounds, and other literacy skills in the kindergarten, or even academic ends. It just doesn't prioritize or decontextualize them in the children's eyes. Fantasy play also provides young children with a motive to pursue things literary (Rosenblatt 1978). All of Paley's classroom studies that touch on fantasy play, from *White Teacher* ([1979] 2000) to *In Mrs. Tully's Room* (2001) represent this vantage point.[4]

We can see fantasy play's superiority in developing young children's capacity for discourse and narrativization when children attempt to define or expand upon the imaginary scene they have in mind so others can make sense of it. Paley observes this happening with three-year-old Mollie, who when she first enters preschool is not yet a fluent speaker in everyday life. When Paley questions her about needing more paintbrushes at the painting table, Mollie tries to formulate her answer: "Do you want . . . do I *not* . . . I do *not* want you." In fantasy play, however, her words flow smoothly. Paley overhears her at the play-dough table: "I'm the mommy snake," Mollie says to the other children as she rolls out the clay. She goes on with her pretend: "'Read me a book,' says the baby snake" (1986, 5). Fantasy play also leads its users away from concrete thinking to problem solving and abstract understanding. Paley gives us the example of Rose, who becomes confused in trying to act out the part of the brother who swallows the sea in *The Five Chinese Brothers*. Unfortunately, she hears "sea" as "seed" and reaches to put a bead she found on the rug in her mouth. The other children want to know what she is doing. Rose, aware of their disapproval, becomes silent and stops listening. Recognizing her distress, Wally intervenes by reinventing the problem as fantasy. "Pretend a fairy changed the seed into a big ocean," he tells her. "They call that a sea sometimes and sometimes they call it an ocean. Now just drink it up like the man in the book. Blow up your cheeks like this. Then blow it out this way" (1981, 50). Rose did, smiling, says Paley.

Vygotsky (1978) distinguished school-age instruction in reading and writing from early childhood education in terms of its meaning for the child. Of central importance is his belief that teaching of reading and writing is appropriate in early childhood education only when it is "organized in such a way as to be necessary for something" in the young child's life. His words cast a long shadow over recent trends.

❖

In a 2006 article called "The Business of Intimacy: Hurricanes and Howling Wolves," Paley recounts a visit to a Wisconsin kindergarten during the first few days after Hurricane Katrina struck New Orleans. In her classic in-the-moment style, she describes how children in the doll corner merge newscasters, a storm, Goldilocks, the wolf, 911, and the Nationals into a spontaneous drama. Attempting to simulate high winds and rain, they send blankets, pillows, and dress-ups flying. One child yells, "The water is coming in." Two children scream, "Get on the roof." Suddenly, cries of "the river is broken" are heard from all over the classroom. Blocks tumble, and waves rise in the water table. The teacher, seeking to contain the storm, joins in. "Let's count to twenty," she says, "So the water can go down. Pretend we're the National Guard. . . . Time to clean up the streets and the houses" (2006, 11).

From the perspective of praxis, a pedagogy of meaning requires the preschool and kindergarten teacher to create classroom life in and across three contexts: the probable, the personal, and the instructive.

To prepare for the probable, she must organize the classroom activities and schedule based on what she knows the children will find meaningful according to the prevailing literature and standards, as well as the cultural milieu in which they take place. This requires her in-depth knowledge of child development, beginning with the premise that she and the children "are not pursued by the same monsters, and do not look for the same escape routes" (Paley 1986, 109). This is reason enough for fantasy play to take center stage. However, this primary role for fantasy play does not exclude the teaching of "content" through such appealing activities as singing the alphabet song or learning to write one's name. As children mature, they may enjoy some further instruction in this area. Art, science, math, and other content-based activities can also be part of the day. But, as Paley reminds us, "There are teacher guides and handbooks for math and science, but none for howling wolves and hurricanes." She quotes Virginia Woolf by way of example: "The writer must get in touch with his reader by putting before him something he recognizes, which therefore stimulates his imagination and makes him willing to cooperate in the far more difficult business of intimacy" (Paley 2006, 13). The fact that Woolf is addressing not what children do in pretend play, but what writers and readers do in story transaction is not off base; it is Paley's very message about the young child's use of story. Young children *are* writers when they use the psychological reach of story-based play to invite others to join them in their living story. But, regrettably, Paley cautions, the children/writers may not find a place in the kindergarten or preschool. They must be invited in by another, more powerful literary figure in the classroom: the teacher/writer. It is she who must first "write" a story about a classroom that has the time, space, and psychological latitude for play to thrive. In short, the first lesson in a pedagogy of meaning requires the teacher to give time for pretend play in the curriculum. This does not mean that nothing else happens, only that fantasy play happens daily and for a reasonable amount of time.

The second lesson in a pedagogy of meaning is the belief in fantasy play's immediate purpose or personal meaning. In essence, this means respecting young children's search for truth or what they know to be true about themselves and the world (Paley 1997). In this sense, a pedagogy of meaning embodies a sociocultural view of teaching and learning that assumes no experience or knowledge is independent of either interest or desire, both of which are shaped by the child's social world. The teacher must therefore incorporate into the curriculum what she knows individual children will find meaningful, including finding ways to formally and informally acknowledge the child's home culture and language. Possibilities range from having family members visit, to providing books in a child's native language in the classroom, to keeping track of world events that may affect an individual family or its subculture. A pedagogy of meaning also means seeing how play can support what makes a particular child's life distinct. The teacher must think to include certain dress-up clothes in the doll corner, such as a doctor's coat for the child who was recently hospitalized, or the dramatization of a book on dinosaurs or race cars for the children fixated on those topics. As the children grow older, attention to personal interests will eventually require not only lessons in how to write their friends' names so they can send notes, but discussions of the latest superhero movies and permission to act out these stories in the block corner. Teaching for meaning in the context of the personal also necessitates that the passions of individual children be allowed to influence the larger curriculum. As Paley documents in *The Girl with the Brown Crayon*, this is precisely what happened when she allowed Reeny's interest in children's author Leo Lionni to spread throughout the curriculum. Paley wonders how Reeny knew that the "whole point of school is to find a common core of references without blurring our own special profiles" (1997, viii). But if Reeny doesn't yet know this consciously, the teacher must.

The third lesson from Paley's pedagogy of meaning is to recognize that pretend play's focus on problem-solving skills, its promotion of a "What if?" view of the world (Paley 2004, 92), brings immediate benefits to instruction. By making the children's thinking public and available in the moment, pretend play gives teachers a laboratory to study what they need to learn next. Pedagogically, this means the teacher must inhabit the zone of proximal development created by fantasy play. It also means the teacher must relinquish control over what the children *should be* thinking and actively embrace what they *are* thinking, individually and as members of a group. This requires that she ask both specific and general questions of what the children do and say. And she must participate in the play in whatever way is necessary to sustain or further it. In essence, Paley says, teachers must agree to "act the part of the Greek chorus" in the children's fantasy play, offering "visible support" through commentary that extends it, even when they are too young to comment on it themselves (2004, 24, 73). A teacher's verbal support of play can extend or deepen the children's social, cognitive, and linguistic capacities. It can also help children manage their ideas within the confines of real classrooms.

3

Storytelling and Story Acting: Meaning Extended

Before he is told he cannot invent the world, he will explain everything.

VIVIAN PALEY, *Wally's Stories: Conversations in the Kindergarten*

In this chapter I examine Paley's storytelling curriculum, offering a methodological overview and considering the role of the curriculum in Paley's pedagogy of meaning of play-based learning. I share my own introduction to storytelling and story acting, before turning to what the experience looks like from the perspective of a New York City teacher who recently became a teacher of stories. I inquire about the research support for storytelling and story acting, as well as its explicit benefits to reading and writing development. In the last section, I look at the lessons learned from a pedagogy of meaning through storytelling.

⊕

The development of Vivian Paley's pedagogy of meaning can be seen in the changing nature of her "contract" with the children in her classroom. In the beginning, she tells us, she agreed to help children with the problems she thought they needed to solve. In time, she rewrote the contract so as to help them solve the problems that were revealed in their play. But even this was not enough. By her own admission, her crowning achievement as a teacher was to create a system through which the children put their play into "formal narratives," which they could then act out and "connect their ideas with the ideas of others" (1990, 18). These formal narratives became her storytelling curriculum.

For the preschool and kindergarten teacher caught between the children's "need" for fantasy play (Vygotsky 1978) and the growing demand for early literacy instruction, Paley's storytelling curriculum stands with arms outstretched in either direction. Like fantasy play, it is steeped in benefits to young children's social, emotional, and cognitive health. And, like fantasy play, it holds implicit benefits for academic preparedness in terms of oral language and narrative development. The storytelling curriculum, however, extends these benefits to directly influence young children's knowledge of a variety of literacy subskills, from letter recognition to vocabulary (Cooper et al. 2007), as well as their control over and response to written narrative. That so much can be accomplished with little more than paper, pen, the child's imagination, and a few friends is the great wonder of Paley's storytelling curriculum, and the second critical tool in her pedagogy of meaning.

STORYTELLING AND STORY ACTING: THE BASICS

To start at the beginning, the storytelling curriculum involves two interdependent and sequential activities.[1] In the first, storytelling, or dictation, the child tells a story to the teacher. (The issue of content is discussed below.) Next, in story acting, the child acts out the story with the assistance of classmates, who are either performers or audience members. Given that any curriculum competes for precious time and resources in the preschool and kindergarten, storytelling and story acting are amazingly efficient and inexpensive. Teachers are always glad to discover the almost negligible cost of materials (paper, pen, large binder, and plastic slipcases to hold stories). And the impact on the schedule is minor compared to the many benefits of the storytelling curriculum. In my experience as a teacher and mentor to classroom teachers, dictation averages less than ten minutes per child and often goes much faster. Dramatization of each story takes only a few minutes. Though some teachers might worry that even twelve or so minutes a day is more than they can devote to an individual child, it must be remembered that no story is experienced only by the author. Ideally, teachers would fit in as many stories as children desire. More typically, teachers fit in two or three stories a day on two or three days a week, depending on the age of the children. (Three- and four-year-olds cannot wait as long between turns as kindergartners, but their stories are usually shorter.) With careful planning, teachers will find time in the schedule to meet the demand. This is not always possible, of course. Thus, the only hard and fast rule when it comes to scheduling is that the children can predict when the storytelling is going to happen and when their turn will be. A predictable, regular routine not only helps them tolerate the time between turns, it suggests to them that stories are synonymous with the lives they lead, and life should not be relegated to special occasions. As to where dictation and dramatization occur in the classroom, the only obvious requirement is that teachers be able to see the rest of the room from where they sit. In some classrooms a "storytelling table" can be set aside or can double up with the art table. In others, space constraints make it better for the teacher to use a clipboard so as to be able to sit anywhere in the room during dictation. Most often, dramatization occurs on the class rug, now renamed "the stage," around which the young audience sits in a circle. Paley reflects on her storytelling methodology in several books (1981, 1992, 1997, 2004). *The Boy Who Would Be a Helicopter* provides perhaps the most useful description (1990, 21–26).

Storytelling or dictation

Most "storytelling" teachers opt for Paley's original vision of a one-on-one experience during dictation, still welcoming, of course, young volunteer listeners and commentators drawn over from other activities. By contrast, in recent years, Paley has felt the advantages of taking dictation from an individual while the class is sitting in a circle, especially when the children are very young.[2] In the original version, a child's storytelling turn takes place when the other children are engaged in free play or focused activities. These range from the traditional, such as the housekeeping corner, to the academic, such as the math center. Taking dictation during this time reinforces the notion of choice and storytelling's connection to play.

In the absence of either a dedicated free play period or center time, or if the teacher does not wish to be occupied during either time, storytelling has been known to occur during independent reading or seatwork time.

What exactly defines dictation varies from child to child, and from age group to age group. Many storytellers just tell their story straight out, and the teacher writes it down with little intervention. More often, however, the teacher acts as a "participatory" scribe during the dictation process by asking question of clarification. This helps storytellers tell the story they mean to tell, and it can greatly extend their narrative skills and understanding. Other forms of participation involve making content or editing suggestions. The teacher often takes the lead:

TEACHER: Do you know how you want your story to begin?
CHILD: My uncle and my grannie . . .

The teacher here might interrupt to ask which grandmother the child is referring to, the one who lives in the city or the one she visits in Ohio. She can also make a comment on the story's content or ask a question to help broaden the young storyteller's original intention. "Ah, another Pokemon story. Will it be the same one you've told before or a new one?" She might offer support throughout the entire dictation in a process I've described elsewhere as the "psychological aside" (Cooper 1993). "Hmm. That's pretty funny. I didn't know Pokemon guys were so silly." Often she will ask the storyteller to clarify a point. "Help me out here. Aren't there lots of Pokemon characters? What is the exact name of the one you're going to tell about?" The children tolerate what occasionally seems to visitors in the classroom as an affront to their authorial rights. According to Paley, the children's priority is having the story make sense to everyone in the class, the actors, audience, and narrator. In other words, they are invested in their story succeeding with the other children. She demonstrates the process of clarification in her responses to Arlene's enthusiastic storytelling:

"Yaash! They falled in a trap!"
"Who did? The witches?"

"No, there is a bad guy in the trap."
"So, there is another bad guy besides the witches?"
"These are good witches." (1990, 22)

At all times, of course, the teacher must indicate that the child has full control over the content of the story.

Paley limits the children's stories to one page, which I also recommend. Children who question the limitation are satisfied when told it leaves more time for other things in the schedule. If a story seems unfinished to the child or the teacher, there is always the option of "to be continued." The story can be reread when the storyteller is finished to confirm that the teacher has captured it correctly or to invite revisions.

Story acting or dramatization

Dramatization can occur after a natural break in the day's activities, after free play, before the read aloud, or before dismissal. It often doubles as a transitional activity between an active period, like free play or lunch, and a calmer one, like seatwork or music. The teacher now turns from scribe to producer. The author and whatever classmates are needed to act out the story are either called to the stage before the drama begins or enter from their space on the rug as their parts come up. The remaining children make up the audience. Actors are chosen in several ways, all of which reflect a view of fairness. I prefer to have the author select any child's name from the class list who has not yet participated. This prevents children from choosing only their immediate friends, mixes up established playgroups, and yet offers some sense of choice. No child from the classroom list, though, may be chosen again until the list has been exhausted. Many teachers I have worked with firmly believe the author has the right to choose whatever actors he or she wants, regardless of the potential for favoritism. Paley herself wants to actively avoid favoritism, and she goes one step further by limiting the author's choice to only his or her own part. All the other parts are assigned by the order of the class list.

Preferably, all stories are dramatized the day they are dictated. Not only does this make the children happy, it invites immediate feedback from the group on their thinking, as the stories often invite discussion. The performance of the story is always a rather low-key affair with no props or rehearsals. To reinforce the sense of narrative and apprise the actors of what they will need to do, the teacher may read the story aloud before the dramatization begins, though Paley typically doesn't do this because of time constraints. She rereads the story only as the actors perform their parts. Ad-libbing of both dialogue and action is common, and generally approved by the teacher, though she rarely calls attention to it. As both director and producer, the teacher offers suggestions to increase dramatic effect. "Is that what a hungry lion sounds like?" she might ask. Expectations, however, are not high. Over time, the children will learn to exploit the content of their stories as they see fit. With few exceptions, dramatizations are staged only once. Early on in my experience with storytelling I instituted a "no touching" rule that is quite valuable in reducing accidents from overenthusiastic actors, whether they are Power Rangers kickboxing or mamas putting babies to bed.

Let me acknowledge that Paley was not the first to invite young children to dictate stories. Dictation has been utilized in language experience approaches to early literacy, in which teachers record children's plans, ideas, responses to classroom events, and so on. Nor of course did she introduce dramatization into the early childhood curriculum. What she is to be credited for, however, is marrying the two activities into an organized, regular event for systematic use in the early childhood curriculum.

It is important to add that Paley strongly advocates the dramatization of adult-authored stories as a complementary activity to storytelling and story acting in the classroom. The regular dramatization of literature not only provides children with vocabulary and themes to borrow for their personal stories, it also provides them with iconic and cultural symbols and images, from wicked witches to tricksters to peacemakers. This cultural information adds to their storehouse of prior knowledge and helps them access all sorts of literature and text over time.

STORYTELLING AND STORY ACTING IN PRACTICE

The storytelling curriculum, like fantasy play, stems from humble origins in Paley's pedagogy of meaning. Wally, of *Wally's Stories:*

Conversations in the Kindergarten, was Paley's first storyteller and story actor. One day, feeling sorry for Wally because he had been on the time-out chair twice, Paley asked if he would like to write, that is, dictate, a story:

> "You didn't teach me how to write yet," he said.
> "You just tell *me* the story, Wally. I'll write the words."
> "What should I tell about?"
> "You like dinosaurs. You could tell about dinosaurs."
> He dictated this story.
> "The dinosaur smashed down the city. And the people got mad and put him in jail."
> "Is that the end?" I asked. "Did he get out?"
> "He promised he would be good so the people let him go home and his mother was waiting." (1981, 11)

It is easy to see how the story Wally told could satisfy a little boy having a hard day. But it was Paley's on-the-spot decision to let Wally act the story out with his classmates that ultimately won the day for him and led Paley to discover that the children were more than eager to further fantasy play's role in the classroom through storytelling and story acting. "For this alone," Paley writes, "the children would give up play time, as it was the true *extension of play*" (1981, 12, emphasis mine). Though sometimes described as a language experience activity (see Van Allen 1976), the storytelling curriculum differs in many ways, beginning with the fact that participation is voluntary and the stories are always dramatized. Many teachers agree with Paley that when dictation is not accompanied by dramatization only a small number of girls, and even fewer boys, appear interested. "It had always seemed enough," Paley says, "just to write the children's words. Obviously, it was not. The words did not sufficiently represent the action, which needed to be shared" (1981, 12). Furthermore, as we have seen, teachers play a much more active role in the dictation process than in traditional language experience activities, not hesitating to suggest changes to the children's language choice or story content.

Wally's Stories is Paley's second book. In one way or another the storytelling curriculum makes its appearance in all the books and articles that follow it. The similarities of the curriculum to informal play are plain to see. For example, Paley's question about whether Wally's dinosaur got out of jail is a totem of how the dictated story creates its own zone of proximal development, which the teacher may utilize to extend the child's thinking (Vygotsky 1978). The dinosaur's promise to be good also allows Wally to practice self-regulation through narrative, to behave more maturely through his story than the boy who had spent the day in trouble. In this way, Wally creates potential for change in the future, despite the reality he cannot escape on the given day. Other similarities between the storytelling curriculum and fantasy play include its dependency on what Paley calls the "social art of language" (1990, 23). This is the language-driven give-and-take and exchange of ideas among friends in the dictation and dramatization processes. For example, when Reeny is dictating her princess story in Paley's *The Girl with the Brown Crayon*, she does not hesitate to reject Bruce's inappropriate suggestion for how the prince should talk to the princess.

> And he says, "Hi, baby?" Bruce snickers.
>
> "Uh-hh," Reeny replies with great dignity, "'cause, see, a prince don't talk that way. He say, 'Good morning, madam. How is your highness today?'" (1997, 3)

We know from the way her larger story unfolds that Reeny's reaction is in part driven by her construction of her racial identity. But Paley further interprets Reeny's position as evidence of the child's belief in the language of story to represent whatever identity she is reaching for in the narrativized play. It says, in effect, "This is who I am and, so far, this is what I know to be true" (4). Paley writes that at first she did not allow other children to interrupt storytelling because she did not understand it as a "shared process" and cultural event (1990, 23). But this understanding accounts for the children's tolerance of improvised dialogue in the dramatizations. It also bespeaks their interest in playing with language as they move both freely and with encouragement from its decontextualized to its contextualized uses.

However, although the storytelling curriculum overlaps with informal fantasy play in Paley's pedagogy of meaning, it also provides new opportunities that have obvious long-term implications for early literacy development. First, much like the best children's literature, the written text offers young children an opportunity to bring order to the feelings, thoughts, and emotions that characterize informal fantasy play. The persistent pursuit of friendship in play is a good example. As we saw earlier, story-based informal play offers many occasions for exploring how to make friends and what friendship means. At the same time, young children are not always able to bring their private feelings to the surface in play, and thus their play is not always as efficacious as they need. The written story, by contrast, is always a public creation and acted out with the group. It essentially functions as an open invitation from the author to the whole class: "Come play with me" (Paley 1981, 167). Shared meaning and participation is the very point of the story. In addition, as Paley notes, the existence of a "script" means that the denouement is guaranteed (122). This certainty not only reduces the risk of failure and enables cooperation, it allows the players, and even the audience members, to safely practice how to be a friend.

Paley tips her pedagogical hat once again when she interprets freely across stories to help children find the invitations to play, the hidden opportunities for friendship. She describes it as her "habit of drawing invisible lines between the children's images" (1990, xi). She believes it embodies her very best teaching.

> "Come listen to Katie's story," I call to Jason. "This mother pig does something that reminds me of you." . . .
>
>> There is the three pigs. And the mother pig is there. Then the wolfs huffs down the brick house. And the mother puts it back together.
>
> "That makes me think of the way you fix your helicopter," I say. (1990, xi)

Paley reports how Jason and Katie then smile at each other, which tells her she is growing nearer to creating the classroom community she is seeking for the children.

Unlike informal pretend play, play in the storytelling curriculum also gives children opportunity to actively reflect on, if not rehearse, a text not one's own. This is a critical element of comprehension that is poorly served in most preschool and kindergarten classrooms by instruction that stresses inappropriate metacognitive strategies following the teacher's reading aloud (Cooper, 2009). Reflection in the storytelling curriculum is promoted through the chance to "eavesdrop" on dictation and to engage directly with questions or suggestions about the plot. Ongoing membership in the theater audience also directs attention to how other children envision the world. The young actors, who are at once removed from the author's thinking and yet expected to embody the text in action, get even closer to what it means to get into someone else's head. Paley says this nuanced engagement with each other's minds is the motivation for joining in the process: "The children's stories, lacking great plots and memorable prose, answered one of the children's most important questions: what do other children think about" (1981, 66)? Of all the contributions of the storytelling curriculum to early literacy development, this may be the most invaluable.

From a purely literary or creative writing perspective, however, the children's investment in what other children think has its limitations. Inevitably, it leads to highly unoriginal stories and the intrusion of popular culture into the classroom, since young children often "think about" what's going on in the world outside the classroom. There is no greater proof of this phenomenon than the superhero story. Nevertheless, many teachers who are open to the storytelling curriculum want to draw the line at superheroes. They complain as much about the repetitiousness as they do about the violence. Paley urges us to offer the superhero a home in the preschool and kindergarten. Her reasoning ties back to young children's unassailable need for friendship: "The stories do not reflect the qualities of a particular child or encourage variations," she writes. "If the child's name is omitted from a superhero story, the authorship is unrecognizable. This must be the point, then, I decided. Such stories are used to mask, not reveal individuality" (1981, 129). I find this an extraordinary insight into the lives of young children. Adults often fail to appreciate that the young child's relationship to other children is rarely casual. In fact, the story that best helps young children gain perspective on their world only *looks* second or third hand. However counterintuitive, all stories are stubbornly personal—including the superhero story—even when they demand sameness (Cooper 1993). The developmental task the superhero story symbolizes is the integration of one's individual and group identities. Early childhood teacher education has for too long addressed this issue only by way of loss, which does not serve or celebrate the process. I explore this idea further in my chapters on Paley's pedagogy of fairness. In terms of early literacy development, however, we should see the young children's unoriginal stories not as a loss of individuality, but as the preservation of their individuality until they are ready to come out from under what Paley calls the "mask" (1981, 64).

In a related vein, Nicolopoulou and her colleagues have conducted several studies on the "gendered subcultures" that the stories of both boys and girls reveal (Nicolopoulou 1996, 1997a, 1997b; Nicolopoulou and Richner 2004; and Nicolopoulou, Scales, and Weintraub 1994). As the authors note, the result is a steady parade of stereotyped characters—from unicorns and butterflies to police and monsters—that any teacher of storytelling and story acting will recognize. This does not mean the children are binding themselves to these stereotypes for the long run. Early childhood educator Connie Floyd has observed that the children use the storytelling curriculum to try on roles needed at that moment, much like clothes in their closets. Some will be discarded; others will be matched with something else. I would also contend that all gendered stories reflect the storyteller's attempt to gain control over stereotypes that threaten to define them.

Nicolopoulou and her colleagues also find that the stories young children tell and dramatize allow them to utilize their "symbolic imaginations" to both appropriate and reinvent gender roles in the service of a large goal they call "worldmaking" (in addition to the works cited above, see Richner and Nicolopoulou 2001). "[P]art of what makes children's storytelling so revealing . . . is that it plays a vital role in their own efforts to make sense of the world and their place in it" (Nicolopoulou, Scales, and Weintraub 1994, 102). The concept of sense-making, which is of course a boost to literacy development, runs throughout the literature on children's narrative (Bruner 1986; Engel 1995). From a sociocultural vantage point, sense-making is always related to the larger culture. As Dyson and Genishi suggest, "Stories are an important tool for proclaiming ourselves as cultural beings . . . That is, we evidence cultural membership both through our ways of crafting stories and in the very content of our tales" (1994, 4).

The merger of written narrative, friendship, bearing witness, and gender development all come together in a story by Martin, a five-year-old boy in a New York City public school, who takes his turn at storytelling and story acting not long after his teacher has introduced the option. Martin's completed story reads:

> Justice League 1
>
> The generals were trying to get the big bad robots. A small robot dog came out and tried to eat Robin's plane. Then the Justice League came. Batman dropped a missile on the big robots and froze them with sonic gas. They were all in a line. All the bad people that were inside the robots came out and started fighting. Then the Justice League started fighting, too. Then, the whole entire Justice League started fighting rough. And the bad guys, too. Then the whole entire Justice League stopped. Then, the bad guys stopped. It was another bad guy. Then the whole entire Justice League came (Batman, Robin, Wonder Woman, Martian Manhunter). And then they all went home, but Martian Manhunter didn't because he had to stay at the watchtower.
>
> The End

Martin's is a fairly typical story for a kindergarten-aged boy. Whatever creative potential was present in the first line was dashed by the introduction of the superheroes in the third. Paley's theory on superheroes has prepared us for its blandness and its boy properties. But Martin's story tells us so much more than the fact that a gendered response to the world is still very much with us well into the first decade of the twenty-first century. I happen to be visiting in Martin's class the day he tells his story. Before he proceeds to the storytelling table, I notice him quietly make a point of telling several of the other boys in the class that he is going to tell a "Justice League" story that day. His tone and body language suggest he is letting them know something very special. The teacher, who happens to catch the same moment, turns and explains to me that *Justice League* is an after-school television show that has caught on with most of the boys in this class. Clearly, Martin is indicating his unity with the group. George, one of the boys Martin has spoken to, comes over to the storytelling table. Martin is still standing up, looking around at the other boys in the room. At the most basic level, Martin is trading well beyond the street value of superheroes in general; he is working with something that will define his particular kindergarten era, just as Star Wars characters and Teenage Mutant Ninja Turtles defined past kindergartens. And so he begins. "Can you make it say Justice League up there?" he asks his teacher. He points to the top of the page. "Make it so you can see it."

After the teacher writes down the first two sentences about the generals fighting the bad robots, and the little robot who tries to eat Robin's plane, George observes (a little harshly, I think), "The Justice League isn't in here." Martin, sitting now, does not look up, but without skipping a beat dictates next, "Then the Justice League came." I am aware of what I've promised here, he seems to be saying. George stays and listens to the rest.

The teacher also has a role in the superhero story: approval and assistance. Both are a blessing to the superheroes in her class, who are banned from most arenas they want to visit. She asks for clarification as to what "fighting rough" means without having to scold Martin for behavior in real life that is too physical. Martin indicates with his arms that it is more powerful fighting than usual. "This is only part one," he says cheerfully, and his teacher smiles and nods. As he gets near the end of his story, his teacher asks which specific superheroes from the Justice League is he talking about. She reminds him that they will need to know so as to choose children to play different parts. He tells her Batman, Robin, Wonder Woman, and Martian Manhunter. The teacher notes that there are generals and robots, too, in the story. There are so many people in his play, she says, they won't all be able to fit on the rug they use for a stage; they will have to imagine some of the characters. Who are the generals, she asks, do you want them to be acted out or imagined? Martin thinks for a moment as if envisioning the drama in his head and says the class can imagine them. Then George and another boy quickly interject to ask if Martin will give them a role in the drama. According to story acting rules, George cannot be chosen, as he has recently had a turn in another child's drama. The teacher assures me he knows this, but, still, he asks. They always do, the teacher tells me. Predictably, Martin casts himself as Batman. When the class convenes for dramatization, the teacher announces that Martin has told a Justice League story. The boys cheer, including George, and Martin smiles. The dramatization comes off without a hitch.

Teachers of storytelling and story acting find that stories that reflect the "truth of children's lives" (Coles 1986) are mostly fictional. Rosenblatt (1978) suggests that the aesthetic stance dominates in early childhood, even in the face of facts. Young children's dinosaur stories are a good example of this. But "everyday" stories are usually fictionalized, too, as real people and real scenarios find their way into make-believe situations. As in informal fantasy play, the written stories offer children opportunities to problem solve, to "be a head taller than" they are in real life (Vygotsky 1978, 102). Also as in informal fantasy play, young children use stories to interrogate what they know about the world—and what they might know.

It is not surprising that the characters and themes of popular culture often find their way from informal play to the written page, but so do external concerns. I have taken stories from young children that involve everything from drug dealers to dead grandmothers to broken promises of trips to Disneyland. I have also taken stories that tell of perfect families, fairytale birthday parties, and only loving siblings. Some are based on truth, some on fiction, but all are based on need. Paley cautions against reading children's plot lines too literally (though we must be alert, of course, for real problems). Like the rest of us, young children seek the universal as often as they seek the particular.

Scribing and directing gives vigilant teachers a front row seat to what Rosenblatt calls the "private overtones" of young children's "entrance into language" (1981, 78). These overtones take their shadings from past experiences that act as reference points in the children's thinking but are unknowable to teachers who have not listened well enough. For example, a wide-awake teacher will realize that a young storyteller's oblique reference to "peoples you don't know" (from a story told by a New York City kindergartner) speaks volumes about her trip to grandma's house in Puerto Rico. A teacher who listens in on parent-child conversations at the cubbies in the morning realizes that the sudden appearance of a carpenter who fixes the chairs and tables in the child's reimagined Goldilocks story is none other than the one putting a new addition on her real house. And if the teacher pays attention to popular culture—as she should—she knows that the scary house that all the children must run past in the dramatization is the same as the one in the movie the storyteller saw over the weekend. Paley understands how important this process is:

> If readiness for school has meaning, it is to be found first in the children's flow of ideas, their own and those of their peers, families, teachers, books, and television, from play into story and back into more play. It was when I asked the children to dictate their stories and bring them to life again on a stage that the connections between play and analytical thinking became clear. The children and I were nourishing the ground and opening our seed packets, ready to plant our garden of ideas and identities. (2004, 11)

Rosenblatt's 1981 analysis of teachers' options in guiding young children's "literary transaction" offers key advice for teachers of storytelling and story acting that speaks to the current rush to literacy subskills and strategy instruction. She writes that teachers have two choices in the use of literature (story) with young children. The first is to pursue conversation that brings forth and cultivates young children's natural predilection toward an aesthetic appreciation of story, that is, their personal understanding of the story. Teachers must ask how the story speaks to what the children are seeking to learn from the story. She calls this method the interpretation of story via the "broad base of the iceberg" and sees it as essential to comprehension. The second choice calls for teachers to direct young children toward an efferent stance, that is, the public meaning they should carry away. This is the "tip of the iceberg" approach (1981, 73). Rosenblatt argues that when teachers move too quickly to press young children to adopt an "efferent" stance toward stories by using them to teach reading skills and other lessons, they risk reducing young children's future interest in literature and story and thus compromise their literacy futures. She also maintains that the "tip of the iceberg" approach is unnecessary in the early years of schooling: "Paradoxically, when the transactions are lived through for their own sake, they will probably have as by-products the educational, informative, social, and moral values for which literature is often praised" (83).

Rosenblatt issued her warning about the consequences of decreasing children's aesthetic response to literature more than twenty-five years ago. How much more significance it holds today in light of recent curricula that replace children's informal, but intimate relationships to stories in the classroom with a more formal program of skill-based instruction around stories.

GOOD NEWS: MORE QUESTIONS THAN ANSWERS

Like Paley, my discovery of the uses of storytelling and story acting for young children occurred while I was still a classroom teacher. I also experienced it as a director of an early childhood program in which all the teachers implemented the storytelling curriculum, and then as director of the School Literacy and Culture Project in the Rice University Center for Education, which I founded in 1990 to help teachers across Houston bring the storytelling curriculum to their classrooms. The School Literacy and Culture Project is the only organization in the country devoted to disseminating the storytelling curriculum.

If Paley credits fantasy play with making her a teacher, I credit the storytelling curriculum with keeping me in teaching and leading me, ultimately, to teacher education. The truth is that in my first few years in the classroom, I worried a lot about being a good teacher. But I worried more that I didn't know how to become one. By good fortune, before I had ever read one of her books, I unexpectedly found myself implementing Paley's storytelling and story acting activities and never looked back.

It was the early 1980s and I had been a preschool and kindergarten teacher in Chicago for about four years. My newly acquired master's degree had taught me to value play as the heart of the curriculum. I can recall the deep satisfaction I felt when the classroom floor filled with the children's block replicas of O'Hare airport or when the domestic drama in the housekeeping corner rivaled anything on daytime TV. Still, I was anxious to be a responsible, up-to-date teacher. In my second year after moving into the kindergarten, I was listening carefully to rumors in the field that the play-based, "academic-free" kindergarten had lost its usefulness. Back-to-basics was on the horizon. Of course, I couldn't know then that back-to-basics was a mere spray of the tidal wave that would come crashing down on kindergarten shores two decades later. In any case, a scouting trip to the first grade in which several of my former kindergartners were students told me everything I wanted to know. The teacher clearly had higher expectations of the children who started first grade with a toolkit of literacy subskills than those who did not. She even seemed to like them better. I was both appalled and nervous. Perhaps hers was just an individual case, but I was still sure I couldn't ignore this information. My school's director gave me permission to experiment.

Luckily for the children, I didn't have a clue how to create an "academic" reading and writing curriculum for kindergarten. The best system I could come up with involved homemade worksheets that emphasized letter sounds, handwriting, and beginning math facts, which the children filled out during table time. In comparing my plans to what kindergarten children are expected to do today, I realize it could have been much worse. But while many of the children easily blew through the tasks on their way to everyone's real interest—free play—too many did not. Those who seemed to crave free play most of all often just gave up. Even today I can see them sitting mournfully as each passing minute at the table meant one less in the block corner. "Finish your work," I'd coax, kneeling beside them. I'd whisper my bribe in to their ears, "Then you can go *play*" (Cooper 1993, 34). In the end, the children's unhappiness at giving up play time bothered me even more than the problems I imagined them facing in first grade as products of the old academic-free kindergarten. I grew dissatisfied and thought about leaving teaching.

My reprieve came when I agreed to be a research assistant to Gillian McNamee and Joan McLane of the Erikson Institute. They were conducting a research study investigating the impact of Paley's work in storytelling and story acting on young children's narrative development (see McNamee et al. 1985). They asked if I would be interested in participating. Among other things, this meant making room in my schedule for children to dictate stories to me and then dramatize them under my direction. I knew nothing about Paley at that point, and only a little more about young children's narrative development. However, a lifelong engagement with stories and children's books, plus my newfound interest in reading instruction, prompted me to think that working with Gill and Joan might carry me another year. Fortunately, I was lucky enough to be co-teaching at the time with Lauranita Dugas, a very experienced teacher who had the wisdom and generosity to encourage my interests. I will be forever grateful to Lauranita for this. Many more young teachers would stay in the field if they could get the type of support I got from her in those years.

Little did I know that becoming a teacher who implemented storytelling and story acting meant that questions I couldn't answer about young children's development would became a routine part of my day. Little did I imagine the exciting breadth of questions I would stumble upon. The ones I liked best exemplified the fusion of children's inner and classroom lives. I remember that after only a month or so of storytelling and story acting, I felt on fire with the need to know just what is a Darth Vader really, and why did the children care so much about him anyway? And what, by the way, is an *aretoodeetoo*? (Obviously, I missed the movie.) I also wondered what "falling in a hole"—a phrase many of the kids injected into their stories—could possibly mean deep down. And why was Christina always chosen to play the princess? Soon I found myself talking to my family and friends about why Nicole would act in stories but not dictate one. Unexpectedly, taking dictation from young children meant I couldn't help but notice and encourage their emerging literacy subskills. Their learning was coming alive right there in front of me in a way I had never seen in the table activities. And the children were learning through each other, as would happen, for example, when Colin would leave his playing just to watch me take down another child's story. I would glance up to see him carefully tracking the transfer of speech to print. I could not reconcile this with his recent classification as "educationally mentally handicapped" by the Chicago Board of Education. Colin's behavior made me decide to keep careful watch on all the children's tracking habits. Soon I moved on to see who could pick out words in isolation. Sometimes I'd pause in my scribing and ask how the storyteller might spell small words like dog or mom, or what sound could be heard at the beginning of certain words. I learned more about young children and literacy subskill acquisition that year than I ever had before.

These may sound like ordinary discoveries to the reader, but they weren't to me. They registered on my young teacher's consciousness with far greater weight than anything before. Prior to storytelling and story acting, there was no regular venue in my classroom that prompted as many questions on so many aspects of children's learning. In this nascent storytelling curriculum, I found the role I wanted as a teacher—the one it seemed I had been searching for in my carefully constructed academic curriculum, but hadn't found. When I took dictation and led the children in dramatization, I went from a mere director of learning to listener, observer, and detective; I became a teacher of stories and a student of teaching. "I don't understand, Thomas," I'd interrupt. "Is Superman in the story, too, or was Batman just thinking about him?" I also became an instructional leader. What might Thomas know or ask or discover, if only I could phrase my inquiries or responses just right? And how might I consider this as preparation for first grade?

In the years since, I have trained and guided many, many teachers in the storytelling curriculum through my work with the School Literacy and Culture Project, and through professional development venues. Along the way, I have had many reminders that my experience as a new teacher of stories is not unusual. They are all a tribute to the power of the storytelling curriculum's ability to help teachers "re-see" the needs of the children in front of her. The latest evidence of this are my exchanges with Laurie Renfroe, a teacher I helped to implement the storytelling curriculum in her New York City Public School kindergarten more than twenty years after my own first kindergarten experience.

STORIES BETWEEN MENTOR AND NOVICE

As always happens when I'm working with a novice teacher of stories, I'm reminded how the passage of time has brought so few changes to the methodology. As I wait for story dictation to begin in Laurie's room one fall morning, I spy the familiar tub of paper, stock of pencils, the clipboard for taking stories anywhere in the room, and the class binder of finished stories.[3] From past experience in this room, I expect the storytellers will come eagerly to tell outlandish stories about their families and treasured superheroes and that they will graciously act in each other's dramas. This is despite the fact that, for all of the reasons I have described thus far regarding the pushdown of academics, Laurie has had more trouble than teachers in the past in squeezing time out of her schedule for storytelling and story acting. Nonetheless, she has been able to settle into a routine that manages to keep the children satisfied, even if it's clear they have to wait longer between turns than they would like.

The only real difference in the way I work with Laurie compared to how I interacted with previous teachers is that she and I are able to communicate regularly through e-mail. In the beginning, we thought it might simply help her to get a few questions answered between visits, but it soon became a way for the two of us to think out loud about storytelling, story acting, and small children. We are now in our fourth year of e-mailing. Appendix D contains many of our exchanges from our first year that highlight the issues and big ideas that occur in "becoming a teacher of stories." I offer a small sample selection below to make the more immediate point that a new teacher's pathway often mimics Paley's discovery of the meaning behind the story, as they also recognize the overlap between the storytelling curriculum and early literacy development. Among other things, Laurie comes to appreciate how the experience stimulates higher-level thinking: "I have heard often that young children cannot think abstractly, but it seems to me that the stories are a place where they are certainly developing/practicing/engaging in the processing of quite deep and abstract ideas."

We start off with an exchange about having the children dramatize an adult-authored story. As noted in the implementation guide in appendix A, it is important to put before children the big ideas and themes in literature that they might want to borrow, either for fantasy play or to put in their own stories. In the beginning, this also serves to orient them to the rules of dramatization before they try to act out the individual stories. My brief assessments of the children's emerging literacy acquisition and Laurie's professional development as a storytelling teacher, (provided here as headings to the e-mails, are meant only to serve as a guide to the exchanges, and don't exclude other interpretations.[4]

The need for stories that feed the imagination
9/17/04
From: Patsy
To: Laurie
Any luck with dramatization?

9/17/04
From: Laurie
To: Patsy
My timing was off on Wed. so I didn't leave enough at the end of the day to do it justice—what I did was just read them *Where the Wild Things Are* and then have them as a whole class be wild things as I read—when the terrible roaring and eye rolling, etc. came up—I'm planning to do it again Monday with different kids being Max etc.—They were very enthusiastic wild things and were irritated at me that I didn't leave enough time to do it correctly! I think I'll shoot for Monday morning to make sure I get it in and leave enough time throughout the week for kids to switch parts, which I can already tell they will want to do. I always forget how small and wiggly they are at the beginning! It is great fun, kindergarten. I feel like I could teach kindergarten my whole life and still have more to learn. I'll let you know how it goes.

Connecting what can be said to what can be written
10/26/04
From: Laurie
To: Patsy
Thanks so much for launching stories in my room—Peter told one today and they acted it out—so interesting—he was so fascinated by my writing down what he said—he was pausing after each syllable sometimes.

The need for mentors: questions about imaginative stories versus those based on real life
10/28/04

From: Laurie
To: Patsy
So. Stories are happening! Thanks again for helping start us off, and for motivating me to try something new. I've taken one dictation each day since Monday and we act it out right after choice time—I love the immediacy of it and so do the storytellers. Most seem to be sticking to real life stories—this must be a result of the writing workshop focus on real life stories. I think it will shake loose of its own accord eventually. (Marisa told a "chapter" in a series of stories she tells at home with her family about an evil being called "Sakemo"—Marisa and her friends lived underground and planned a plan to steal Sakemo's breakfast when he wasn't looking.) Do you recommend telling them outright that they can make a made up story if they seem to be sticking to real life ones? Marshall, who never draws at all (he just sits there during writing workshop unless I work with him for a long time) told a story today about winning a flag at a baseball game—this seems to be much more where he is at than the writing workshop. I wish I didn't have to ask him to write every day.

I have some questions about what kinds of things to keep an eye out for as I'm taking dictation, too, in terms of how they tell their stories. I am watching to see where they are looking, if they are modifying the speed of their speech, etc. What else?

10/29/04
From: Patsy
To: Laurie
I wouldn't attempt to influence the content except where the kids seem stuck or bored. No doubt fantasy will arrive on its own. ("Sakemo" may have done it already. Marshall can be encouraged to tell more abut the flag, even if he just wants to make up some more.) On the other hand, if you're simply curious, you could attempt to lead them out of personal narrative and simply remind them in group that the dictated stories can be about anything they want (except bathroom stories and those that are too—judgment call—violent).

Things that are true and not true: I think I'd stop short of anything more specific. I want to know what kinds of "non-true" things they think about.

The influence of imaginative literature on storytelling; dealing with bad guys
Turn-taking and storytelling
10/29/04
From: Laurie
To: Patsy
Aisha told a story today about a fish whose whole family went on vacation without him and while he was alone he made friends with a good shark and when the bad shark came, the fish and the good shark and the other little fish made a big shark together and chased him away. *Swimmy*-esque. I read *Swimmy* to them yesterday. Interestingly enough, Aisha chose to play the part of the fish's mom who went on vacation—a small part—and wanted Drew (a very calm boy) for the main little fish.

Re: storytelling turn taking—I have just been taking kids that ask about stories and checking them off on the class list—but today both Manuel and Jasmine asked during Aisha's turn if they could tell stories on Monday so I put them down on a list. First Manuel is up and then Jasmine.

10/30/04
From: Patsy
To: Laurie
Re: stories and personal narratives. Enough said. The kids found the loophole.

The attraction of storytelling and story acting
Struggling with writer's workshop in kindergarten
12/21/04
From: Laurie
To: Patsy
We have not done stories for two days because of various holiday choice time projects that needed my full attention. Anyway, the kids have been asking nonstop for stories—I'll do them again

tomorrow so they don't get out of the groove. I wish I could quit doing writing workshop with them—they are so much more interested in writing when they write signs or cards or notes or lists that have to do with their play. I think they would learn to read and write just fine if stories were the literacy program. But I can't.

It's the stories that captivate them and drive them, it's the stories that they ask for. On days we don't have writing workshop it is rare for a kid to ask about it. Hmmmmm.

Imaginative stories
12/23/04
From: Laurie
To: Patsy
It was a delicious day in the kindergarten. Andrew's story was about going swimming at the ocean in Jamaica and seeing an electric eel. When he went back to his house, the lights were busted because the eel had shocked everything. Andrew's Mommy called the Light Man, who put the lights back on. Then everyone went to sleep.

2/10/05
From: Laurie
To: Patsy
Little Blake—you remember Blake—told (surprise) not a superhero story today, but a gingerbread story—the gingerbread man stole a carriage from a lady that had three babies and a fox in it, and then he took it back to the lady at her home. She cooked him and he jumped up and ran away to the fox's home, which was in the water. He melted and the fox ate him. When he first started telling, he said, "No girls is gonna be in this story," but then he wanted Marisa, Emma and Jasmine for the babies, and Kia for the lady. Serious Marshall was the fox. Blake was the gingerbread man. He was so happy, he grinned for the next hour. Rare, for him to grin that much.

2/12/05
From: Laurie
To: Patsy

My friend Susan next door is starting stories in her classroom next week. She has her book all set up. Oh, you would have loved seeing Luke's story yesterday—it was called "THE ORGINAL SPEEDRACER." He fills his stories with dialogue. There was a part where the Speedracer song had to be sung—he asked as I was writing it down if the audience could do that part, "Because we're all actors here," and then before acting the story he taught them how to sing it. They were most obliging and when Luke gave them the cue (it was the part where Speedracer jumped into the car) they all went, "Go Speedracer, all around the town," just as he'd taught them. It was a beautiful moment—funny, but also really beautiful—all of them were so intent, so focused, so absolutely absorbed in creating the world of the story—not one child was off task. That almost never happens during other parts of the day. Except when we are having a discussion about things that matter tremendously to them—like whether or not someone should have to be a bad guy in a game if they don't want to—they all decided emphatically no on that one.

Becoming a knowledgeable teacher of stories

2/13/05
From: Laurie
To: Patsy
I've been working on my list about why stories are so important. Here are some thoughts.

Assessment/Promotion of literacy development

- Children practice making sense
- We support and validate the sense they make in stories
- We notice and support the child's interaction with the dictated text—Does he track? Does he notice letters, spaces, familiar names, sight words, punctuation, left-right motion? Does he slow to match his telling speed to our writing speed?
- We support grammar development as child tells
- Before becoming writers themselves children must have models—they need to see us writing words down often. They are absolutely involved in watching this happen because the stories are their own.

- Children come to understand that writing is for catching meaning on paper.
- Dictation/dramatization helps kids fall in love with storytelling and stories—or rather, they already are in love and we provide space, time, attention (both individual attention while taking dictation and group attention while dramatizing)

Assessment/Promotion of social development

- Stories address issues of fairness; everyone gets a turn on the list both to tell and to act
- Stories provide an opportunity for community building through working things out together (is it too sad to tell a story about a party that not everyone was invited to? Etc.)
- Each child has multiple opportunities to be publicly cherished and celebrated
- Children assert control within the group
- Children see themselves as individuals with individual stories to tell (and direct) and also as members of a group, as audience members and actors. With stories, the idea of individuality and community are not mutually exclusive
- Children tackle/process issues of good/bad, deal with things that frighten them, stories validate this
- Non-threatening forum for children to share their real selves with us/each other

Also—

- Acting the stories fits with their developmental level—out loud, physical
- And the realm of fantasy can enter the room through the structure of storytelling

Assessing stories in context

4/16/05

From: Laurie

To: Patsy

I was looking over the year's stories yesterday and I was noticing just how many real-life stories we were getting at the beginning of the year—it really did take a while for them to bust out—now the balance has tipped in the other direction. Do you think that they were influenced by the heavy doses of personal narrative they were getting at the beginning of the year? Is that typical, for classes to start out with more true-life stories?

Sharing the storytelling experience with beginning teachers
Muddying the waters

5/24/05
From: Patsy
To: Laurie
I hope you realize how important it was for my students to hear you last night. I'm throwing them a curve with storytelling, since all of their placements or experience is either in workshop schools or ones in other states where invented spelling is the sum total of the writing curriculum. I do feel like I've muddied the waters for you. I really wish you could know the Houston group.

5/24/05
From: Laurie
To: Patsy
It was so fun to meet your students.—I feel like we barely touched the surface of the deeper issues. As for my staff meeting, there was, eventually, a lot of interesting thinking through of basic observations of all of our kids on the playground, talking through the kinds of play we see, the kinds of play in dramatic play or in the Duplo center . . . people were wondering how to support superhero-type play within the kind of curriculum we're expected to enforce—I talked about stories and how engaged they are during those times, how important the stories are—easy to fit in! We also talked about how that kind of play is about being on a team, being part of the group—not about being an individual so much. And I wish I could see some other, more developmentally appropriate examples of kindergarten. And yes, you HAVE muddied my waters, and I thank you for it!!!! More mud means more suspended sediment which means . . . my metaphor is dwindling . . . more thinking going on, at any rate. A child development/ed class seems important.

TRANSITIONING TO READING AND WRITING: EVALUATION AND ASSESSMENT

If *Wally's Stories* brings us the origins of the storytelling curriculum, it also signals Paley's initial decision not to engage in the conversation about the formal teaching of reading and writing:

> Visitors were often puzzled to see dozens of stories tacked and taped all over the room, each story dated to show when it was written and acted out. The children left their stories in school if they wanted them to be acted out again. . . .
>
> "Do you teach reading, then?" a visitor asks. "Are these stories the methods you use?"
>
> "Not really," I respond, "although some children do learn to read. We think of ourselves as actors. These stories are our scripts." (1981, 166)

A decade later, Paley is willing to go so far as to recognize the formal learning opportunities that storytelling and story acting comprise, including the development of rules that make the creation of, listening to, and response toward story possible. Tying this to what is required in learning to read and write, she says, "The [telling and performing of stories] encompasses all of language and thought. *It is the academic inheritor of the creative wisdom of play*" (1990, 35, emphasis hers). Finally, although she never reviews the impact of the storytelling curriculum on literacy skills per se, Paley provides in *A Child's Work: The Importance of Fantasy Play* (2004) a formal defense of play's contribution to early literacy development..

Informal fantasy play and the storytelling curriculum share the same theoretical profiles when it comes to language and narrative development, two key requirements of literacy learning (Dickinson and Tabors 2001; Halliday 1973; Snow 1991; Snow and Dickinson 1991; Wells 1986). Both depend on and simultaneously contribute to vocabulary development, extended discourse, and a sense of narrative. The storytelling curriculum, described by Wiltz and Fein (1996) as a "narrative curriculum," entails additional components of written language, such as concepts of print and comprehension of text. (Please see appendix B for the example of five-year-old Mark's stories, which reflect growth in language and narrative development over the school year, as well as various stories from young children in a three-week summer camp prior to their kindergarten year. These samples represent how quickly young children start to mine one another's stories for vocabulary, language, and ideas.) Though empirical studies are limited, my conceptual analysis of the storytelling curriculum's components reveals that when compared to objectives of early literacy instruction found in the literature (see Cooper 2005; Au, Carroll, and Scheu, 2001; Cowen 2003; Dickinson and Tabors 2001; Morrow 1990, 2002; Sadoski 2004; Xue and Meisels 2004), the storytelling curriculum addresses all of the significant indicators of early literacy development, as outlined below:

Early Literacy Development Indicators: Dictation

- Motivation
- Oral language development: verbal expression, vocabulary, sentence patterning, home language, standard English
- Narrative form: how stories work, where stories come from, what stories are composed of, sequencing, plot development, characterization, writing process, authorial intention, and use of imagination
- Conventions of print: how print functions, including directionality, spaces between words, letters, words, and punctuation
- Code: basic principles of encoding and decoding
- Word study: sight words, phonics, spelling comprehension: reading for meaning

Early Literacy Development Indicators: Dramatization

- Motivation
- Narrative form: how stories work, where stories come from, what stories are composed of, sequencing, plot development, characterization, writing process, authorial intention, and use of imagination
- Comprehension: reading for meaning

Using a variety of standardized early literacy measures, a small but growing body of empirical research examines the storytelling curriculum's impact on particular skills and finds promising results. McNamee and colleagues (1985) find that the stories young children tell and act out demonstrate greater narrative growth than stories told by children in a control group. Applebee's 1978 adaptation of Vygotsky's stages of concept development provides the schema for evaluation. More recently, my colleagues and I (Cooper et al. 2007) report on a quasi-experimental study of the storytelling curriculum's impact on young bilingual children's vocabulary development, as well as on their acquisition of literacy subskills. Our findings suggest the curriculum significantly affected growth on both measures.[5] In addition to her work on gender and identity, Nicolopoulou's work on the storytelling curriculum's relationship to narrative development is particularly compelling (Nicolopoulou, 1996, 1997a, 2002; Nicolopoulou, McDowell, and Brockmeyer 2006). [6] Among her key findings, as we have seen, the storytelling curriculum offers opportunities for the peer group to scaffold children's thinking.

The importance of these studies is twofold. First, they make evident that authentic, or contextualized, literacy-related activities, like the storytelling curriculum, can improve young children's language and narrative skills. This has substantial import for the design of early literacy curricula in general, but also for the preservation of fantasy play activities in the early childhood classroom. Second, the studies directly refute critics of such activities, who insist that low-income children cannot afford a curriculum so deeply rooted in their everyday and family lives. Given the long-term consequences of language and narrative development on reading and comprehension, we should ask instead how they can afford a curriculum that lacks this contextualization.

COMPOSING THE MEANINGFUL

The impact of the storytelling curriculum on vocabulary, oral narrative, and literacy subskills through an aesthetic engagement with stories that will lead to reading is but half its contribution to young children's early literacy development in a pedagogy of meaning. Its effect on their identity as storytellers who write is the other half. By "writing," I don't mean Paley's description of the children's "writing" scenarios for free play that other children read and participate in. Those child writers are figurative. In the storytelling curriculum they are quite real, and what they accomplish is an essential first step in preparing for the later task of becoming expository and creative writers in the literal sense. But the goals of the storytelling curriculum speak to a very different perspective on young children as writers than do other strategies directed to developing writing skills. I speak here specifically of the push to require "writing workshops" in the kindergarten and, in some schools, the prekindergarten early literacy curriculum. This trend in early childhood education has received much less attention than the focus on subskills instruction, but it is just as troubling, for it too runs counter to the early literacy needs of young children.

Early childhood writing workshops rest on the assumption that no time is too soon for children to value and adopt the habits of mature authors. But from a developmental perspective, this is a highly dubious proposition for children under seven or eight years old. I think there is a reasonable case to be made for forestalling a writing workshop until second grade. Despite young children's ability to create psychologically meaningful stories, as we have seen in their fantasy play and storytelling, they are not disposed to hone their narrative craft or express themselves creatively with *intent*. The stories they tell and act out constitute writing in the Vygotskian sense of "written language," which reflects the attempt to participate in the culture, not the presentation of a set of skills. Young children tell stories—write—and act them, as I've discussed, to know and be known. A premature emphasis on how well they do it seems to miss that point entirely. Judging by the sample stories in appendix C, sameness, even dullness, is not a problem. Interesting twists on language or even plot lines are to be appreciated, but we err in assuming they are deliberate creations. The fact is, preschoolers and kindergartners do not need to be "writers" yet. They need to be storytellers, who use the written narrative to advance their personal causes. A premature focus on the subskills of composition won't achieve this.

At the early childhood level, the writing workshop curriculum is largely, though by no means exclusively, associated with the work of Lucy Calkins and her staff. Her books on subject, *The Art of Teaching Writing* (1994) and, more recently, *Units of Study for Primary Writers: A Yearlong Curriculum (K-2)* (2003), have been widely disseminated. Briefly, in Calkins's version of the writing workshop, all children are helped to identify as authors immediately upon entering school.

More important, they are expected to act like authors. They must write often and independently. Dictation is not permitted regardless of their skill level, though drawing is allowed until they possess some rudimentary knowledge of sound/symbol correspondence. Work around the craft of writing and revision is expected early on. A writer's notebook and writer's folder are standard in almost all the classrooms I have visited. Finished products and works in progress are "published" by way of reading aloud or creating in-house books.

In my experience, writing workshops below the second-grade level demonstrates a problematic, and potentially harmful, disregard for what young children are inherently interested in when it comes to writing. It also convolutes the teacher's expectations. Just as Vygotsky said young children's use of symbols does not mean they are mathematicians (1978, 94), their use of practices well beyond their actual needs does not mean they are authors. We use the term affectionately only because, as Dewey writes, we aim to see the "end in the beginning" of their education. We mean no harm by bestowing the title on them, and we cause no harm, except when we confuse young children's potential selves with expectations of what they can do in real time. Vygotsky tells us that "[a] contradiction arises in early childhood when writing is taught as a motor skill and not as a complex cultural activity" (1978, 118). Indeed, there is strong ethnographic evidence that middle-class home environments offer children as young as a year-and-a-half opportunities to write or draw freely either in imitation of what adults do or in response to something on their minds (Clay 1975; Schickendanz 1999; Teale 1978; Taylor 1993, 1998). This is a good reason for early childhood classrooms to be filled with writing materials, have a dedicated space for writing, and make time for independent explorations. Shared writing, in which the children and teacher write together, and other similar activities are wonderful components of an early writing curriculum. The problem with the writing workshop is that the "cultural activity" it relies on—the author as artist—is not the aspect of the writing culture young children most need at this time in their development.

Let us consider some practical distinctions between the storytelling curriculum and the writing workshop for young children, beginning with the ban on dictation. As the experienced teacher knows, the younger the children, the harder it is for them to encode individual words, let alone whole thoughts. First, there is the physiological matter of maintaining a grip on the pencil for the length of time required to get their ideas down on paper. Kindergarten children write slowly, and for some even a 25-word story can be physically demanding for a long time. Martin's story has 135 words. Another problem related to encoding is that, by virtue of normal language and cognitive development, the stories young children would like to tell will always include words they know to speak but can't begin to spell. This often creates anxiety in young children, especially kindergartners. Developmental theory tells us that they are just beginning to discover rules in general and are pleased by spelling words correctly, even if that means they need help. Writing workshop teachers usually suggest children "sound out" the unknown word or consult a friend. Of course, sounding out not only interrupts the flow of young children's thoughts, it proves unproductive when the word in question is well beyond what they have been taught thus far about sound and symbol correspondence. Consulting with a classmate rarely offers a better alternative. I have seen many young children in writing workshop classrooms too shy to ask another child for help or who have met with rebuff when they do. The stakes are raised on getting the spelling right when, as often happens in writing workshop classrooms, there is a "no erasing" rule. Interestingly, neither the dictation component of the storytelling curriculum nor the generous offer of help with spelling seems to inhibit young storytellers' interest in independent writing. Nicolopoulou, McDowell, and Brockmeyer (2006) offer compelling evidence that young children's participation in storytelling and story acting is tied to significant gains in independent journal writing.

Another critical element of the writing workshop that is at odds with Paley's philosophy is the teaching of writing as craft. For example, Calkins (2003) recommends that teachers conduct mini-lessons in craft around the use of literary elements, such as metaphor and simile. Presumably, this is to improve the quality of the writing. But while young children may produce metaphors spontaneously that teachers write down in storytelling, their control over language has not reached the metacognitive level to produce them deliberately. We must ask how necessary such lessons are to either the stories young children want to tell or their future as writers. As for revision, the writing workshop usually demands that children return to their work to edit and revise if they intend to "publish" it. Again, this requirement is justified only if we assume that children are naturally drawn to perfecting their story form.

But if the goal of independence in writing and working on their craft does not serve young children well, its limitations pale in comparison to those of the content-driven mandate outlined in "Small Moments: Personal Narrative Writing" (Calkins 2003). According to this unit of Calkins's writing workshop curriculum, the most acceptable path to becoming a writer is paved with what's "true" in our lives and, better yet, the particulars we have examined ("stretched") in detail. Obviously, this perspective eliminates all fantasy-based stories, as it also works to draw children's attention away from things that may be true but that they can't "know" firsthand. The following excerpt, taken from the introductory unit "Launching the Writing Workshop," makes this point clearly. It describes a teacher who hopes to help kindergartners avoid choosing a topic based on what they like to draw (in this case rainbows) by acting out her thoughts and feelings of "what authors do" when they are choosing a topic:

> "Hmmm. What should I write about?" Pausing, she said, in an unenthusiastic voice, "I could write about rainbows . . ." Shaking her head as if to dismiss that very bad idea, she said, "But you know what, I never did anything with a rainbow! I want to write about what I know. Hmmm. I know! I go running every morning, and funny things happen to me when I'm running. I can tell about what happened one day on my jog." (2003, 3)

Leaving aside the inauthentic quality of the teacher's voice and story, the idea that young children will find "what happened one day on my jog" more compelling than rainbows goes to the very heart of why the writing workshop is simply of out of place in preschool or kindergarten classrooms. As a pedagogy of meaning implies, the *true* stories young children want to write (or tell) are the things they are reveling in right now or feeling a need to become more familiar with—like rainbows. This does not mean the things they tell or write are literally true or globally interesting. And whether the desire to write about rainbows is tied to things that they are capable of drawing or to the very real but elusive phenomenon of colored stripes in the sky, young children, especially girls, do indeed like to tell rainbow stories. "They woke up and saw a rainbow and went to school" comes from a storytelling session in one of my classes. Other topic choices drawn from real storytelling classrooms include how to come alive after dying and how a teacher lives both in the Bronx and in Haiti at the same time. Then there are the stories of a green witch, a laughing tiger, time travel, all the characters on Sponge Bob, and the Dark Knight. That the world makes a practical distinction between knowledge of the real and knowledge of the imagined is not confusing to children even as young as four and five. What is confusing to them is why anyone would care to insist one is better than the other.

Shelley Harwayne (2001) suggests that the writing workshop has lost its way around the issue of imagination. She argues that not even older elementary school children should be pushed to write what's literally true or culturally more significant and urges teachers to take a stand against such requirements. Despite hers and others' words of caution, there is plenty of evidence that imaginative story lines are systematically shut down on young storytellers in writing workshop classrooms all around the country. Some kindergarten teachers I know implement the storytelling curriculum two days a week because they want to, and the writing workshop on the other days because they have to. The "real stories only, and kids do all the writing" days are ones that follow writing workshop rules. The "tell whatever you want, and the teacher will write" are storytelling days. The children sometimes get confused. I've heard many children check with the teacher as to whether it was a day for real stories or for their own.

Vygotsky describes writing as "organized development" (1978, 118). From this view, it seems obvious that the rush to have young children acquire the habits and practices of older authors is ill-considered at best. But the insult to young children's imaginative lives, their "need for story" and for the aesthetic violates the very essence of the early childhood years (Dyson and Genishi 1994; Rosenblatt 1978). According to Vygotsky, the achievement of "written language" is the result of reading and writing instruction based on "something the child needs," something "meaningful." The best source of meaning is the environment and imaginative play (1978, 118). This approach resonates with Dewey's theory on where to aim instruction. "What teachers need to learn," Dewey wrote, is that the activities we ask children to engage in should reflect what their "culminating power and interest" is today, not tomorrow:

> To them applies the maxim of striking while the iron is hot. As regards them, it is perhaps a matter of now or never. Selected, utilized, emphasized, they may mark a turning-point for good in the child's whole career; neglected, an opportunity goes, never to be recalled. Other acts and feelings are prophetic; they represent the dawning of flickering light that will shine steadily in the far future. As regards them, there is little at present to do but give them fair and full chance, waiting for the future for definite direction. ([1900] 1990, 192)

Storytelling and story acting supremely embody language development and imaginative thinking in four- to six- and, in some cases, seven-year-olds. These qualities must be indulged if early education is to serve what lies ahead, including the writing workshop. It's hard to pinpoint exactly when children will be ready to take advantage of the many virtues offered by the writing workshop curriculum. But it is safe to say that most will be content to wait until they have said good-bye to Santa Claus, lost babies, and the Batman self. In due time, they will allow their fantasies to go where all fantasies go in middle childhood: underground, down the rabbit hole, or over the rainbow. The concept of genre writing, and the literary elements associated with each style, will even become interesting to them. Insisting on this knowledge too early, however, will not make them better—or more satisfied—writers, readers, or thinkers.

⚙

Paley's educational philosophy yields to specific pedagogical practices around storytelling and story acting that both support young children's search for meaning and advance their early literacy development. The superiority of these activities in the preschool and kindergarten curriculum is found in their essential elements, from giving young children's imagination free reign to offering them assistance with literacy-related issues through questioning, editing, and directing techniques. Participation in storytelling and story acting extends the virtues of fantasy play for young children by providing additional opportunities for them to practice oral discourse, vocabulary, narrative construction, and concepts of print in scaffolded interactions with their teacher and peers. Participation also enriches young children's concept of story, narrative construction, and written language as a culturally meaningful activity. The lessons that embody Paley's pedagogy of meaning in the storytelling curriculum, as in fantasy play, reflect its probable, personal, and instructive contexts.

First, since the teacher can expect the children to be drawn to storytelling and story acting, much as they are drawn to fantasy play, she must "write" the classroom schedule so as to make room for it on a regular basis. She must be ready with supplies and lists of names for keeping track of turns.

Second, since storytelling and story acting are highly personal activities, the teacher's first priority is to help the young children create the story they mean to tell, that is, the story that's in their heads. At the most basic level, this means the teacher must ask questions and find other ways to make sure that what she is writing down adequately captures a given storyteller's intentions. She must be prepared to make connections in a child's life that the child is not even making. (Teacher: "And then the boy says, 'Wa. Wa'? Is that what you want me to write? Is the boy crying? I wonder if your baby cries a lot.") Helping young children tell the personal also means the teacher must come to a decision as to how she will receive their interests. Although there is always the possibility of an inappropriate topic (such as "bathroom" stories, which I tell the children I will not write down), the teacher must have a well thought out response to those that are not so much offensive as they are less preferable, for example, superhero stories. There is also the matter of delicate topics, such as trouble at home. These should be handled by the same standards that the teacher would handle them at circle time or at the snack table. On the other end of the spectrum of questionable topics is the bland story, where nothing much happens. It is often referred to by storytelling teachers as the "and then, and then" story. Once the teacher decides it no longer serves a developmental purpose for the child, but rather reflects a stuck gear of sorts, she can help the child move on. Direct instructional opportunities in narrative construction, as well as literacy subskills, is the third lesson we can draw from the storytelling curriculum.

Paley says that fantasy play allows young children to reflect, to ponder, to wonder "What if?" (2004, 92). Storytelling and story acting, by extension, allow them greater control of their thoughts. These activities also create a zone of proximal development that the teacher can use to great advantage when she scribes or directs stories. As I've suggested, she can provide basic emotional assistance around such philosophical problems as how one feels about a colicky baby brother. She can also help young children untangle a narrative by, for example, putting down her pen to pause and say something on the order of, "I'm thinking you have a different picture in your head than this story is turning out to be. Would you like to stop here and tell me more about . . .)?" Then, there is the help she can provide around specific literacy skills. Both storytelling and story acting offer many instances in which the teacher can casually reinforce concepts of print, word study, subskills, and comprehension. She might simply call the child's attention to a feature of something she has written down, a repeated word or how a period is used. She can also follow the child's eye movements to see how and where he or she is in tracking print. Comprehension skills are boosted in storytelling and then again in story acting when the teacher, storyteller, and class engage in discussion about intention and point of view among the characters in the stories.

PART II

Relational Matters: A Pedagogy of Fairness

4

Teaching as a Moral Act, Classrooms as Democratic Spaces

In each, it seems there is a struggle between self and community; the conflict is acted out in a dozen different ways.

VIVIAN PALEY, *The Girl with the Brown Crayon*

In this chapter, I examine the theoretical foundations that support fairness as a pedagogical priority. By some definitions, the goal of complete fairness is an oxymoron in the classroom. Sacrifice of some will always be required in order to meet the needs of others. How fair is that? This is the challenge to fair teaching that cuts across all the topics that Paley investigates. Fair teaching also means we seek out the individual child's story; that is, we do not wait for it to find us. I draw from my own teacher's story to examine the inadvertent consequences of not teaching fairly on young children's experience of school.

❖

The concept of fair teaching influenced Vivian Paley's work from the start. She writes that *White Teacher*, her first book, was inspired by the question of fairness toward black children. She carried this question into all her future studies, as each year she asked herself, "Is this classroom in which I live a fair place for every child who enters" ([1979] 2000, xv)? What I describe as Paley's pedagogy of fairness addresses what she says is the young child's greatest fear about starting school—being alone—in light of the cruelest truth about the way schools work: not everyone is welcome. However vigorously denied by the cultural myth that portrays schools as fair places and early childhood as a time of innocence, Paley makes visible how exclusion is built into the very fabric of early schooling, from expectations of achievement to who gets asked to play. In doing so, she uncovers early childhood education's willingness to tolerate exclusion. The implications of this are obvious in many ways, but Paley digs deeper. *"[T]he child is lost at school,"* she tells us. "[A]side from all else we try to accomplish, we have an awesome responsibility. We must become aware of the essential loneliness of each child. Our classrooms, at all levels, must look more like happy families and secure homes" (1990, 147, emphasis hers). She also argues that if teaching is to become a "moral act," the "goal of fairness," her response to the lost child, must surpass even fantasy play and story as a priority in the early childhood classroom (1990, xii).

Though a pedagogy of fairness can surface across the curriculum, my analysis finds its primary focus in the ecosystem of relations that make up classroom life: teacher and child, teacher and children, child and child, child and group. From a methodological perspective, a pedagogy of fairness is, simply, teaching to include within and between all of these relationships. Some may question how a focus on fairness falls into the category of pedagogy. Paley asks, how can it not? How can we not teach, as best we can, to a universal experience that we know substantively affects young children's developing identities and quite probably their long-term school success?

A pedagogy of fairness is not to be confused with more familiar goals in early childhood education, such as sharing and cooperation. These are important civic standards of classroom life, of course, but they are outcomes of fair teaching, not one and the same. Fair teaching encompasses all that honors young children's need to be sought out and valued, to be remembered, by the teacher and the group regardless of their race, gender, popularity, or developmental difference. Viewed this way, a pedagogy of fairness manifests itself in very concrete ways. A straightforward illustration is the issue of who gets to participate in the storytelling curriculum. Fairness demands that teachers understand classroom life well enough to know how much is at stake for those children who do not tell or get chosen to act in stories. In effect, they are absent from the collective class-consciousness that participation in the storytelling curriculum creates. The problem for those left out is therefore even greater than the inevitable sadness and disappointment they feel about not having their story heard or not being asked to play. It is the lost opportunity to be psychologically connected to the group. To counter the possibility of this exclusion, the fair teacher does not leave young children's participation up to chance. Rather, she takes responsibility for monitoring the class list closely to see who needs to be reminded to sign up for a turn. Or she might keep a list of class names in the storytelling box of materials, and cross off the children's names after calling them to the storytelling table. When she has run through the whole class, she starts again. She goes through a similar process for dramatization, allowing the author to choose actors from the list of children who have not had a turn yet (appendix A offers several other turn-taking options). To the untrained eye, these decisions may appear mundane strokes of pedagogy, but to the children who are at risk of being excluded, or who are on the verge of disappearing from group life, they are gifts.

Another example of fair teaching that addresses group membership directly is Paley's classroom dictum "you can't say you can't play," which targets the force of popularity in school by disallowing rejection of other children in all corners of classroom life. As I discuss below and more fully in chapter 6 regarding Paley's 1992 book of the same name, "you can't say you can't play" famously goes against the traditional view that young children have the right to play with whom they wish. Unsurprisingly, "you can't say you can't play" is not a philosophy to which all children (or even all teachers) intuitively gravitate. Paley nonetheless makes the case for it as fair teaching at its best.

To be sure, Paley's pedagogy of fairness is also concerned with less transparent issues involving gender, developmental difference, and race that compromise the possibility of full inclusion in classroom life. I begin chapter 5 with race because it is where Paley's own exploration of fair teaching and subsequent development as a fair teacher begins, and I take up her well-developed critique of teacher attitudes toward gender and developmental difference in chapter 6. But neither Paley's contribution to teacher education as a white teacher of children of color nor her analysis of gender and development in the classroom can be fully appreciated unless we consider her story over time and in the context of her original goal of fairness.

THE BUILDING BLOCKS OF FAIR TEACHING

Given what should be the integrated nature of teaching and learning, a certain theoretical overlap between Paley's pedagogy of meaning and her pedagogy of fairness is to be expected. Fairness, like meaning, finds support in social constructivist and sociocultural learning theory in the call for teachers to take responsibility for scaffolding children's learning and development. It also draws on a developmentalist perspective in its respect for young children's internal drives and innate needs and differences at a given time. Interestingly, it, too, is responding to critical issues in early childhood development that are receiving insufficient attention in modern classrooms. But here the difference between the pedagogy of meaning and the pedagogy of fairness can be observed. A pedagogy of meaning focuses on curricular matters that affect young children's pursuit of truth in the classroom. A pedagogy of fairness, while obviously not external to the curriculum, concentrates on relational matters that influence the teacher's sense of moral purpose in the classroom. Paley's work targets very specific issues in this regard. As I have suggested, these include the insidious bias toward some children by teachers and early childhood educational tradition, the indifference to the sensitivity of this period in terms of young children's separation from home and mother's lap, and the purpose and potential of early schooling in a democratic society.

With respect to the issue of teacher bias, Paley's pedagogy of fairness begins with a self-examination of her teaching practices in the context of larger cultural norms (Banks 1988). From a sociocultural perspective, a pedagogy of fairness recognizes that who young children are coming in the door must not be redefined by school or societal biases. Again, while some measures of attention to children's cultural differences (including gender) may overlap with the curricular program, such as inviting a grandparent in to read, fair teaching roots the effort in feelings of respect. It also requires that the teacher be scrupulously honest in assessing her own beliefs and practices around culture. And she must look past loyalties of any kind to scrutinize what effect the other children, their families, or institutional norms may have on classroom relations. Categorically speaking, a pedagogy of fairness has much in common with Noddings's views on the relational ontology of care in education. As Noddings writes, "When I care, I really hear, see, or feel what the other tries to convey" (1992, 16). The assumption is one of reciprocity in the classroom. Echoing Noddings, Paley says teachers must first know what it feels like to be a child in school. She also says they must know what it feels like to be a teacher ([1979] 2000, xvii). Paley's attention to what teachers feel is key to implementing a pedagogy of fairness. Too often, external demands and control over teachers' time and decisions suggest that teachers' feelings are somehow irrelevant to children's learning. Nothing, of course, could be further from the truth. According to Paley, teachers who are sensitive to feelings (and actions) that even hint at a disconnect between the children's experience of school and the teacher's own will be alert to any bias, superimposed expectation, or measure of success that preordains who young children should be, what they should feel, or (as increasingly and aggressively suggested by the pushdown of academics) what they should know and become.

In terms of its focus on the children as psychological beings, a pedagogy of fairness built on caring also serves a different purpose in the classroom than does a pedagogy of meaning. Whereas the latter looks to create concrete opportunities to engage young children's interests, fairness demands that teachers focus on the developmental challenges involved in coming to school in the first place, challenges that began with the move out of the baby years. The preschool and kindergarten years roughly overlap with Erik Erikson's third stage of life, "Initiative vs. Guilt." According to Erikson, a successful resolution of this stage requires that children develop a psychological sense of individuality, while they simultaneously make significant progress away from home and primary caretakers toward group membership. They must also become confident that their evolving intellectual powers will be well received. Erikson writes that young children can achieve these goals by exercising their newfound control over their bodies, along with their impressive powers of language. Their rich imaginative lives also increase their problem-solving capacities. In these ways, Erikson says, young children in this stage "become bigger," "cooperative," and more "purposeful" in everyday life. Success enables them to profit ever more from interactions with parents and teachers, and to become assured of their future acceptance among their peers (([1950] 1985, 255). A cornerstone of Erikson's developmental theory is the idea that the accomplishments of any one stage of life are preparatory for the next. For the preschool and kindergarten child, he says, this means "entrance into life"—or schooling (258). The fact that Erikson was writing in an era when preschool and kindergarten were much more distinct from elementary school than they are today only increases the pressure on today's teachers to make the preschool and kindergarten experience as welcoming and productive as possible. Erikson's focus on psychological development and social relations also provides the teacher with a lens to look at the significance of developmental differences during these years, which, if ignored, might compromise a successful effort to integrate into classroom life.

The fair teacher of young children makes every attempt to capitalize on young children's growing physical, linguistic, and intellectual powers. She is also mindful of the limits of young children's capacities that might inhibit their explorations. For example, she recognizes that young children's bravado in these years is sometimes a cover for the immature logic skills that can sometimes leave them feeling unsafe away from home. She also knows she must directly assist their efforts toward self-regulation over physical, social, and intellectual skills if they are to avoid feeling guilty about their progress.

If there is a hierarchy to Paley's pedagogy of fairness, it is likely to be topped by what teachers assume to be the purpose and potential of early schooling. Paley adopts Dewey's belief that the moral and social aims of education are inseparable and democratic. For Dewey, as for Paley, morality is to be found in actions between and among people. He writes, "Morals are as broad as acts which concern our relationships with others. And potentially this includes all our acts, even though their social bearing may not be thought of at the time of performance" ([1916] 1966, 357). As I discuss in the ensuing chapters, there are many different ways in which Paley demonstrates the teacher's obligation to act from and work toward a moral code in the classroom if she is to be a fair teacher. The epigraph for her book *The Kindness of Children* (1999) captures why we must begin with children so very young. "The moral universe," she quotes an ancient Hebrew text, "rests upon the breath of schoolchildren." However, as Dewey argues, the traditional notion that cultivating a democratic electorate involves merely creating an informed electorate falls short of school's potential. The result is schools become mere transfer stations of information. Instead, writes Dewey, what a democracy really needs from its schools are persons of democratic character, who can exercise intelligent judgment and who are capable of looking beyond self-interest (Boisvert 1998, 98). True democracy, according to Dewey, will always require more than external trappings and superficial knowledge. It requires an "atmosphere of trust" that invites the free exchange of ideas among people. It means uncensored news, neighbors in open discussion, and the pursuit of truth. Dewey warns against forces that threaten free exchange. "Intolerance, abuse, calling of names because of difference of opinion about religion or politics or business, as well as because of race, color, wealth or degree of culture are treason to the democratic way of life. For everything which bars freedom and fullness of communication sets up barriers that divide human beings into sets and cliques, into antagonistic sects and factions, and thereby undermines the democratic way of life" (1939, x). These are the very same concerns embodied in Paley's pedagogy of fairness.

Though Paley is clearly indebted to Dewey regarding the goal of moral and democratic classrooms, it is important that we appreciate the original aspect of her educational philosophy. Whereas Dewey gives us "school as society" in general terms, Paley gives us "school as classroom" up close through intimate portrayals of classroom-based fair practices. In doing so, she moves the discussion from the idea of classrooms as the mirror of society's better self to classrooms as a mirror of the teacher's very soul. She is, as LaCorte and McDermott (2004) suggest, a model of moral-decision making that forces teachers to confront new standards by which to measure themselves as teachers. Paley's focus on classroom relations and fair teaching promotes her vision of the ideal classroom as an "island of safety and sensibility" (1990, 1), in which young children can be emotionally and intellectually free to practice and develop democratic habits.

What I am describing as Paley's pedagogy of fairness has attracted an unusual amount of attention across disciplines. Interestingly, a significant proportion of that attention comes from outside the field of teacher education. Much of this commentary, though not all, has been instigated by the radicalness of Paley's "you can't say you can't play" in the context of character education. But any criticism of a pedagogy of fairness and character education must acknowledge that Paley implicates herself in the process, even before the children. She also follows Dewey's recommendations ([1916] 1966, 340) and focuses on experiences that help the children acquire habits, not simply beliefs, which will pass into the children's subconsciousness as necessary and good. In view of these refinements, the overwhelming response to Paley's pedagogy of fairness is that, despite being inconvenient and at times problematic, it is also a moral imperative from which we cannot turn our backs in early childhood education.

THE PARADOX OF FAIRNESS

Given Dewey's influence on education, the idea of a fair, that is, a moral and democratic classroom, is not groundbreaking. Little evidence exists, however, that such classrooms abound even under the best of circumstances. Paley fully admits the ways in which her own working conditions are privileged to the point that no obvious obstacle stands in her way. Yet she also shows that her classroom was often not a fair or democratic place for young children, especially in the first half of her career. For many teachers who aim to be better servants of the democratic ideal, the problem is manifested by what Covaleskie describes in reference to Paley as the "paradox of education," that is, the understanding that while democracy theoretically guarantees individual liberty and freedom, it is equally about the common, as opposed to individual good" (2003, 330). This common good demands sacrifice from the individual. The result is an inescapable tension between the needs of individual children and the needs of the group. Reason tells us that the two will often be at odds. This tension may also be exacerbated by Paley's willingness to exercise her moral authority in defining what a "good childhood" means in her classroom. Dahlberg, Moss, and Pence (2006) describe this as an inevitable task of early schooling in general, but few teachers are willing to declare such a personal vision. *You Can't Say You Can't Play* confronts the paradox directly and incurs the condemnation of some (Goodman 2000) and respect of others. Ultimately, it is in her efforts to reconcile the issue of race in the classroom that Paley first learns how the power of her moral authority enables her to address democratic goals through her teaching. As Banks writes, "We can create an inclusive, democratic, and civic national community only when we change the center to make it more inclusive and reflective of our nation's diversity" (2006, 195). Understanding the teacher's moral authority begins Paley's release from that "cloud of giveness" that Maxine Greene (1995) warns is a limit to our teaching imaginations.

TEACHING TO INCLUDE

Whether the transition away from home begins with infant day care or is put off until kindergarten (a rare case these days), early childhood educational research has long recognized that most young children do not automatically trust new teachers and new settings. Paley says the children are smart to be on their guard. Though there are many traditional activities and rituals designed to ease the children's adjustment, such as home visits and abbreviated days during the first few weeks of school (Balaban 1985; Laverick 2008), Paley offers us ample evidence that young children do not always find the classroom door fully open. She shares the story of Alma, the only black child in her class one year, who says nothing in the first two weeks of kindergarten but "Ysm." We might think her merely quiet, but as Paley finally realizes, she is afraid of her white teacher ([1979] 2000). Paley also tells us about Clara, a white child, who is not popular with her peers. Clara's situation is not an unusual one, but her pain is all too personal when she tells Paley, "It's more sadder if you can't play" (1992, 20).

All teachers carry the burden of the children they somehow did not manage to include. I often wonder what happened to Fabian, from one of my first kindergarten classes. He started school late in the fall, as his family had just moved to Chicago. It happened that the girls greatly outnumbered the boys that year, and I remember being pleased at how thrilled the other boys were to add Fabian to their ranks. His storehouse of prior knowledge, particularly about dinosaurs, was also very impressive and initially appealing to all of us. It did not take long, however, for Fabian's star to fade. He had a tendency to stand too close, to talk too much, to touch other people's bodies too often. For some reason, it also annoyed the boys (and me) whenever Fabian would proclaim them his *best* friends, all of them, which he did regularly and loudly. He was, in short, too needy. In time, the boys withdrew their offer of friendship, and Fabian grew confused by their remoteness. He turned to the girls, with whom he fared only slightly better. By year's end, he was mostly a child apart.

Many years later, the excluded child was Raisa, a student in a kindergarten room I observed while supervising a student teacher. She rarely spoke to her classmates, and almost no one spoke to her. I could never pinpoint what was wrong exactly except that she was so clearly intimidated by the others. It's possible they found this an unattractive trait in a playmate. Unfortunately, I had no words of wisdom to help her teacher. The truth is, I have probably observed scores of Fabians and Raisas over the years, young children lonely in a classroom full of children. Teachers talk to their parents about their inevitable lack of friends. The teachers attempt to be objective, though they seldom implicate themselves in the problem.

Traditionally, early childhood educators have responded to children who don't fit in with an eliminate-the-problem approach. The idea is to make the children more likable to other children by correcting unpleasant habits. In more recent years, it has become common to advocate tolerance of differences, rather than the elimination of them. But here's the rub in either case: The practice of including children that no one likes, admires, or envies is uniformly understood as pity in any true sense of the term. If this weren't the case, few teachers would recognize the phenomenon that Paley lays bare in *You Can't Say You Can't Play*: "By kindergarten," she writes, "a structure begins to be revealed and will soon be carved in stone. Certain children will have the right to limit the social experiences of their classmates. Henceforth a ruling class will notify others of their acceptability, and the outsiders will learn to anticipate the sting of rejection" (1992, 3). Yet most teachers instantly recognize Paley's description of a ruling class and the parade of unpopular children who are forced to sit "outside the circle" of classroom life (11), to borrow a metaphor from her own biography. We also know that many unwelcome children don't even make it all the way to kindergarten before they are informed of their outsider status. The graver reality is that most teachers are stumped as to what to do about it. As I show in teachers' responses to the "you can't say you can't play" rule in chapter 6, many believe they cannot make an unwanted child likable. Whether this is actually true is beside the point. According to Paley, what we can do is accept the moral responsibility to eliminate the option of exclusion. "You can't say you can't play" and other practices of fairness are a far greater challenge in early childhood education because, unlike expectations for the teacher in regard to early literacy development, there are few public consequences if she reneges on her commitment to equal opportunity play.

FAILING AT MEANING THROUGH FAILING AT FAIRNESS

Long after I had left the kindergarten classroom for teacher education, I came face to face with my failure as a fair teacher in a way that I will never forget. Ironically, it also involved my failure to follow the basic principles of a pedagogy of meaning in storytelling and story acting. I refer to my utter deafness to what a little girl was trying to tell me about Princess Leia.

It was the late 1990s, and the movie *Star Wars* had just been rereleased. My husband was eager to take our children and me. I hadn't seen the movie the first time and I assumed I wouldn't like it. (It turns out, I was wrong.) Despite not having seen it before, I had become well acquainted with the characters and basic plot structure through the stories my kindergartners had told me—or so I thought. At lunch, prior to the movie, I told my family about a kindergarten class I had once, whose fascination with the movie seemed to know no bounds. I recounted for them all the sword fighting and how one little girl in particular, Abby, had been fixated on Princess Leia. I laughed as I told them about her coming to school with her hair styled over her ears in imitation of those notorious buns, and how all the other girls admired her, which made her smile. She had a beautiful smile.

I forgot about Abby by the time the movie started. Then, as the story unfolded and I saw Princess Leia on the big screen, I found myself back in that long-ago kindergarten. Suddenly I was crying. How had I missed it? How had I not realized that Abby didn't just *like* Princess Leia? She *needed to be* Princess Leia. Even more, she had needed me to know it. But of course, I thought as I watched the movie, Princess Leia was the perfect soul mate for my sad-eyed Abby, who had been orphaned as the result of a train accident not six months before. She was living in Chicago with an emotionally distant and demanding relative. It wasn't working out. Yet while I knew her personal story was unique, I had assumed the truth of her life was no different than most little girls with respect to princesses with long hair and princely interests. That is, I assumed I had interpreted her Princess Leia stories correctly as a girl story, developmentally appropriate but not exceptional.

Clearly, I was wrong. Until that moment in the theater, I never realized just why Abby never tired of telling and acting out Princess Leia's daring and courageous biography. Princess Leia was strong, smart, and in control, claims I could have made about Abby. But the spaceship princess was also unquestionably lovable enough to be worth rescuing. In this, she epitomized Abby's need and her dream. I had missed it entirely. I might have investigated Abby's fascination by simply going to the movie. But I wasn't curious enough. I arrogantly misused my teacher knowledge to see only Abby's generic interest in *Star Wars*. As a result, I missed the chance to learn directly what I only stumbled upon more than fifteen years later. It never occurred to me that Leia's story might have been balm to Abby's deep wounds, that it created a space in her life in which she could rise above her everyday self and reality. I never attempted to look at it from her point of view, despite all the signs she was giving me. I also had not fully understood how the children who were such willing participants in Abby's never-ending drama could see what I could not. She had reconstructed a family for herself through dictation and dramatization, and they graciously went along.

My error in appreciating Abby's story but not the storyteller was the moral equivalent of what Paley means by "confusing the extraordinary with the mundane." The cost to Abby was so much more than she should have had to pay.

5

Race, Pedagogy, and the Search for Fairness

I did not want to feel a stranger in a culture not my own.

VIVIAN PALEY, *Kwanzaa and Me: A Teacher's Story*

In this chapter, using multiple perspectives relative to the notion of teachers' racial and ethnic identity development (see Banks 1988; McAllister 2002), I look at what Paley means by fair teaching as a white teacher of black children. I begin with an examination of several vignettes from *White Teacher* ([1979] 2000) that reveal Paley's initial and naïve assumptions about being a fair teacher in an integrated school. As we see, she quickly learns that her avowed interest in being fair to black children is not the same as fair practice. I ask how Paley's self-identified kinship with children who feel different by virtue of her own ethnic identity clears or muddies the fair teaching waters, a controversial issue in teacher education. I then consider the special legacy of *White Teacher* in teacher education, including the controversies it has raised despite its ongoing use in the field. I follow Paley's development as a white teacher of black children through two subsequent books, both of which take separate tacks and represent a new stage and level in her thinking on race and fairness. *Kwanzaa and Me: A Teacher's Story* (1995), written some sixteen yeas after *White*

Teacher, cedes center stage on the subject to black community members and teachers across the country. It is therefore not a study of race and fair teaching per se, but a study of necessary conversations that have informed Paley's understanding. Her last book centering on race is *The Girl with the Brown Crayon* (1997), in which she lets a black child—five-year-old Reeny—have the last word on what is fair. I close the chapter by considering what lessons we can learn from Paley's pedagogy of fairness when the fact that children and teacher do not look alike presents either a barrier to effective teaching or an opportunity for teacher development. For this reason, I have chosen not to include Paley's *In Mrs. Tully's Room: A Childcare Portrait* (2001) as part of this discussion, although Paley clearly admires and learns from Lillian Tully, an African American teacher, whose stories of her childhood in the segregated South form the core of her pedagogical approach. Furthermore, written five years after Paley retired from classroom teaching, *In Mrs. Tully's Room* does not provide additional insight into Paley's development as a white teacher of children of color. Its central focus is not race, but storytelling and, in particular, the valuable role of classroom teachers who are also storytellers.

✲

Any analysis of Vivian Paley's pedagogy of fairness must give a prominent role to her work as a white teacher of black children, reflecting the time Paley spent teaching first in the South and then on the South Side of Chicago. As I have noted, her desire to investigate her performance as fair teacher of black children was the impetus for her first book, *White Teacher*, and it propelled her through *Kwanzaa and Me* and *The Girl with the Brown Crayon*, the last book she wrote while still a classroom teacher. In different ways and to surprisingly different ends, each book offers teacher education an unusual lens through which to look at classroom practices and professional development relating to race and its corollaries, racial identity and racism. Though Paley's focus is on black children and their families, the discussion has obvious implications for white teachers of other children and families of color.

Paley could not have chosen a topic more ripe for investigation in the later 1970s, when she began the self-study that led to *White Teacher*, focusing on her experiences in a newly integrated school.

Central to her story is the fact that integrated schools in the decades following the civil rights movement did not reflect neighborhood populations, but were affected by a variety of external factors, such as court and district orders, community outreach efforts, and the desire of parents of color for a higher-quality education than their local schools could provide. Arguably, these same factors lie behind the majority of integrated schools today. As Paley describes, one upshot of this was that many of the so-called integrated schools might have been identified more accurately as "white integrated schools" ([1979] 2000, 10), meaning the white culture still dominated, as it does to this day, and the majority of teachers were white. This had and, as we shall see, still has particular consequence for black children, for whom, traditionally, black teachers have figured significantly in development beyond as well as in the classroom, often serving as role models, community leaders, activists, and substitute mothers (Brooks 1987; Foster 1997; Irvine 1990; King 1993; Ladson-Billings 1994a; Lipman 1998). To what extent the important teacher-student relationship changes when the teacher is white is a question that in light of current and projected classroom demographics cannot be ignored.[1]

WHITE TEACHER, BLACK CHILDREN

In *White Teacher*, Paley takes us through the several iterations that represent the first phase of her identity as a white teacher of black children, all of which have clear implications for fair teaching in the new millennium. I begin with her initial commitment to "see no color, hear no color, and speak no color" ([1979] 2000, 7).[2] This was a practice commonly embraced by many white educators in the 1970s and well into the 1980s. It was, theoretically, displaced by the multicultural education movement, which called for open conversation and acknowledgment of race in the classroom (Banks 1988, 1994; 2006). But, as Paley's story of Alma shows, acknowledging race in the classroom also means taking responsibility for how children experience it, a commitment that she was not prepared to make then and, I argue, that many white teachers find difficult still.

Alma is Paley's first black student. We learn that Paley is determined not to recognize Alma's race in what she thinks is Alma's best interest, but Alma apparently cannot get past it. Paley finds herself disturbed that after two full weeks in school, the little girl seems afraid of her. Her racial politics called into question, she writes, "I knew that the relationship of a white teacher and a black child could be traumatic, but it was intolerable that a black child should fear me" ([1979] 2000, 2). Paley's honesty here exposes a common flaw in the thinking of many white teachers who, although cognizant of the cultural hurdles faced by children of color in dominant white institutions, wish to be personally viewed as an exception to perceived threats of bias or disrespect. In other words, she is willing to acknowledge the problem as long as she is not seen as contributing to it. Paley realizes her silence is contributing to it, however, after Alma accidentally knocks over a white boy's block structure.

> The tower came crashing down, one block hitting Donald. Red-faced, he jumped up and pushed Alma as hard as he could into the closet door. He yelled, "You bad brown doody!"
>
> Alma's head caught the edge of the door. She screamed in pain and grabbed for her head. When she saw the blood in her hands she began to wail and shake. I ran to Alma and frantically hugged her. I rocked her back and forth as she moaned. I could feel her rage and fear. Poor baby, what was she doing in this sea of white faces? (4)

Paley's confusion and anger at herself is evident in her response. She knows instantly that her silence on race has made her somehow complicit in the slur and in the injury. Her instincts take over, and she rushes to take Alma into her arms, unconsciously lapsing into rocking and a "sing-song tone" that she thinks sounds like the black women she had heard in New Orleans (4). She reports that only then does the little girl relax.

Some black scholars suggest Paley's attempt to speak to Alma in a more culturally congruent way is not really an option open to white teachers (Boykin 1992; Hale 1986). Others, like Irvine (1990, 2003), press for cultural congruence whenever possible. In either case, Paley makes no claim that the moment worked any miracle in her practice. Unlike what would follow next in a movie about a white teacher's enlightenment, Paley admits that she continues to practice the "creed of color blindness" (9) through that year and also the next, when she has two black children in her class. At this point in her development Paley, like many white students in my teacher education classes, finds the open acknowledgment of race in the classroom, particularly on a personal level, far easier said than done. Her commitment to color-blind teaching doesn't meet its demise until she moves north in the mid-1970s and begins teaching at the University of Chicago Laboratory Schools where a number of experiences force her to become not only more open, but more honest about her role as a white teacher of black children.

Her new kindergarten class consists of nineteen white, three Asian, and eight black children. She recognizes that the children will be asked to adjust to a white institution (the "white integrated school"), and not the other way around, but she is nevertheless very excited by what the diversity can mean for her own classroom. Also, a number of events support her in the process of abandoning color-blind teaching. One is a conversation she has with Mrs. Hawkins, a black parent in her classroom who asks Paley to publicly recognize her children as black. "It's a positive difference," she tells Paley, "an interesting difference . . . if you teachers could learn to value differences more. What you value, you talk about" ([1979] 2000, 12). Delpit makes a similar point in *Other People's Children: Cultural Conflict in the Classroom* (1995). Paley embraces Mrs. Hawkins's advice immediately. It helps her, for example, find words to admire the beautiful brown of a child's skin when the little girl expresses a desire to look like a blonde child in a book. But whatever progress Paley has made thus far around race-based conversation, an important lesson for teacher education is that it is not enough. Simply talking about race is not fair teaching.

In the new preface to the 2000 edition of *White Teacher*, Paley tells a story she had left out of the original volume. The story involves the book's origins, and its initial omission suggests that she was too self-conscious of its implications to include it at the time. She writes that six African American parents had requested to talk with the faculty about their children's experience in school. Expecting to be praised, Paley and the other teachers are not prepared for the parents' accusations of "prejudice and unfairness" (xii). The parents say their children are singled out when they should not be, and overlooked when they should be recognized. Paley is shocked at the charge. In response, she starts keeping track of her reactions to the children's behavior. She is humbled to find the black parents have reason to worry; she is not always a fair teacher of black children. But even with new resolve, Paley is not initially equipped for the lessons yet to be learned, beginning with Steven, whose language shocks her and tests her authority.

Steven is as unprepared for the integrated classroom and the middle-class school environment as Alma had been, though he is not so quiet about being there. He not only openly resists his new environment, he uses reverse racial slurs with Paley, like "fuckin' honky" and "white motherfucker," and edicts like "Don't nobody white look at me" ([1979] 2000, 13). Paley's attempts at behavior modification for Steven, including positive reinforcement, do little to stop the flow of invectives or his anger at white people, including her. When Steven begins to attack other children, Paley becomes desperate and tries several new tactics. First she takes a page from Steven's playbook. Rather than just talking about race naturally as Mrs. Hawkins had suggested, she brings race into her conversations with him and other children every chance she gets: "Steven, that orange shirt looks good on your brown skin." "Charlene, your Afro is so soft and round" (18). She also engages Steven in a compromise that limits his saying *fuck* to twice a day, thereby allowing him some control. In response to Paley's new attitude and practices, Steven not only calms down physically, but also soon stops the offending language.

Many white teachers can learn from Paley's willingness to engage with, not against, Steven's behavior, which however problematic clearly signals his need for her to find a way to include him as a valued member of the class. But most teachers will never have a young child whose language and behavior test their racial sensitivity this much. A more common dilemma from a fair teaching point of view is how Paley's racial consciousness affects her relationship with two of Steven's black classmates. The first is Arlene, whom Paley describes as "the smartest five-year-old she ever had" (24). She not only has very high expectations of Arlene's academic achievement, she finds herself hoping that Arlene's behavior will offset Steven's in the white children's minds, and as a result head off the potential for a negative view of blacks. Then she catches herself. Why doesn't she worry about black children's perceptions of whites when the most difficult child in the class is white? Up until that moment, she had assumed that no child, black or white, would judge the entire white race by the behavior of just one child. Why then would they judge the whole black race in this way? With some injury to her self-image as an equal opportunity supporter, she realizes she "was confident of the staying power of whites" (26). Obviously, she has lower expectations of blacks as a group.

Arlene's story poses yet another problem with regard to the fair teaching of black children. This is the merger of racism and classism. While Paley is happy to confirm Arlene's academic superiority, she must go further and admit that Arlene's professional parents and middle-class behaviors, especially her use of standard English, make it a straightforward proposition. It's not as automatic, she realizes, to appreciate Kathy, another black child in the same class, who uses nonstandard English and whose parents did not go to college. In fact, her bias is revealed in her reaction to learning from another teacher in the school that Kathy's older sister is at the top of her class. She suddenly sees Kathy's potential in a new light. "I began to look more closely at Kathy, and I felt my expectations changing," she says (27). She begins to interact more expansively with Kathy and demands more of her in play. What Arlene and Kathy teach Paley and us about fair teaching is that to have high expectations of middle-class Arlene, but not of lower-class Kathy, is as much if not more of a crime against pedagogical fairness than if she had simply underestimated Kathy alone. Again, for many teachers of children of color, the lesson is as relevant and difficult today as it was then.

Claire brings another quandary to Paley's attempts to find a role for race and fairness in pedagogy, only by this time Paley has learned enough from her experiences with black children to push back from first impressions. Claire, the child of immigrant parents, speaks English, French, and Creole, but she talks rarely and often nonsensically. She often seems confused by what is asked of her. Besides her language issues, Paley cannot help but notice that Claire does not seem to know how to play imaginatively or collaboratively with the other children, who keep their distance from her. Paley consults a learning therapist friend and is advised to have Claire tested for learning disabilities. After some thought, however, Paley refuses. She tells herself quite simply that she does not yet know enough about what

Claire *can* do. As she had learned with Kathy, to make any assumption about the child's competency would not be fair. The first problem to tackle, Paley decides, is to help Claire learn how to play with others. Given her belief in the power of play to further both language and social skills, Paley creates a plan with Claire's parents for Claire to stay after school and play with just a few children under Paley's guidance. In only four weeks' time, Claire's play, language, and relationships with the other children begin to improve dramatically.

There are other lessons Paley learns about fair teaching and race in her year with Steven's class. But it is her unconscious search for the perfect black child that reveals the limits of her pedagogy of fairness at this stage of her thinking. Soon after school starts, she gives the "perfect" role to Ayana. Tellingly, this status is not based on Paley's assessment of Ayana's academic potential, though she seems highly capable, but on her social and emotional precociousness. Paley writes that Ayana possesses a gift for comforting or soothing her classmates, especially the other black children, when they are under stress (71). At one point, Paley herself accepts Ayana's comfort as well. She also deeply admires Ayana's highly developed racial identity, on display when she talks candidly and self-assuredly about the differences between blacks and whites. But in the end, Ayana tests Paley's view of black children in a way the others do not. The girl steps back from her assignment as class guru and starts to gravitate more toward some of the other black girls in the class. In doing so, she becomes less ideal to Paley. "When Ayana first entered our class," she writes, "I misjudged her compassionate behavior for being all there was to know about her. I wanted this to be the real Ayana because I still needed to have black children justify themselves by behaving better than whites. As Ayana and the other girls strengthened their bonds, Ayana began to act in more ordinary ways. I was disappointed. Where was my perfect child?" (106).

Paley's admission that for her the perfect black child is one who somehow transcends racial identity is a critical step in her development as a fair teacher of black children. It forces her to confront her underlying preference for black children to be less black, and in doing so, she is finally able to break away from this denigrating attitude. The most critical lesson is her willingness to learn from Ayana, to be persuaded of the girl's point of view about her own racial priorities. For it is Ayana, not Paley, who recasts herself in Paley's eyes as a little black girl like any other, unpretentiously trying to find her way in a white school. Watching her, Paley finally realizes that the only fair view of black children is to see them the way they want to be seen—as black. Reeny, the black child at the center of *The Girl with the Brown Crayon*, reminds Paley of this lesson many years later, making her realize that she must accept and "consider, quite simply, the way people are" (1997, 15). Research suggests that openness to a child's racial identity is critical to effective teaching and success with black children (Cooper 2003; Foster 1997).

There are more vignettes in *White Teacher* that trace Paley's development as a teacher of black children and the evolution of her pedagogy of fairness, including Paley's realization of how much she and the white children in the room benefit from the black children's presence. There are also many questions still to come for Paley. The important thing for now is that a pedagogy of fairness neatly aligns with Paley's search for meaning in the children's fantasy play and storytelling in the classroom. But it is also clear that a pedagogy of fairness is much harder to adopt and refine in the classroom than a pedagogy of meaning. For unlike in fantasy play and storytelling, teaching for fairness is not a matter of discovering things children do naturally; she must reinvent the established order of social relations. Nowhere has this proved more difficult in American schools than in race relations. It is for this reason that *White Teacher* has proved such an important book to teacher education, though as we have seen, it is not Paley's last word on the subject of race and its lessons are by no means incontestable. Indeed, we shall see that its ongoing role in teacher education both overestimates and underestimates Paley's vision of fair teaching.

THE LEGACY OF *WHITE TEACHER*

Paley was not the first white teacher to put race before the American public. Herbert Kohl's *36 Children* (1966) and Jonathan Kozol's *Death at an Early Age* (1967) had started the conversation more than a decade before. Both books had the desirable effect of stirring up public outrage about conditions in schools for poor black children.[3] By contrast, in *White Teacher*, Paley focuses on the black child ill-served by a seemingly supportive and well-endowed environment, and her outrage is directed at herself. To a great degree, *White Teacher*'s significance to teacher education is captured by its disarmingly blunt title. For almost thirty years it has called attention to a stark, seemingly intractable reality in American education: the teacher who looks like over 90 percent of all the other teachers in America, but unlike the children at the center of the achievement gap crisis.[4] *White Teacher* was the first time a white teacher asked, not how are black children being cheated by white America, but in what way am *I* cheating them? It is this question specifically and significantly that begins Paley's pedagogy of fairness.

Even more impressive than its aims or even its accomplishments some thirty years after its publication is *White Teacher*'s sheer endurance in the conversation on teaching children of color. It has reached an iconic status and continues to be widely cited in books, articles, and other forums that focus on teaching for social justice, critical pedagogy, and multicultural education. It is still regularly found on course syllabi for teacher education, sociology, and psychology. This is not to say *White Teacher* has endured without criticism. Some scholars of color have questioned Paley's authority to speak for the needs of children of color and whether she has served them effectively in her own search for identity. As in the previous discussion on early literacy development, we must consider these detractions thoughtfully or risk misunderstanding Paley's particular contribution. In order to do so, however, we must also consider these objections, as they rarely are, in the context of Paley's subsequent work on race and fairness in *Kwanzaa and Me* and *The Girl with the Brown Crayon*.

In brief, objections to *White Teacher* run on two tracks. Some scholars of color, including Ladson-Billings (1994b), object to giving Paley expert status in teaching black children. They caution that the foremost authority on teaching black children in America is always a black teacher. This is not a casual observation, but a true shading of the effectiveness of white teachers in general. Delpit (1994) goes further and finds that Paley's lack of insider status results in racially insensitive pedagogy. Delpit refers us to the block corner scene toward the end of *White Teacher* in which Rena and Ayana are talking between themselves, as Paley assists them in putting away the blocks.

> "White people tell lies," said Rena.
> "That's right, they do tell lies," Ayana agreed.
> "Do all white people tell lies?" I asked.
> Ayana read my face. "Uh . . . no. Not all white people." She looked guiltily at Rena . . .
> Once Ayana had said, "There are angels in the clouds blowing the wind," and I had responded, "Do angels make the wind blow?" She did not take my question as criticism. She described fluffy angels bellowing forth puffs of wind. When I asked her about white people telling lies, she knew this was not a safe thing to have said. There was apparently no way I could keep a neutral look on my face. ([1979] 2000, 104)

Delpit, empathizing with Ayana's discomfort, guesses this can't be the first time Ayana had become anxious about offending her white teacher. How much easier it would have been for her to explain herself if Paley were black, Delpit says. Minimizing a white teacher's ability to make black children relaxed around racial issues, Delpit suggests the burden will always fall on the children when their teachers do not look like them. Then, powerfully, she adds that she would not put her own black child in such an environment. "Paley praises the integrated kindergarten environment," she writes. "But she does not have to worry about being a minority of color" (1994, 132).

In more recent years, *White Teacher* has come under even harsher criticism when lumped with the books on white teachers that followed it. Willis and Harris, among others, blame it for starting a highly dubious trend, arguing that since its publication "there has been a plethora of seemingly endless personal narratives that detail how unaware many white researchers and educators are of the role they have played in the miseducation of students from cultural and linguistic backgrounds that differ from their own" (2004, 294). The basic claim here is true. *White Teacher* has been followed by many similar first-person accounts of the learning curve for teachers of diverse children, especially since the mid-1990s (see, for example, Dilg 1999; Howard 1999; Landsman 2001; and McIntyre 1997).[5] And the claim that children of color are being miseducated must be taken seriously. This is reason enough for me to point out these objections to *White Teacher*. It goes without saying that scholars of color are in a better position than white teachers to speak to the needs of children of color. They also offer us a more contemporary platform from which to ask whether the lessons in fair teaching we draw from *White Teacher* yield to what Sartwell (1998) calls the highest authority of the community. I refer to the now well-established standards for effective teaching of black children by black scholars that did not exist when Paley wrote *White Teacher*, such as Ladson-Billings's tripart model of culturally responsive pedagogy (2000).

Culturally responsive pedagogy links effective teaching of black children with, first, the teacher's high expectations of the children's academic achievement; second, her support for black children's cultural competence; and, third, her cultivation of their sociopolitical awareness.[6] This might seem a somewhat heavy system to impose on Paley's homey discourse and narratives of preschool and kindergarten, but it proves quite helpful in the end. We know from the vignettes describing her response to Arlene, Kathy, and Claire, for example, that though Paley initially meets the principle of high expectations with varying degrees of success, she is not indifferent to its consequences. Her ongoing search for fairness is a natural ally of high expectations. As for the second principle of culturally responsive teaching, cultural affirmation, we learn that with time Paley shows great latitude in her outlook on differences that black and white children manifest in language, play, and problem solving, not to mention hair, dress, and so on. She even learns not to overreact when Kenny comes to school in a shirt on which "SUPERNIGGER" is emblazoned, a statement not likely to be allowed in today's schools. We also know she regularly thinks to invite all families to share stories and special aspects of their home cultures. Again, her commitment to "equal say" serves her extremely well.

Whether Paley sufficiently meets Ladson-Billings's first two principles of culturally responsive pedagogy is no doubt open to interpretation, especially by the more exacting standards of multiculturalism. The narrative structure of *White Teacher*, however, does not lend itself to further analysis. At the same time, one has to say in Paley's defense that there is every indication that she anticipates the direction Ladson-Billings's research will take the conversation. For this reason, I think we cannot accuse her of deliberately miseducating black children, pace Willis and Harris's suggestion above (though this does not deny their claim that Paley conflates her journey as a white teacher of black children with her personal search for identity). However, there is less evidence in *White Teacher* that Paley addresses Ladson-Billings's third principle, cultivation of the children's sociopolitical awareness, in any real depth. We know that she defends Sylvia, a black child, against a white parent's insinuation that she is disturbed and does not belong in the school, but this is not the same as engaging Sylvia in her own defense. We learn through her black teaching assistant that she handles Martin Luther King's story admirably, but we hear no more about explicit lessons on the politics of injustice. Sociopolitical awareness is, of course, the most difficult of Ladson-Billings's three principles to teach in preschool and kindergarten, given the children's level of cognitive awareness. But as I have argued elsewhere (Cooper 2003), it is also the most difficult for white teachers to achieve generally. This is because white teachers (including myself) not only have to privately admit to their failings in regard to race, they must publicize those of whites as a group. It is therefore possible that Paley may indeed fall short of fully realizing the principles of culturally responsive pedagogy in *White Teacher*.

The more important question to the present discussion is whether Paley's contribution to the conversation on educating black children—on being a fair teacher—changes when we consider her later books on race, *Kwanzaa and Me* and *The Girl with the Brown Crayon*, as well as the race-related fantasy she intersperses throughout *You Can't Say You Can't Play*. In addition, we must ask whether Paley's agenda is the same as that of her critics. This is to say, perhaps everyone has some right on their side. Even if Paley is able to meet the criteria of culturally responsive pedagogy in her later books, she makes very clear that the black children's stories that line *White Teacher*, while distinct in their own right, also stand in for a broader conversation on difference, beginning with her own search for inclusion as a Jewish child in a Gentile world. Though Willis and Harris (2004), for example, suggest this is a wrongheaded appropriation, Paley comes down hard on the side of human similarities over human differences, as the black scholars James Comer and Alvin Pouissant acknowledge in the foreword to *White Teacher*. Paley reexamines her unapologetic belief in the special power of the integrated classroom to place children of color in a reciprocal relationship with all types of outsiders in *Kwanzaa and Me* and then refines it in *The Girl with the Brown Crayon*. In the end, this belief is a defining characteristic of her overall pedagogy of fairness, the roots of which are traceable to her own experience as an excluded child.

IDENTIFYING WITH DIFFERENCE

"I have always identified with children who felt different," Paley writes in *White Teacher* ([1979] 2000, 22). It is a theme that recurs throughout her books, though it is true her identification as an outsider might have seemed more potent when she first started writing in the late 1970s. She is referring to her experience of being a Jewish child in classrooms with Gentile teachers and Gentile agendas, like holiday parties.

However, Delpit's assertion fifteen years after *White Teacher* was published that Paley can praise the integrated classroom only because she does not experience it as a minority *of color* is a direct refutation of the importance Paley places on her identity as a religious minority. For Delpit, Paley's whiteness trumps her Jewishness and denies her the racial sensitivity needed to teach black children well. It seems plausible, though, that Delpit misreads Paley. If we look again at the example Delpit cites in condemnation—Paley's response to Ayana and Rena's labeling of white people as liars—we see that Paley is not claiming to be an insider in the black community, that is, to know what it means to be a black child scolded by a white teacher. She claims only to know what it feels like to be an outsider in mainstream white society, to self-identify as different. This perspective offers a different reading of the block corner scene, especially when we read on in *White Teacher*. Contrary to Delpit's interpretation, Paley does not resist or resent Ayana and Rena's racial categorization of whites as liars. She tells us that her grandmother had engaged her in similarly sweeping generalizations about Gentiles when she was growing up. It's clear from Paley's story that she learned over time to put her grandmother's pronouncements about non-Jews in the context of the larger Jewish experience. But she also writes that she had been taught to hide her Jewish identity in an effort to avoid victimization by Gentiles. It is precisely because Paley identifies with the girls' struggle to defend themselves against past or future injustices that she cannot keep a neutral look on her face or help pressing them on their views of white people as liars. That this is not an excuse for making Ayana feel unsafe is a point well taken. But Delpit's complaint that Paley's Jewishness is irrelevant to her reaction goes too far.

On the other hand, Delpit may not go far enough for those who see Paley's claim to white non–majority status as an oxymoron or who reject her overall message of inclusive classrooms. This cannot be avoided. Paley's focus on race is at once specific and general in *White Teacher*, fused as it is with her vision of the black child as "Every Child" (xix) in the larger sense of equal treatment, opportunity, and value. She is also resolute in her belief in the integrated school as the apogee of an educational experience in which all are accepted, known, and thrive through the restorative power of teachers to do what the outside world cannot. As Comer and Pouissant write in their foreword to *White Teacher*, "Paley does not believe in preparing children for a society that is so recognizably imperfect" (Paley [1979] 2000, vii). This belief in the power of school to act as a buffer to racism, ethnocentrism, and other forums of exclusion, is tested and refined—and again refuted by some—in important ways in Paley's later books, and whatever other significance Paley holds in the dialogue, we cannot go forward from *White Teacher* without acknowledging it.

PURSUING FAIRNESS FURTHER

Kwanzaa and Me, published in 1995, picks up where *White Teacher* leaves off.[7] Race and fairness are still central, but the better part of twenty years has passed, and Paley's beloved integrated school is under fire. It is for this reason, perhaps, that *Kwanzaa and Me* is Paley's most unsettled book. In it, she explores race and fairness not through the "equal say" she attempts to offer the children, but through the adult voices she seeks out to help her revisit the question of the classrooms young black children need. These voices principally include Lorraine, a black teacher in her school, and the black parents in her classroom. She also consults with teachers of color and teachers of children of color around the country. *Kwanzaa and Me* thus signals a huge step in Paley's pedagogy of fairness from teacher of children to teaching within a community. This is a common characteristic of effective teachers of black children (Cooper 2003).

Unfortunately, *Kwanzaa and Me* has been much less visible in the research than *White Teacher*. Whether this is due to the era in which it was published, or the fact that without the children as main characters, it loses the singular immediacy of Paley's earlier book, is hard to say. However, any legitimate attempts to describe what Paley's work on race or fairness means for teacher education will not ignore it. For one thing, by placing classroom life at the edges of her stage and ceding the center to the community at large, Paley exposes herself even more than in *White Teacher*, as those she turns to force her to reexamine her qualifications as a white teacher of black children. However vulnerable this makes her feel, it is an appropriate step in her development as a teacher and classroom researcher.

The book opens with a visit from Sophie, a college student and the former kindergartner identified as "Ayana" in *White Teacher*. Paley is eager to talk. She tells Sophie that the community controversies regarding black children and the integrated school have left her "inhibited on the subject of black children" (1995, 2). It's obvious she wants to be to be relieved of her doubts of what she had been so sure of in that long ago kindergarten. "I want her to tell me that this is still a good place for Ayana, this integrated classroom, because a lot of people are sure it isn't. And probably never was" (1).

Paley tells Sophie about the feedback she's been getting on the integrated school experience. She says a black teacher in the high school has written an article advising black parents to keep their young children away from the school, especially the boys, and to send them to a black school to secure their racial identity. In the same vein, a black professor with whom Paley serves on a panel has angrily stated that the integrated school can only succeed in making black children feel "dumb and ugly." Paley wants to hear from Sophie that this is not so. Sophie cannot help her out. Looking displeased, she asks Paley, "It never occurred to you that we might question the integrated school?" (2).

Paley, taken aback, says it is the one thing she took for granted. Sophie then tells her that she is transferring to Spelman, the historically black college for women in Atlanta (the implication is that she currently attends a mostly white university). She apologizes to Paley for upsetting her, but finishes with a hard thought: "I'd have done better in a black school. I'd have been more confident. I was an outsider here" (6). Her words clearly call into doubt the efficacy of Paley's efforts at fair teaching, at teaching to include.

Sophie's conversation with Paley is emblematic of the external and internal attacks on the integrated school that started to surface in the mid-1990s, as the promise of the early years gave way to difficult realities. These ranged from a lack of scholarships in private schools, to a lack of financial support for magnet or specialized public schools designed to appeal to the white community, to resistance from some pockets of the black community, including, as Delpit's 1994 review exemplifies, black scholars who questioned the impact of the "white integrated school" on black children's self-esteem.

If in *White Teacher* Paley overestimated the power of the integrated school to buffer black children's status as outsiders, she does not hesitate to admit it in *Kwanzaa and Me*. Nor is she unwilling to admit to her own distress. As Lorraine, her black coworker, and black parent after black parent challenge the idea that black children need the integrated school, Paley says frankly that she does not know how to respond. She has for so long assumed integration to be an unmitigated good in early education. Her critics offer her several lessons, however, which she takes to heart. Forcing her to revise a claim from *White Teacher* that the most essential lesson is to keep "up to date" on what it feels like to be a teacher and child (and also a parent), Paley acknowledges that she has "underestimated the changes taking place in the black community" (1995, 26). In confronting them now, she must accept the possibility of irreconcilable differences between herself and many of its members. For example, she may want to fight racism in the classroom (85), but black parents may not want their children at the center of the fight. She is also reminded in so many ways that a single classroom, a single teacher, is not a school. She cannot keep the children safe all day. And while

Paley wants to lessen the importance of color (53), some of the black parents tell her they want a school that prioritizes blackness. As she learns from Lorraine, there may be a place for the segregated school after all.

The influence of these voices on Paley's growth as a white teacher of black children is lost when analysis of her work is limited to *White Teacher*. This is not to say that all of the lessons of that first book are void, or that her Jewish identity no longer figures in her learning and teaching. She has simply broadened her definition of what's fair teaching to accommodate voices of authority greater than her own. We see this when, near the end of *Kwanzaa and Me*, Paley talks with a black mother in her class who is thinking about withdrawing her son from the school for one with more black children and teachers. Paley asks why, and Mrs. Arnold tells her, "Look, I know teachers here mean well. But, it's still *them* defining *us*." She then turns the tables on Paley and asks her to look at the problem from a different perspective. "What if you Jewish people had been defined by others over centuries, some of whom were anti-Semites" (1995, 134)? Despite the irony of the question given the stereotypes Jews have struggled against, Paley takes Mrs. Arnold's comments in a different direction. She wonders if her Kwanzaa stories, a very deliberate attempt for her to connect with the black children in her classroom, have also insidiously represented an attempt to define them.

Kwanzaa and Me is the only one of Paley's books to end on an ambiguous note, and it is perhaps a lesson in the extreme complexity of the subject of race and fairness for Paley. On the last page, she asks Lorraine what she thinks the value of her book might be. Lorraine answers that Paley is encouraging a dialogue. Paley accepts this faint praise, and then, paradoxically, Lorraine adds that the dialogue requires an integrated environment. In something of an about face then, Paley retreats to her earlier endorsement of the integrated school by concluding with a story about Kesha, a black child in her kindergarten, who dictates to Paley a story about a black princess, who can speak any language "because she asked everyone to teach her" (1995, 140). It seems that by the book's end, Paley has accepted the limitations of the integrated school for black children, but she cannot give up her belief in its potential.

To bring Paley's work on race and fairness full circle, I turn now to her 1997 book, *The Girl with the Brown Crayon*, her last book to target race directly, and the last she wrote before she retired from teaching. By the late 1990s, Paley's main fear for the future of the integrated school has come to pass. Eight of the thirty children in the classroom she describes in *White Teacher* were black. By the time of *The Girl with the Brown Crayon*, there are only three children of color in her kindergarten, two boys and one girl. One family is thinking about leaving, again for an all black school. The engine that drives Paley's exploration this time is not her role as a fair white teacher of black children, but her role as a fair teacher of Reeny, a particular black child with a brown crayon for the many self-portraits she literally and figuratively creates in her kindergarten year in Paley's classroom.

Beyond her clearly extraordinary gift for story and literature, Reeny is also extremely confident of her racial identity. Paley notes that where she herself could never have mentioned her Jewishness openly in school, Reeny proudly announces she is black, and within that identity also demonstrates her sense of her own uniqueness. When one of the black boys calls her a "short-haired black girl," or when he says "Hi, baby" as he walks by, Reeny tells on him immediately (1997, 2). She does not want to be categorized or stereotyped. By contrast, Paley recalls that when she was a child her own "face burned with shame" after a boy in her first grade called her "Kinky-stinky" in reference to her tightly wound head of curls. She never told anyone, let alone fought back (3).

In yet another serendipitous curricular move on Paley's part, Reeny's story unfolds in a yearlong class exploration of Leo Lionni's many children's books. This is the "invented" classroom Paley loves to preside over. The idea is inspired by Reeny's instant identification with Frederick, Lionni's individualistic brown mouse in the story of the same name (1967). Next comes the reading of, acting out, and writing about Lionni's many other stories. As it happens, a major theme throughout Lionni's work is the role of the outsider. Reeny chooses *Swimmy* (1963) as the book to be read when her grandmother visits the classroom. *Swimmy* is the story of a little black fish who organizes all the red fish in defense against their larger predators.

At one point, he becomes the "eye" around which all the other fish gather in the shape of a larger fish to scare off predators. Reeny's grandmother tells Paley her grandchild is sending her a message. "I believe it's this: Tell me, Grandma Ettie, if I belong here where I'm so different. Or should I still be with my own people like I was in pre-school and the way I am in church?" Miss Ettie also informs Paley that Reeny is aware that her grandmother wants her to go to a school with more black children. "[S]he will not become a leader of her people if she stays here" (1997, 63), she says. To illustrate her point, Miss Ettie tells Paley about the time Reeny's father was mistaken for a computer repairman by a school secretary, despite his dress clothes. In the same instance, another father, a white man in khakis and a t-shirt, was automatically assumed to be a parent in the school.

By this time, Paley no longer questions black families' experience of racism. She responds to Miss Ettie, "I think no white person is in a position to argue with you about this. Your story happened here, and there is no guarantee it won't happen again" (64). Yet her response is again a concession to a world she clearly wishes weren't so. For however open she is to the reality of black families' lives, Paley's belief in the integrated school is shored up in a new way by Reeny's investigation of her racial identity. It has fostered her awareness of how black children's racialized sense of the world is an essential lens through which to see the world. It is Reeny, for example, who shows Paley and the other children that they have been undervaluing Walter, a classmate whose English is very limited. Recalling one of the Leo Lionni books, Reeny points out that no puzzle piece is worth more than any other. They are only different.

To conclude, though Paley remains, stubbornly, as Blum (1999) notes, a "committed integrationist," her multiple investigations into being a fair white teacher of black children leave us no choice but to accept the paradox she accepts for herself. This is the fact that the black community knows more about what's best for their children than she does. She may long for the integrated classroom, but it is not her right to assume it is the best defense against the problem of racial discrimination, whatever her individual commitment or abilities to counter it. It is a powerful lesson for multicultural educators, learned over time by Paley, and one that is often ignored by critics who look only to *White Teacher* for evidence of her culturally responsive pedagogy. It is also an essential lesson in adopting a fully realized pedagogy of fairness.

⯐

"Every Child" may not be the label contemporary multiculturalists might put on the black child, as Paley does in *White Teacher*, if they mean to honor the black culture's particular significance. But "valued" is surely a word they would accept, a word Paley also uses to describe the black child throughout her work. The labels are less important to teacher education, however, than Paley's reminder that teachers must take responsibility to look beyond their self-interests to ask what it feels like to be a child in school, as well as a teacher, the first lesson in a pedagogy of fairness. This question is all the more important when teacher and child do not share such a critical characteristic as race (or, Paley would add, religion).

Paley's pedagogy of fairness cannot make racism go away in schools. But it does embody lessons that work to hold racism at bay. Unlike in fantasy play and storytelling, though, the lessons are not curricular—except insofar as we take for granted that teachers will never expect less of any child in any area, as they simultaneously learn to incorporate the best culturally based activities, books, or special events in the classroom. But although a pedagogy of fairness is not curricular, it is not amorphous. Paley understands the need for the concrete.

Resting first on the assumption that black children, like children of all colors, must be valued in the classrooms, the next lesson in Paley's pedagogy of fairness is to acknowledge that racism exists in America in small and large ways, between people and in institutional norms. This requires that teachers eschew a color-blind stance in teaching and at faculty meetings. It also requires open discussion with both children and parents and other faculty members.

Third, as teachers we must accept responsibility for eradicating racism both in schools and, whenever necessary, in ourselves. This obviously means we must be willing to be surprised by our own racism, as Paley was when she began the self-study that became *White Teacher*. Without the possibility of surprise, we will not look deeply enough into our beliefs or far enough behind our practices.

Fourth, a pedagogy of fairness requires that teachers not only welcome conversation about race in school, but also affirm race-based behavior. This includes everything from different learning and language styles to different styles of dress. Children must be allowed, as Paley says, to show us who they are.

The fifth and perhaps most difficult lesson of all in a pedagogy of fairness is that teachers must be willing to learn from children of color and their families. The lesson may include cultural information, like the holiday Kwanzaa, but it is hardly limited to such things. The requirement entails a fundamental willingness to see children of color and their communities in general as contributors to classroom life and concerns.

In sum, Paley's pedagogy of fairness makes it possible for teachers to embrace race in the classroom as both a direct and nuanced phenomenon. It asks them to celebrate race, as it holds them accountable for racism that they ignore or perpetuate. Paley makes clear that a pedagogy of fairness centered on race is easier and harder at different times over the course of a teaching life. But it must always be, she says, on the horizons of teachers' imaginations.

6

Fairness Extended: Superheroes, Helicopters, and the Unchosen

Magpie, is there such a thing as too many tears?

VIVIAN PALEY, *You Can't Say You Can't Play*

In this chapter, I look at fair teaching as it applies to boys in the feminine-normed kindergarten, which Paley explores in *Boys and Girls: Superheroes in the Doll Corner* (1984). I then turn to her study on developmental isolation—although Paley herself refuses to use such labels in the case of Jason in *The Boy Who Would Be a Helicopter: The Uses of Storytelling in the Classroom* (1990). Following upon this, I look at her novel and controversial attempt to help children recover from the habit and consequences of rejection in *You Can't Say You Can't Play* (1992). I close by considering the remaining lessons to be learned from Paley's pedagogy of fairness.

⊛

Just as Vivian Paley's views on being a fair (white) teacher of black children evolved over the years, so did her views on being a fair teacher of other children outside the classroom circle. Unlike the issues of race and the integrated school, however, the other matters in which fairness dominates Paley's work did not advance in response to "the outside world struggling to get in" ([1979], 2000, 9). On the contrary, it might be said, her concerns took shape as she observed the inside worlds of the classroom struggling to get out. Each of these internal issues had been widely ignored by teachers for so long that she might have looked past them all with impunity. In pursuit of the fair classroom that all young children need, however, she could not. The first problem she addresses hides in plain sight every day and in every early childhood classroom. It is the psychosomatic and social distance between small boys and their female teachers and classmates. The second is one we like to tell ourselves we've solved by providing "mainstreamed" and "inclusive" classrooms. It is the distance between developmentally different children and their teachers and peers. And, the last problem is so insidious that for the most part early childhood teacher education refuses to recognize it. It is the distance between unpopular children and those who wear the mantle of the chosen.

All of these issues obviously capture the relational nature of life in classrooms. Along with racism, they provide teachers with a fairly comprehensive inventory of why it sometimes does not feel good to be a young child starting school. The effects of these problems in the classroom provide all the justification teachers need to battle them, despite their apparent intractability. Paley's pursuit of fairness writ large leads us full circle back to her philosophy of education and the ultimate purpose of schooling: democracy in action. The democratic classroom weighs heavily on Paley's mind throughout her writing, but it is in her discussions of fairness regarding race, gender, developmental difference, and inclusion that it is best realized.

NOT LIKE US

I have always found *Boys and Girls: Superheroes in the Doll Corner*, the name of Paley's third book and kindergarten study, an enigmatic title. On the one hand, it conjures images of kindergarten girls who dress up as Wonder Woman to put the baby to bed. On the other, it brings to mind crusaders eager to trade in their capes for neckties. Actually, neither scenario is correct. The title refers to a doll corner seriously divided (literally and metaphorically) along gender lines and gender roles. Superheroes who act like superheroes are no more welcome in the kindergarten doll corner than mothers tending babies are in the blocks corner. This, of course, is not news to a seasoned kindergarten teacher like Paley. The gendered play of boys and girls in the doll corner is no leftover habit from preschool. If anything, she writes, "kindergarten is a triumph of sexual stereotyping" (1984, ix). That is, young children seem to revel in the playing out of different gender roles at the extremes. Lest we be inclined to rationalize this development as the result of socialization not of either gender's choosing, and therefore somehow undesirable, Paley warns us off: "Adults may approve or disapprove of certain behaviors and gather explanations from psychologists, but the children watch one another and synchronize their movements. It is the most exciting game in town" (xi). As certain as Paley is of the gender roles unfolding in her classroom, she is less sure of what the significance is to her teaching. This is what she aims to uncover.

Though somewhat more understated than the other books in which Paley's pedagogy of fairness is front and center, I would argue that *Boys and Girls* competes handily. As always, Paley captures the children's play evocatively. Noting the relational differences at work in the children's play, she writes that of any event the boys inevitably ask, "Who won?" They seek proof of evil. Girls, by contrast, seek proof of goodness and ask, "Who's happy?" When it comes to the doll corner, Paley writes, kindergarten superheroes don't so much come to visit as to invade. They're good guys looking for bad guys, or they're bad guys on the run. By contrast, the doll corner matriarchs don't so much invite the superheroes to play as attempt to domesticate them. Don't disrupt, they scold the intruders, be fathers. For the girls, the doll corner is the culminating phase of pretend play around family life. Though they may venture forth from the house to the forest, they don't leave the old family roles and obligations behind in their play. For the boys, the doll corner and its stock characters are things from which they must run. They want to trade in that domestic world for the universe, preferably a universe at war.

Paley admits that that the further the boys get from the doll corner, the closer they get to "rhythms and images" bursting with movement, noise, and mock violence that displease her (xii). Worse, even when the girls' play is loud and rambunctious—as it undeniably can be—she gives it a pass simply because its themes are less aggressive. This may not be fair teaching, but the truth is Paley's reactions are so commonplace in early childhood education that on one level they hardly register. It is simply not unusual that the more boy-like the boys' play grows—as it inevitably does—the less teachers find their preferences attractive. Most would agree with Paley: "When the children separate by sex, I, the teacher, am more often on the girls' side. We move at the same pace, and reach for the same activities" (ix).[1] But the first lesson of *Boys and Girls* is that Paley does not let teachers off the hook. In effect, she asks us to consider what it means when teachers begin to psychologically pull away from half of the children who have not yet learned to tie their shoes. The doll corner is Paley's metaphor, but the segregation of the boys' interests from her own is not limited to fantasy play. The "activities" she refers to include arts and crafts and the typical "school work" involving fine motor coordination that takes place at the tables.[2] She makes the further observation that girls are attracted to table work additionally because the teachers are there, establishing early their acceptance of how school works over the long haul. As I discuss below, given the pushdown of academics into the preschool and kindergarten, early childhood educators must be concerned with the ramifications of this split between boys and their teachers now more than ever.

Some might say that boys have been fleeing the classroom and their female teachers in American schools since before Huck Finn. Modern literature and popular culture, from Dennis the Menace to Holden Caulfield to Harry Potter, celebrate nonconforming, singular young males. Others argue that girls have been even more discriminated against by schools and teachers throughout American educational history. Thus, the full weight of Paley's admission of discrimination may not be readily apparent. But what if we paused a moment and substituted black children for boys? Or brown children? Muslim? Or Jewish? Would we celebrate then? By what standard can we honestly look a child in the eye and say, "I may not like you but I will teach you if I must"?

Like Paley's books that focus on race and fair teaching, *Boys and Girls*, too, has its place in history. But it is not the one we might expect. To appreciate what prompted Philip Jackson to describe Paley as "unflinching" and "courageous" in tackling gender bias against boys in early childhood, we must consider it in light of the gender identity wars that raged in the last quarter of the twentieth century. Some developmental and psychoanalytical corners championed the argument advanced by Bruno Bettelheim that archetypal, gender play represents the final phase in young children's sex role development. Responding to an earlier article Paley wrote on gender-based play, Bettelheim (1975) argues that extreme sexual stereotyping by the young self is an unavoidable phase of late early childhood in order to unequivocally secure the girlness or boyness that will become essential in later sexual development. Bettelheim goes on to say that the latency period that follows this phase contains both time and room for children to make their way back to the center to more nuanced gender roles. From this perspective, there is no need to worry that the well-acknowledged exaggeration in the doll corner will translate into long-term occupational or social destiny. Permission to engage in sex-typed play should therefore be a matter of course.

In the feminists' corner are those who have examined how schools shortchange girls in the long run, leaving behind the very success Paley says they enjoy in the early childhood years. Carole Gilligan's field-changing feminist treatise *In a Different Voice: Psychological Theory and Women's Development*, published just two years before Paley's *Boys and Girls*, provides the historical context by which we can judge the boldness of Paley's effort. Gilligan argues passionately that gender differences are not "biologically determined or socially constructed" but are a combination thereof (1982, xix). The long-term problem for girls, she says, is that the social construction of gender as manifested in school expectations has historically favored the analytical thinking more typical of boys and systematically disfavored girls' more relational view of events. Though Gilligan's work attracted its own share of controversy, it was the fire starter for a surge of research that points to the losses girls, not boys, suffer in schools under gender-normed expectations, especially in the middle-school years. *Failing at Fairness: How Our Schools Cheat Girls* (Sadker and Sadker 1994) and *Reviving Ophelia: Saving the Selves of Adolescent Girls* (Pipher 1995) are two examples. Derman-Sparks's influential anti-bias curriculum (1989) serves up many warnings against a benign view of gender-based play in the preschool and kindergarten classroom.

Let me be clear. Nothing Paley argues in *Boys and Girls* suggests that girls' development is any less precious or less in need of caretaking than boys'. She is mindful of what happens when girls indulge only in stereotypical play. She points out, for example, that their commitment to the doll corner often steals time from other learning opportunities that have real implications for learning. One example is the logico-mathematical and spatial lessons to be garnered through block play, of which most girls do too little. And, to her chagrin, she discovers that she hadn't realized that girls can be just as physical as boys, how much they like to run, for example, though she has not provided them with the opportunity to do so. It is extremely humbling information to the teacher who prides herself on her observation skills. The elegance of *Boys and Girls*, however, is that without detracting from what girls need from their schooling in the beginning or in the long run, it leaves no doubt that boys receive short shrift from their first teachers for no other reason than *they are not like girls*. In this sense, it can be argued that Paley took an even greater risk in *Boys and Girls* than she did in *White Teacher*. In the latter, unfair teaching based on race was a topic on many minds. But in the furor that Gilligan's work ushered in, Paley's was a lone voice for boys. With the passage of time, she has also proved something of a seer. Much has been written in recent years on the problems boys have in school. Research has shown they now lag behind girls on almost every measure of school success, from reading scores to dropout rates. Sadly, the fact that they are most associated with the rise in school violence has contributed to their newfound time in the spotlight. There is also an increasing awareness that the problem resides as much in school as out of it. For example, in a 2008 study on young boys' relationship to their teachers, Raider-Roth and colleagues find that teachers, acting out their own gendered identities, too often attempt to enculturate boys away from their boy-like tendencies, thus setting them up to resist school and teachers from the beginning. Newkirk (2002) offers a thoughtful analysis of the genres that boys are attracted to, such as video games and television, which are generally devalued in both reading and writing curriculums, leaving them to put their natural interests on hold for years until they have more control over their literacy lives. Of course, by then they may no longer be interested. Booth (2002) details an approach to teaching reading and writing that employs typical boy interests, such as comics, action-oriented stories, and drama to counter boys' perceptions that reading and writing is what girls do.[3]

The radical assumption that Paley makes in *Boys and Girls* is that what young children are inclined to do must contain some truth that holds the clues as to how to best teach them fairly. If this is so, then it appears the key to a young boy's learning is a teacher who not only tolerates his interests in louder, noisier, aggressive play and genres, but also asks why he finds it meaningful (bringing us back to Paley's pedagogy of meaning). By the study's end, Paley is compelled to wonder if her kindergarten has been an unsafe place for boys. Beyond the advantages that her preference for doll corner play, metaphorically speaking, brings to the girls, there is the matter of table work. This has never been an insignificant fact of kindergarten life for boys, even when it was more or less restricted to arts and crafts activities or school readiness activities. Table work typically relies on two skills: fine motor coordination (including holding a pencil) and the ability to sit still for fifteen or more minutes. Most often it does not call on the child's imagination. On average, boys are less proficient at these skills than girls, a fact that most have known about themselves since entering preschool. When called upon at the height of their interest in being not like girls, they are primed to run in the opposite direction in more ways than one. But, as Paley makes clear, the "rules" of kindergarten say no running, and preferably no superheroes. We could probably add no roaring to this list, though, as Paley writes, "the more unprotected boys feel" in kindergarten, "the louder they roar" (1984, 50). This leads to the next question in fair teaching: Should the teacher grant boys the protection they need?

By study's end, Paley not only learns to find empathy for boys seeking the psychological safety of world dominance, she finds its purpose. For boys, she realizes, "There cannot be too many superheroes once you leave the doll corner" (99). Boy play is the protection they need in response to what they cannot do right, at least not yet. Paley concludes that the balance of free play and table activities in her kindergarten favors the girls' natural tendencies (85), and she makes a decision that will affect her teaching forever. Since boys need more, not less, time to enact the dramas of boyhood before they can settle down and take their seat at the table with the girls, she will give it to them. She makes a substantive and, by today's standards, subversive change in the class schedule: she doubles the time for free play. In doing so, she proves her hunch that boys will be "less like boys" when they have more time to be boys. That is, they participate cooperatively in activities at the table and engage in more school-friendly behaviors once they have had sufficient time to run, to be loud, and most of all, to engage in fantasy play. In an equal display of fair teaching, the girls spend more time in the block corner.

Boys and Girls: Superheroes in the Doll Corner remains ahead of its time still. Until we, as Paley suggests, admit that the fundamental problem is not the profiles of particular boys or their overall incompatibility with the demands of school, but their incompatibility with the feminized norms of early schooling, we have done little to give them a fair start. We will continue to send them into the upper elementary school grades on edge and out of sync with school norms and teacher expectations. That the vast majority of them manage to make the adjustment is of course a testimony to their resilience and not to our collective teaching imagination. It also tells us nothing about the ones who don't.

VEHICLES OF THEIR OWN

As its title suggests, Paley's 1990 book, *The Boy Who Would Be a Helicopter: The Uses of Storytelling in the Classroom*, has much to tell us about stories and storytelling. In many ways, it is a useful follow up to *Wally's Stories: Conversations in the Kindergarten* (1981), where storytelling and story acting first surfaced in her work. Even more important, it deepens our understanding of Paley's pedagogy of fairness, as her philosophy solidifies around Jason, the helicopter boy. Many first-time readers wonder why Paley doesn't seek a special placement for Jason. She certainly gives many details that would seem to warrant such a decision. She notes that he is unable to engage in normal conversations and social relations, though she shows us that he is capable of speech. He seems indifferent to invitations to play. Paley details Jason's apparent determination to remain a solitary player on the fringe of classroom life, creating a private world around a toy helicopter with a broken blade. Indeed, we learn that when Paley or the other children attempt to interact with Jason, he often responds angrily. At other times, he withdraws, as if overstimulated by their questions and interest.

Paley anticipates the concerns Jason will raise among readers in the book's preface, but she asks that we put them on hold. "There are labels that might be attached to Jason," she writes, "but we'll neither define nor categorize him" (1990, xii). What she means by this is that although there are the usual labels, she has a different one that speaks to her work in fair teaching and the purpose of schooling. Jason is not a special education student to Paley, but he is an outsider, in fact, he is "the quintessential outsider, beyond race, place, or age" (xi). But not even this explains why Jason's story moves Paley's theory of fair teaching forward so dramatically The fact is, Jason exemplifies a most critical, if typically unexamined, conundrum of fair teaching: the child who most needs to be included, but who refuses our invitation to join. Paley, however, tells herself that her theories of teaching are "unreliable if they do not include Jason" (31). Her willingness to take the plunge into the uncharted waters of working without labels, of teaching only to include and understand, demands our attention.

The Boy Who Would Be a Helicopter is not the first or last time Paley throws the classroom door wide open so that everyone can play inside the circle. It is, however, unique in her repertoire of work on fairness in that it is not Jason's background, gender, skin color, or even his personality that distances him from his teacher and his peers. Although it is possible he could represent any subset of these groups, Jason's role in Paley's teaching life is not what he (and his helicopter) represent. Instead, she finds, she has no choice but to follow him and his helicopter wherever they go (57). Paley describes this as her pedagogical move from theory maker to storyteller. Eventually, Jason's helicopter-based play reveals that his communication problems may be tied to his fear of abandonment, including a fear of being left at school. This does not signal a happy ending for Jason. He is not suddenly free of all his isolating behaviors. As the year progresses, he seems less glum, but he has not been relieved of his differences.

This is Paley's point. It is not within her power to fix Jason. Her job is to believe in his right to be cared for and valued in school, and to make school a safe place, as it must be for all who enter. "He is the one we must learn to include in our school culture if it is to be an island of safety and sensibility for everyone" (xi). It is in this sense that Jason's story extends what Paley had learned earlier about children ostracized by race or gender or, as we shall see, by unpopularity. "The story of Jason and his helicopter reminds us that every child enters the classroom in a vehicle propelled by that child alone, at a particular place and for a particular purpose. Here is where the fair study of children begins and where teaching becomes a moral act" (xii). Sidorkin's analysis of *The Boy Who Would Be a Helicopter* picks up on this as well. He borrows from Bakhtin's theory of polyphony (multiple voices, multiple claims) to describe the Paley's book as a novel (it is not) in which the teacher's role is to help the children "combine their strengths against the common enemy of isolation, muteness and incomprehension" (2000, 6).

In the next and last section on classrooms as fair places, I turn to Paley's controversial experiment in her classroom requiring the children to take up this charge. "You can't say you can't play" is the rule behind her plan, described in her 1992 book of the same name. Just as Noddings suggests that teachers must help students develop the capacity to care (1992, 18), Paley comes to believe that fairness that resides only in the teacher is not enough. For Paley, more than most, understands that the teacher is but half the classroom story.

PARADOXICAL FAIRNESS: MANDATING INCLUSION

You Can't Say You Can't Play functions as something of a sequel to *The Boy Who Would Be a Helicopter*. Its epigraph immediately alerts us to Paley's continuing focus on the outsider with a quote from Leviticus 19:34 that begins "The stranger that sojourneth with you shall be unto you as the homeborn among you." This time, however, the outsider and stranger is not the unknown child, but the *uninvited* one. The book opens with a rueful comment from Paley: "Turning sixty, I am more aware of the voices of exclusion in the classroom. 'You can't play' suddenly seems too overbearing and harsh, resounding like a slap from wall to wall. How casually one child determines the fate of another" (1992, 3). The problem, Paley soon decides, is the children's "habit of rejection," which suddenly, and it seems unexpectedly, she can no longer tolerate. And so she bans it with six simple words on a sign she hangs in her kindergarten classroom: YOU CAN'T SAY YOU CAN'T PLAY. With this, she launches her investigation into mandated inclusion.

In many ways, *You Can't Say You Can't Play* is Paley's most atypical book. That is, rather than seeking to unveil young children's development or experience in school, she actually attempts to change its course. It is also her most radical book, for its mantra is a direct challenge to some of the established building blocks of early childhood education, including the child-centered curriculum, the socially competent child, the teacher as facilitator, and schools as preparation for real life. This may account for why so few teacher educators have attempted to adopt it and why replication studies are so limited in number and sample size. (Two of the few examples are Harrist and Bradley 2003 and Sapon-Shevin et al. 1998.) At the same time, what Paley's idea has lacked in followers or imitators, it has gained in sustained attention as a perennial presence on course syllabi and in articles on education and social justice. Always a favorite topic of debate, it suggests that few of us have forgotten the pain of rejection in school.

You Can't Say You Can't Play brings Paley's pedagogy of fairness to full bloom. Whereas she earlier took responsibility for understanding and teaching to young children's racial, gender, and social identities, she now ups the ante by asking the children to take responsibility as well. This vision of a teacher guiding young children to universal fairness offers a serious challenge to contemporary classroom practice. It is one thing for teachers to have high expectations of their own inclusiveness. It is quite another to require that the children do so as well. But Paley's philosophical commitment to fair classrooms cannot stand without this proposition. This is not to say that she draws upon widespread support for her innovation, as my analysis below shows. I rely on two sources for evidence. The first comprises findings from my survey of thirty-five teacher education students, teachers, and teacher educators. The survey calls for a written or oral opinion following group discussion, and responses run the gamut from supportive to resistant. The second involves arguments from the literature, both for and against the rule, as well as an exploration of its implications for a democratic education.

Beginning with the survey, it is clear that those who favor the "you can't say you can't play" rule find it long overdue. They see no positive side to allowing some children to act as gatekeepers in classroom play (including recess). In fact, many connect exclusion with greater long-term interpersonal and social problems. One survey respondent writes, "If we don't also teach or facilitate affective content (like 'you can't say you can't play'), then I don't think we have any right to be distressed about rising levels of violence and alienation in our society." Others in this group take a more personal perspective; they echo Paley's own recollection of never being at ease in the shadow of more popular children. They are grateful for her innovation and share her idealism in building a world in which rejection is not only eliminated, but also unimaginable. I might note that this was a common response in popular reviews of the book when it was first published.

Other survey respondents are attracted to the idea in theory, but view it as unrealistic in practice. Objection centers mostly on the intense monitoring it requires: "My first thought is that it is an appealing rule because it provides a structure, without any allowed loopholes, for instituting system-wide fairness and access for all students. . . . Is it practical?" This sentiment reflects the views of the four elementary school teachers in the 1998 replication study by Sapon-Shevin and colleagues. The reaction should not surprise us. Teachers dislike practices that must be heavily monitored. "You can't say you can't play" most certainly falls into this category, at least at first. Other members of the survey group hesitate because they fear the resistance they will meet from the children. Their intuition tells them that most will react like Paley's Lisa, who complained, "But, then, what's the whole point of playing?" rather than like her "sad-eyed" and excluded Clara, who welcomes the change (1992, 14). Teachers dislike having to talk children into things, especially children who hold some status in the class. Finally, this skeptical group also express doubt as to whether it's ethically fair to impose their worldview of personal relations on individual children, even in the name of fairness to all children.

With regard to this last point, Paley, too, has her doubts about the ethics of forced inclusion and acknowledges that it feels counterintuitive. After all, she notes, teachers themselves prefer to sit among friends in the lunchroom. She does not judge, admitting only that there is a "natural desire to include certain people and exclude others" (73). But after much reflection, she is not deterred by either the impracticality of her mission or her own misgivings. Instead she allows herself to be swayed by Angelo's assessment: "People that is alone they has water in their eyes." In doing so, she decides "to set out specifically and openly to make children less sad by giving them the keys to the kingdom" (74). In the end, she is energized by the potential changes that "you can't say you can't play" can bring for all children, including the Lisas. To her delight, the children in her kindergarten classroom adjust rather quickly to the rule, dispensing worries of both impracticality and top-down management.

Convincingly as she makes the case for herself, however, Paley does not persuade all. The third type of response to "you can't say you can't play" has several different voices in both the survey and the literature, but all essentially oppose the rule on merit. At the very least, according to Goodman (2000), it is "simplistic," an extreme and shallow form of indoctrination into the code of "niceness" captured in such familiar norms as be helpful, share, take turns, and so on (as contrasted with don't be mean, fight, or bully). Others don't see the rule as simplistic as much as merely ineffective. Forcing someone to play with someone else won't solve the problem of rejection, one of the survey respondents writes, adding, "I'm *not* going to play nicely with someone I don't like, no matter what the teacher said." Other respondents worry whether the rule itself will only intensify a child's feeling of rejection by calling attention to his or her rejected status. Paley's own coworkers raise a similar objection.

Goodman goes on to offer yet a second objection to the rule. This one suggests far more dire consequences. If Paley sees the rule as a reasonable effort to right an unqualified wrong, Goodman sees it as a slippery slope toward the forced acceptance of not just unpopular, but truly antisocial behavior. Through this lens, the rejecter becomes the victim of the rejectee's bullying. Goodman writes, "Although of course we want children to be caring, considerate, tactful, and understanding of others, we also want them to be honest, strong-minded, and bold. We want them to resist peer pressure, to speak out against wrongfulness, to refuse to go along, even at the cost of offending. An honorable child, standing by the truth, must risk hurting, perhaps alienating, another" (2000, 30).

In some sense, Noddings anticipates Goodman's concern about bad influences in her discussion of friends whose behavior betrays the guidelines for friendship. However, Noddings suggests that the real test of a caring relationship comes not in the offense, but in the response. Real friends, she says, do not turn their backs on the offenders; they do what they can to help them. "From the perspective of caring, there is no inherent conflict between moral requirements and friendship, because we have a primary obligation to promote our friends' moral growth" (1992, 99). Furthermore, Noddings does not suggest that friends, especially children, forgo common sense. If a break proves beyond repair, she writes, the offer of friendship may be withdrawn. From Noddings's perspective, then, Goodman's concerns about the potential consequences in a "you can't say you can't play" classroom are overblown. To this I would question Goodman's presumption that things could ever advance to this state of alarm. There is no evidence that Paley intends for teachers to ignore real and serious social transgressions among children (though I doubt she can imagine children capable of committing truly antisocial acts). She only intends to counterbalance the meanness of exclusion that surfaces in all early childhood classrooms. Should her effort replace the habit of rejection with the habit of moral indifference, Goodman would indeed have a case. But nothing in what Paley writes encourages the children or the reader to turn a blind eye toward dishonesty, disobedience, or dishonor.

Yet, as extreme as Goodman's warning is about the potential harm the rule could cause young children's developing psyches, it is still less puzzling than her third reaction, and the one most prevalent among the education respondents. This involves the benefits of exclusion for the excluded. I refer to what one respondent calls the "silver lining" of rejection and what Goodman calls the "morally productive lessons" that would be lost in a classroom in which all children can play. Goodman writes of the rejected child, "Rejected may learn that exclusion by a child is not so terrible, that he can shrug it off and play with more accepting children, that he need not see himself as victimized"(2000, 30). For some, Goodman is apparently on to something here. The majority of survey respondents proposed that rejection should be not only tolerated, but also actually welcomed in the classroom because of its positive impact on the rejected child's "character." Even more fascinating, the stronger the writer's objection to the rule, the more experience with rejection he or she admitted to. One teacher education student, for example, wrote that he had been rejected in middle school for being very overweight and a bad basketball player.

> This idea, you can't say you can't play, has now consumed a major part of my thinking. I have been wavering back and forth on what I have thought about it, and I have recently come to a new hypothesis: [Shouldn't] survival of the fittest dominate? By forcing everyone to let everyone play, no one has to improve.

As a result of his experience with rejection, the respondent said, he lost weight and got better at basketball. Another student teacher wrote a "personal story of successful exclusion."

> When I just started to play baseball I was terrible and therefore excluded from the group of boys who played [well]. I went to my Dad who spent time with me, and taught me to play. Once I learned to play I was no longer excluded. If those boys had been forced to accept me I never would have learned the game as well, and I would not have those memories with my father.

A third wrote of her fifth-grade group's rejection of another classmate.

> This one girl named Jenny tried time and time again to get into our group. We occasionally played with her, but most of the time we just played the four of us and excluded her. . . . If we would have been forced to play with Jenny, we probably would have ended up being mean to her, and making her feel worse. . . . I definitely believe that rejection is wrong and that no child should be made to feel like a complete stranger, but I don't think that a rule like Paley's is

> the solution. In my situation, Jenny was better off not being friends with my friends and [me] because we never would have been her real friends [even with Paley's rule]. She came to find other friends who were her true friends.

Finally, a fourth education student wrote that when it came to rejection, well, "That's life."

The students' perceptions of the value of rejection are undoubtedly shaped by myriad factors, from family to class to culture. But just as surely, school played a pivotal role, beginning in kindergarten. Paley writes that by kindergarten a social hierarchy has settled in that gives some children permission to determine the popular fate of their classmates, meaning some will be allowed to play, while the others "learn to anticipate the sting of rejection (1992, 5). We know from Paley's own survey of students in her elementary school that the aftereffects of early rejection don't wait until college or even high school to emerge. They start as early as first grade, as some of the reactions to the "you can't say you can't play" rule that Paley obtains from the older children demonstrate:

First grade
"[S]omeone has to be the one who tells everyone [who can or cannot play]."
"[The excluded] person just walks away. That's better."
Second grade
"Yeah, [the rule] is fair, but some people don't like other people. So it would spoil the game."
"That would be more fair, but it would be impossible to have any fun. It is a good rule, though."
Third grade
"They don't want people they don't like. They don't want me."
"The rule won't work. If people don't like them and don't let them play, and if there's a rule, they'll tell the teacher and if the teacher makes them do it they just won't be nice to that person."
Fourth grade
"[The rule won't work.] We're meaner than when we were young."
"The boys accept themselves much more. A girl is more likely to tell another girl she can't play."

Fifth grade

"In your whole life you're never not going to go through life not excluded. So you may as well learn it now." (1992)

So it is little exaggeration to suggest that when Paley asks, "Must it be so?" she is doing more than asking to let all children play. She is more than disagreeing with Goodman. She is asking why it is we have not galvanized ourselves to oust rejection from our classrooms before it becomes an end in itself, before it obscures the insidious result of not disallowing it. She leads us to understand that long before they have lost their teeth or stopped believing in Santa Claus, all young children discover that some of them are more valued than others. How fair is that?

I suggest that there are several possible reasons why we've allowed social rejection to flourish in the early childhood classroom, all of which go to the very need for *You Can't Say You Can't Play*, and hence to the success or failure of Paley's challenge. All are well known in their own right, and all share one common assumption: the inevitability of the popular child and its correlate, the unpopular child.

Empirically speaking, early childhood authorities have long suggested a social bell curve by virtue of the concept of normal social development, which includes the concept of the child who does not fit in (Spodek 1993; Williams and Fromberg 1992). Ladd and Coleman's 1993 review of the literature finds that, first, children are capable of forming peer relationships at early ages; second, there are important pathways to friendship and peer acceptance for young children; and, third, peer relationships are significant in children's lives and may make important contributions to their development and well-being. Studies of rejected children, who by definition fall outside the range of normal, suggest that peer rejection begins early in life (Coie and Dodge 1983; Howe 1988; Ladd and Price 1987, as cited in Ladd and Coleman 1993; Spodek 1993; Williams and Fromberg 1992). Teachers' evaluations of these children are likely to include language such as "lacking social skills" or needing "help and support from teachers in developing positive relationships with others" (Bredekamp and Copple 1997, 123). However, the research also suggests that rejected children often maintain their status throughout childhood, leading to the obvious conclusion that the recommended "help and support" is not adequate to the task.

The image of the unpopular child is so powerful in our collective imaginations, so much a part of our collective definition of childhood, that, as the earlier testimonies reveal, it is even embraced by the unpopular children themselves, as if it were a law of nature. To add insult to injury, the very young unpopular child need not exhibit anything like the gross antisocial behavior Goodman warns against. Nor does she need to be the victim of cultural bias, racism, or other more overt forms of rejection, though it might be argued that such biases have their natural roots in the very fact of an acceptable social hierarchy. What Paley makes so heartbreakingly clear is that in the preschool and kindergarten, it is already more than enough that the rejected child is not appealing—perhaps not verbally adept, not quick, too fat, not well dressed. In other words, not like the popular children.

Another well-recognized force at work in the type of classroom that Paley is struggling against and that helps maintain the status of popular versus unpopular children is the belief that young children cannot be expected to accept their peers until they have first accepted themselves. This conviction has led to familiar practices aimed at developing children's self-esteem based on their individual profiles, an approach embodied in the recommendations of the highly influential *Developmentally Appropriate Practices in Early Childhood Programs (DAP)*, published by the National Association for the Education of Young Children. Consider the following directive concerning classroom community building from the second edition:

> Teachers use many strategies to help build a sense of the group as a cohesive community. The children sometimes work on group activities that all can identify with. . . . Teachers engage children in experiences that demonstrate the explicit valuing of each child. (Bredekamp and Copple 1997, 124)

DAP further recommends that pedagogical decisions be based on "what is known about the strengths, interests, and needs of each individual child in the group to be able to adapt for and be responsive to inevitable individual variation" (9).

There can be no doubt that teachers who subscribe to *DAP*'s recommendations aim to ensure the healthy development of all children, including the very same children Paley means to rescue by declaring "you can't say you can't play." Yet it seems obvious that the road to full inclusion cannot rely on group activities that "all can identify with." Practical participation in community life requires that, if not all, at least many individual strengths, interests, and needs be suppressed for the common good. It is also not clear that the explicit "valuing of each child" leads to the explicit valuing of *all* children. For example, "I Am Special" or "I Like Me" activities are common to kindergarten. The idea is to help young children recognize their own uniqueness, as well as to appreciate the uniqueness of others. Implicit in this view is the belief that a suitable level of self-worth will lead to an in-kind embrace of others' special qualities. Assuming for the moment that this is true, we must not forget that acceptance of someone else's differences is not the same as an invitation to play. But, in fact, if love of self easily translated into acceptance of all, then there would be no social bell curve, no need for "you can't say you can't play." The brutal fact of schooling is that some differences are more appealing than others.

Another problem with the self-worth proposition is that most teachers testify that children who exclude others often exhibit plenty of self-worth. They appear to have secure friendships, perform well at school tasks, act generally happy, and take on leadership positions in the class. Furthermore, in addition to picking and choosing playmates discriminately, they are careful in the maintenance of their own status. In a kindergarten classroom I visited recently, for example, two boys with clear social standing in the room had excitedly selected the Duplo center during free time. A few minutes after they started, Samantha, a child with no reliable playmates, showed up. "Samantha's here," Jordan told Michael with a note of uh-oh in his voice. Then, easily forsaking what he had coveted just a moment ago, he announced in a pseudo-casual voice, "We don't want to play with Duplos, right, Michael?" Off they went. As I see it, teachers' attempts to increase the self-worth of children like these are unnecessary. Their respective sense of self is quite good. Moreover, any increase in self-worth is highly unlikely to increase their tendency to include those toward whom they are naturally disinclined.

Paley's decision to remove the individual child from the center of the curriculum and replace it with the included child not only brings about a sea change in the children's lives, it asks something very different of teachers. Paley makes crystal clear that the new order will not result from mere modeling or long-term cultivation, two traditional tools of the early childhood teacher. It requires teachers' direct meddling in children's interpersonal affairs, immediately, boldly, and steadfastly. Via "you can't say you can't play," Paley openly exchanges the historical role of teacher as facilitator of children's relationships for one of teacher as moral authority. Young children, she decides after decades of observation, cannot be depended on to act in the interests of those who seem different. "We must be told, when we are young, what rules to live by. The grownups must tell the children early in life so that myth and morality proclaim the same message while the children are still listening" (1992, 110). The question here, linked to Vygotsky's theory of scaffolded learning, is not what children do naturally, but what they can do with assistance (Bodrova and Leong 2007; Vygotsky 1978). Implicit in Paley's direct approach is the idea that classroom teachers who fail to create inclusive classrooms or implement a curriculum that focuses on the rejected child's deficits only serve to normalize rejection in the classroom. They fail to make it necessary for us to even consider whether sanctioned exclusion may *in and of itself* be the problem.

In the end, Paley easily accepts Noddings claim that power is not only unevenly distributed between the teacher and child, it must be so in order for the teacher to serve the best interests of the child. Noddings cites Martin Buber's reference to teachers' "special responsibilities" to see the world as the children see it. This would mean, of course, as all children see it, even the rejected children. She says, "The teacher-student relation is, of necessity, unequal. Teachers have special responsibilities that students cannot assume. Martin Buber . . . wrote that teachers must practice 'inclusion,' teachers must, that is, take on a dual perspective: their own and that of their students" (Noddings 1992, 107).

The decision to prioritize the needs of rejected children challenges the usual progressive practice of letting self-interest drive the curriculum and leads to questions of what we mean by democracy in education. Mayhew and Edwards, founding teachers in Dewey's

University of Chicago Laboratory School and authors of *The Dewey School* (1936), offer some insight as to the relationship between banning rejection and the progressive tenets of choice. According to Mayhew and Edwards, the child is always "an individual in relationships . . . [and is] always a member of a society which in turn had powerful influences upon him. It is also conceived that a person finds his best expression when his interests and purposes are identical with those of a group as they put through a common project together" (1936, 427). In Paley's kindergarten classroom, the children's "common project" is not based on math or science, but on play. Play, she writes, is as singularly suited for the purposes of inclusion for children on either side of the inclusion fence as it is for other purposes discussed in chapters 2 and 3. As I see it, for a child to include another in play does not require acceptance of difference, as it does when predicated on the first child's self-interest, but merely the *practice of acceptance*. Simultaneously, it allows a formerly rejected child to practice being included.

I see this process as similar to Vygotsky's 1978 description of what happens in imaginary play. In essence, the acceptance and inclusion practice provides the opportunity for all children to embody not their actual selves, but their potential selves or, in this case, their group selves. Paley's "you can't say you can't play" argues for early childhood educators to go beyond the question of how and when they support children's individual development to ask how and when they support group membership for all. This view, as Mayhew and Edwards suggest, allows us to see the group as empowering rather than threatening, as welcoming rather than rejecting. It could further be argued that the role of the group is so significant that the optimal development of all children, even the popular ones, can flourish only when group membership is guaranteed (Erikson [1950] 1985, 85). Thus, teachers who skirt its role in the name of the child-centered classroom run counter to the children's long-term interests. Noddings turns to Dewey on this: "[Dewey's] child-centered followers . . . too often concentrated on the child's past and present expectations, forgetting that the teacher bears major responsibility for the child's future experience or growth" (1992, 64).

Without question, then, "you can't say you can't play" challenges the traditional balance of power between teachers and children around social relationships in school. It also challenges the very purpose of schooling. With one rule, Paley upends the long-standing belief that the best preparation for real life is the school's imitation of it. In fact, school as a democratic institution is the tipping factor in her decision to go ahead with the ban on rejection in the first place. First, she wonders, "I want to do a favor for Clara, but is it fair to spoil Lisa's and Cynthia's play?" But then she remembers where she is. "Is it fair for children *in school* to keep another child out of play?" In school is clearly the distinction here. "After all," she goes on, "this classroom belongs to all of us. It is not a private place, like our homes" (1992, 16).Community ownership implies community, not select participation. Just as we do not construct buildings merely to test the hurricane's strength, a "you can't say you can't play" agenda means we do not create classroom environments so that only the strongest members survive. In the end, Paley decides that the right to inclusion trumps the right to preference in school. The right to play trumps the right of refusal in school. The teacher, in school, gets to decide this. Of course, some rejected children—though decidedly not all—display off-putting behaviors. Their inclusion in play, forced or unforced, probably will change the dynamic. They indeed might need some assistance in entering the play without threatening its dissolution. But does any of this negate their group membership in school? Paley says no. Covaleskie (2003) agrees.

The benefits of systematically disallowing rejection seem obvious for the rejected child, but there are benefits for others as well. One surprising result is the impact on the needs of those seemingly fortunate members of what Paley calls the "ruling class." If we look closely, we may find that some young children, though of course not all, can feel burdened by too much popularity and too much power over others. Even as they profit from their position, the tears of exclusion and the habit of rejection can weigh heavily on the ruling child's shoulders. "I don't want to be the boss," Curtis tells Paley. "*They* say I am." Sometimes children turn their power into self-rejection. As we saw above, a fourth-grade girl tells Paley that boys don't inflict this kind of pain on one another. "We're definitely meaner to each other." Another says that "we get more practice being mean" as time goes on. "We're much meaner than in kindergarten."

Often children end up trapped by their favored status. I am reminded of Renee, an overweight, unpopular six-year-old in one of my own kindergarten classes, long before I had encountered "you can't say you can't play." Parts in our class stories at that time were assigned by the author of the day, not the teacher, as they were later. After months of dramatizing stories about kingdoms and castles, common interests of kindergartners, Renee suddenly erupted as she was once more passed over for the most coveted role. "Why does Lauren *always* get to be the princess?" I checked my notes and found that Renee had never been chosen to be the princess by her classmates and that no more than three other girls had been chosen only once. Lauren, an exceptionally beautiful child, whose looks were recognized by children and adults alike and were no doubt part of her appeal, had been chosen all the rest of the times. I asked Lauren if she would mind taking a break from the princess role to give the other kids a chance. Lauren looked surprised, and then decidedly relieved. She said, "I wouldn't care. I'd be glad." The children took Lauren at her word and thereafter chose her to be the wicked stepmother and even the prince. She appeared to flourish in her new range of dramatic options, as did Renee and the other girls in their new role as the princess.

Additionally, a "you can't say you can't play" classroom resonates with research on non-Western child-rearing practices suggesting that, outside the United States, many cultures look to schools to indoctrinate young children into group membership before they seek to distinguish them as individuals in the group (Bernhard et al. 1998). Tobin, Wu, and Davidson's 1989 cross-cultural study of preschools in China, Japan, and the United States finds that parents in the first two countries just assume their young children will do the same thing as everyone else in such activities as exercise or dance. American parents and even school personnel, on the other hand, express "ambivalent" feelings about such uniformity. An emphasis on individual children's rights even surpasses democratic goals for many, except with regard to policies that might interfere with their own child's individual rights. The authors of the study write, "The emphasis Americans give to the importance of individualism, freedom, and self-actualization displaces discussion of equality. Egalitarian concerns emerged clearly only in discussion of administrative policies, not with regard to the treatment of children in preschool" (Tobin, Wu, and Davidson 1989, 146). It remains to be seen whether yet another fallout of globalization is the exporting of this child-centric approach (Dahlberg, Moss, and Pence 2007). Although in time, we may find immigrant families in our preschools and kindergartens embracing the child-centric view, as our classrooms include more and more cultures from all around the globe, early childhood educators must continue to examine what we mean by group membership, egalitarianism, individualism, and other assumptions about classroom life.

Neither Paley nor her supporters claim that "you can't say you can't play" will eliminate rejection. However successful we may be in shaping children's earliest social experiences, we cannot protect them from the other forms of institutionalized rejection that unquestionably await them. All too soon, the preference for individual children becomes not just a response of the educational system to individual variation, but a requirement of the system. For example, where some young children lack the social skills necessary to fit in, others will be found to lack the cognitive. Pull-out programs begin separating the nonproficient from the proficient, and the gifted from both. By fourth grade, all children know who is smart, artistic, and athletic, and who is not. Eventually, race becomes a factor, as Paley reminds us in *Kwanzaa and Me*. Institutionalizing fairness by way of "you can't say you can't play" won't eliminate racism in our classrooms, of course, any more than it will always save the unpopular child from an undeserved fate. That said, we must not become blind to the enormous burden children carry when they are excluded from the classroom in explicit and insidious ways. In the end, both Paley and the children found it "far easier to open doors than to keep people out" (1992, 118). There may be other lessons to be learned in the kindergarten year, but surely there are no more important ones.

✧

The lessons in teaching that Paley learned over time as a white teacher of black children are highly compatible with those she advocates for the fair teaching of all the children in her classroom. It bears repeating that these lessons are as morally persuasive as they are stunningly self-evident: teaching to include is the first obligation of all teachers. What makes Paley's approach so accessible is that it embodies what makes us human as teachers and actors in a common enterprise. For Paley, "doing school" is never a matter of what young children are asked to do (though this is no small matter, as we have seen). It is, first and foremost, a matter of being who you are, or rather, being who your teacher allows you to be.

Adapting the lessons of fairness Paley has given us in her studies on race and the necessity of eschewing a color-blind stance, we learn first that teaching to include when it comes to gender, developmental difference, and popularity requires that teachers be equally direct about exclusion. That is, they must be willing to talk about similarities and dissimilarities and to recognize their impact on teaching and learning. They cannot pretend any longer that distinctions don't matter.

Second, teachers must accept responsibility for the ways in which the class schedule, curriculum, and most important, habits of interacting prevent the full inclusion of all children in all activities. This leads to the practice of "you can't say you can't play." Whether teachers actually post a sign, as Paley did, or simply apprise the children of the classroom rule is up to the individual.

Third, related to the practice of including all, but aspiring to full participation, teachers must work to create classrooms as democratic spaces, where all "stories" are heard, and where exchange of ideas is valued and cultivated.

Finally, if a pedagogy of fairness requires that the wisdom of black children and their families is to be respected and learned from, we must be willing to learn from all the children who sit outside the circle. It is in this way, Paley says, that the "fair study of children begins and where teaching becomes a moral act" (1992, xii).

Epilogue

The Classrooms Young Children Need —an "*N* of Many"

As Vivian Paley shows us, beyond anything else, the classrooms all young children need in the twenty-first century must be fair and meaningful. In these classrooms, a teacher waits for children to arrive to tell her who they are today. With her help, they will learn who they might be tomorrow. I'd like to close by reiterating my earlier claim that we make a mistake if in our appreciation of Vivian Paley, we fail to ask what lessons her story holds for young teachers just starting to form their teaching habits, as well as for experienced teachers stuck with a pedagogy that no longer serves the children or themselves. Most of these teachers will never be recognized beyond their school buildings. Most will not have the time to write and publish in order to analyze their work. But most will care enough to borrow a good idea when given the option.

In the twenty-five years since my first "storytelling classroom," I have had the privilege of working directly with several groups of teachers around Paley's endeavor in Atlanta, New York, and, most often, Houston. We have all learned many lessons along the way. One teacher told me recently that most important for her was learning to see herself and the children in relation to everything that happens in school. "I want to comment on everything in the classroom," she told me. "There's nothing that anybody says or does that doesn't have meaning to me. Recess. Lunch. I'm constantly wondering about all the little things that don't seem to fit, and how they fit." When I asked others what they had learned from Paley, one mentioned she couldn't get away from thinking about "you can't say you can't play." Could it be possible for teachers to crash the popularity game? In this vein, another said she was learning to indulge her young children's need to belong, and to embrace her role in making this happen. Others talked in different ways about learning to be a teacher of children first, and a teacher of academics second. One teacher said she had learned to resist what didn't make sense in the lives of the children before her.

I find these are fairly common reactions among teachers after they have been exposed to Paley. I believe their enthusiasm is essential to attracting—and keeping—the next generation of early childhood educators, perhaps now more than ever. When I asked teachers about the conflict between Paley's philosophy of play and learning and the sweeping changes taking place in early childhood education—from a longer school day to demands for more skills instruction—a veteran teacher observed that none captured anything close to the need for fairness or inclusion. I asked, "Is Paley relevant, then?" She hesitated and then answered, "Relevant to the ages."

I wrote in the prologue to this book that Paley's legacy will be squandered if we see it as something precious or idiosyncratic. Rather, we must see its general applicability to early childhood praxis now and in the long run. I have attempted to fuse the practical with the theoretical to make the case for the pedagogies of fairness and meaning in teacher education. I want to close by emphasizing that when all is said and done the best methods of pedagogy are those that raise questions, not answers. Paley's evolution as a teacher reminds us that we may not be able to predict the journey, but our teaching would only be poorer if we try to avoid it. Paley inspires us to believe that teaching must stand for something. She chooses fair and meaningful. Through these lenses, she discovers, not the composite children and teachers of manuals and social proclamations, but, to paraphrase Reeny, *teachers and children the way they are* (Paley 1997, 15). It is a moral beginning.

Appendix A

Guide to Implementation of Paley's Storytelling Curriculum

This guide represents the collective experience of many teachers over the years who have successfully integrated storytelling and story acting into their preschool and kindergarten curricula. Invariably, individual teachers modify the process to suit their preferences and needs. In this sense, it in some ways varies with Paley's implementation process. I'm especially grateful to all the teachers and staff in the School Literacy and Culture Project for their contributions to this guide.

PLANNING

Frequency. Ideally, teachers should offer storytelling and story acting daily to as many children as are interested. This is not always possible, given other constraints on teachers' time. Storytelling and story acting must occur often enough to have an impact on children's development. Given the demands of the classroom, a base line schedule is as follows: three- and four-year-olds need the chance to dictate a story at least every other week, and to act a story at least once a week. Five-year-olds can go quite a bit longer between turns for dictation, but they, too, need to act in a story weekly.

Materials. Teachers will need to have a steady supply of pens and blank paper on hand. The right size paper seems to be 8½ × 11 inches, though teachers should experiment. Carbon paper is recommended to make an instant copy of the story, so that the child can immediately put one away to take home, and the teacher has one to read to the class (and for assessment purposes). Many teachers put their copies in plastic sleeves that are alphabetized by name in a binder they keep in the class library for children to refer to all year.

Location. Teachers should choose a place for dictation that allows them to see all corners of the room. Most prefer sitting at a table, but the use of a clipboard allows dictation to take place anywhere. In either case, there should be enough room for drop-in listeners. Dramatization usually occurs around the classroom rug or gathering space. It is helpful to have a small, uncluttered space adjoining this where the actors can wait "offstage" until their turn comes to enter the drama.

STORYTELLING (DICTATION)

Seating. The child/author should sit to the left of a right-handed teacher/scribe and to the right of a left-handed one so that the teacher's arm does not block the child's view of the writing.

Name and date. Before the dictation begins, the teacher writes the child's name in the left-hand corner and the date in the right. The teacher should say out loud what she is writing.

How to begin. First-time storytellers, and children who are very shy, might need some help to get started. It's OK to offer suggestions until the child gets used to the process. ("I really like those new sneakers. Would you like to tell a story about the day you went shopping?") Sometimes it's merely a matter of offering a beginning or a way in. ("Some stories begin 'One day' or 'Once upon a time' or 'Once there was a little boy.' Would you like to start that way?")

Length. Because of time restrictions, stories are limited to one page. Children who press to tell more should be taught about installments, sections, and "to be continued."

Subject matter. The fewer the restrictions on subject matter the better (except the obvious—bathroom stories, explicit sexuality, unkind descriptions of other children, and so on).

Echoing. As the teacher writes, she repeats back to the child what he or she has just said. ("One—day—a—bear—came—to—dinner.") This keeps both teacher and child on track and calls the child's attention to the words being written.

A hesitant storyteller. If the child hesitates between thoughts, the teacher should be casually encouraging. ("Yes? And then what happened" or "OK. Go on. I'm ready.")

Writing and narrative development. The teacher helps the child expand on thoughts by engaging in a conversation about the story. ("Wow! You must have been really scared when the monster came. Did you scream? Would you like to put that in the story?" "What did the baby do that made everyone laugh?") Sometimes it helps for the child to think ahead to the dramatization. ("Tell me what the kids are going to do when they are tigers in the play. Maybe you could put that in your story ahead of time.") Teachers should be upbeat, involved scribes. ("*No* kidding? Oooh, that's scary." "Hey, I *like* this part where the fire engine talks." "A deep blue, gooey-gobbly day?—I *love* it!")

Skill development. The teacher indirectly points out or asks questions about decoding, such as beginning sounds, double consonants, and rhymes. Occasionally she asks the child to spell a word that is more of a challenge. ("Do you remember how to spell floor?") Grammar and punctuation mini-lessons can also be easily inserted. ("Where should I put the quotation marks?")

Editing and revision. Editorial questions regarding sequencing, narrative development, and so on can be asked of the storyteller at any time. ("So, your mama took you to the store and then to school. Is that right?"). Dictated stories are rarely revised, though they can be if a child desires to.

Rereading. When the child is finished dictating, the teacher immediately rereads the story to make sure she "got it right." She makes any changes the child requests.

Choosing the cast. After rereading the story, the teacher reminds the child about choosing a cast. First, she calls attention to the possible cast by underlining the characters in the written story. It is assumed that the author will play the lead, though this is not a requirement. The child chooses the cast from the class list, noting who has not had a turn yet in this cycle. As many characters may be chosen as there is room on the classroom's "stage." Four to six actors will cover the main characters in most stories. When necessary, the audience is asked to imagine the rest of the characters. Because it may be difficult to remember who's who when it comes time to dramatize later in the day, the teacher writes the cast names and their parts on her copy of the story.

STORY ACTING (DRAMATIZATION)

First rule. Keep it simple. Do not think in terms of rehearsals or props.

Preparing the class. The teacher gathers the children in a semicircle and begins by announcing who wrote a story that day. She asks each author in turn to come stand beside her while she reads the class his or her story.

Calling the cast. The teacher announces who in the class will play which roles and asks them to come stand "offstage." (A small rug helps to mark the spot. Actors move onto the stage as required.)

Performance of the story. As the teacher rereads the story once more, the chosen actors act as the story line dictates.

Dialogue. The teacher pauses before any dialogue to see if the actors have remembered their lines. If not, the teacher simply repeats them, and the actors repeat after her. Improvisation is welcome, except where it changes the author's intent or distracts from the overall play.

Directing the performance. The teacher should feel free to interrupt the dramatization with suggestions. ("Laura, the little bear is very upset to find his porridge eaten all up. Can you look upset like the little bear would?")

Curtain call. After "The End" the actors join hands and take a bow while the audience claps.

OTHER DRAMATIZATIONS

In addition to their own stories, children also love to act out books and stories written by adults. This is a key opportunity for them to learn how good stories are constructed (beginnings, middles, ends, problems, solutions, and so on). It also extends their vocabulary and knowledge of sophisticated sentence structure. The method is the same, except usually the teacher, not a child, chooses the cast. Dramatization of a favorite book can occur as many as five to a dozen times before the children want to move on.

Appendix B

Sample Stories

The following stories, shared by teachers who implement the storytelling curriculum in their preschool and kindergarten classrooms, represent a variety of ways to think about the uses of storytelling in the classroom.

DEVELOPMENT OVER TIME

The stories children dictate typically reveal true growth in language and narrative development over the school year. Of course, age, gender, cultural background, and group life will always have an impact on the children's progress, as suggested by the stories below.

Mark's Stories

Mark, age five, is in the classroom of a veteran storytelling teacher.

September 1

Driving over Stuff

I would drive a car in the mountains. I ran over stuff.

The End

October 23

The Power Rangers Battling Bad Guys

The Power Rangers were doing something. On the next day, they woke up and the bad guys came and they started battling and the good guys had a power sword and one had a special gun with special bullets and one bad guy died and then all the bad guys were dead except one was still alive. The blue guy stuck his sword in and the last bad guy was dead now.

The End

Blue guy: Mark
Red guy: Stevie
Bad guy no. 1: Dillon
Bad guy no. 2: Marshal

February 5

The Dog and Cat

One time there was a dog and there was a cat and they played hide-and-seek. The cat counted and then they started chasing each other and then they started looking for something to eat. They looked in the backyard but then they didn't find anything. Then they went into the house and went outside. They jumped on the trampoline for a while and then they got off and they went on the play structure at their house. They slid down the slide and swinged on the swing and got off the swing and ran around. They were playing "Guess Who." They went inside again. They took a nap.

The End

Cat: Mark
Dog: Thomas

May 1

The Wild Jungle

One time there was a cheetah and then he saw an elephant coming towards him and the cheetah had a mighty bird called the cock-of-the-rock. The elephant had a frog. They all charged together and said, "I think we should go exploring together." They went off into the dark rainforest and saw a predator coming towards them. The cheetah noticed it was an Indian and the Indian was carrying a long pointy stick and a really sharp knife. The cock-of-the-rock was very strong and said, "Giddy-up all animals, let's get that man!" so they all ran after him and the man said, "If you get me, I'll get you." Then the other animals in the rainforest heard the four animals getting in trouble and they all came to help. But there were 100 Indians but they became friends together and said, "You want to come over to our house?" The animals said, "Not until you come to our house first."

The End

Cock-of-the-rock: Mark
Man: Thomas
Cheetah: Henry
Elephant: Laura

Federico's First and Last Stories

Federico is in prekindergarten and is learning English as his second language.

October 14
I played in the block center. Build car. Right there game center. Bus bumpy. Play cars. I like play dough. Library. Sand table. Play outside.

The End

April 27

The Running Big Bad Wolf

A big bad wolf killed all the people. He ate them. He went to the park and ate the fish. The shark was in the water. The shark ate the bad wolf. The shark was playing with him friends. The alligator was in the water, too. They were fighting. The alligator won. He went to drink from the water fountain. He went to the park doing exercise. The daddy at the water fountain said, "Stop fighting."

The End

Benjamin's Stories

Benjamin is almost three years old. These are his first three stories.

February 2
Benny. It's two.

March 12
Mommy, Daddy, Johnny, Sara, they stayed home. They did nothing. That's it.

The End

May 2
Mommy was playing with me. John was playing in his room. Daddy was napping in his bed.

Kathryn's Stories

Kathryn is also almost three years old. Here are her first three stories.

January 22
Daddy. Mitchell.

March 12
Mitchell played with me. Daddy played with me. Mommy played with Sadie. Sadie jumps. Sadie bites. Sadie wear down. Sadie is a big dog.

The End

March 26
Daddy play with Sadie. Sadie bites Daddy. Sadie played with me. Sadie go to Mitchell's room. Sadie bites Mitchell. Sadie go downstairs. Sadie don't like the cage. Daddy goes upstairs. Mitchell play Monopoly. Sadie went away.

The End

BORROWED STORIES

These stories, dictated and dramatized in a kindergarten classroom within the same three-week period, reveal how young children willingly borrow ideas from each other. They also reveal their keen attraction to fantasy stories. The stories are categorized by theme, not in the order in which they were told.

Forest Stories

Paris's Story

The Kids That Went to School

Once upon a time there was two little girls and one little boy. The first little girl was named Rainbow. The second little girl was named Rainbow Dash. The little boy's name was Lightning. They were in the forest picking food. They went deeper and deeper into the forest. Then a fox came and a wizard came with the fox. The fox said, "Hi!" Then the mom came and her name was Julia. And the three kids' mom said, "Let's go back home so we can cook the food." So they went home. And then the dad came and he said, "What's for dinner?" It was chicken nuggets and French fries. Then the three little kids went tot bed. The next morning they went to school. Then they came home and went to Sea World. They went on lots and lots of roller coasters. Then after the roller coasters they went to go swimming. Then they went home.

Mom: Julia
Rainbow: Paris
Rainbow Dash: Preston
Lightning: Malik
Dad: Aidan
Fox: Stephen
Wizard: Mika

Janna's Story

One day in the woods there was a cow and he was walking in the forest. He didn't hear the coyote howling because he didn't have that big ears like the coyote, because the coyote has the biggest ears. The coyote was sick. The coyote was lying in the leaf pile. And when the cow listened really hard he could hear the coyote howling. Then he ran saying, "Moo, I'll help you!" The coyote went "Ahroo!" (He had an earache.) Then the coyote talked to the cow and told the cow that he had an earache. The cow helped the coyote by giving him a nice bowl of porridge. And the coyote felt much better and thanked the cow and asked him if they could be friends. The cow said, "Yes!" Then the cow and the coyote went home to the coyote's house which was a cave and they lived happily ever after.

The End

Cow: Anna
Coyote: Janna

Stephen's Story

The Two Kids

One day a little boy whose name was Malik was walking in the forest and his mom and dad told him to be careful. Then he saw a witch and the fox appeared with the witch. And then there was a wizard. The wizard was trying to catch the boy. Then the boy was running away and then he saw a little girl. She was a policeman's daughter and she said, "Why are you running away?" The boy said, "Because a wizard's chasing me!" The fox and the wizard was trying to catch the boy and the girl. Then the policeman saw that the wizard and the fox was trying to catch his little girl and boy. Then the policeman chased the wizard and the fox and the witch appeared. Then there was another policeman and the other policeman helped chase them. And then the mom helped chase them, too. Then the mom and dad that had the little boy, they were trying to find a way to see if they could get on the mountains to see their child. They saw the child and they got down and swam through water and they got out and dried off. Then they got everyone and saved them.

The End

Boy (Malik): Stephen
Mom: Julia
Dad: Conner
Witch: Preston
Wizard: Janna
Girl: Paris
Police: Lucas, Jared
Mom: Mika

Julia's Story

The Three Kids Face the Wizard and the Fox

Once upon a time there was three kids and they went out to the forest without their mom and dad. They got in trouble because they were faced by a wizard and a fox. The wizard and fox took the three kids away. They were deciding to cook them up as a stew—and for the fox, a big brunch! The fox and the wizard threw the kids into the dungeon and the kids were scared and the big sister screamed! The wizard and fox heard it and they disappeared. Then they all went home happily ever after.

The End

Three kids: Julia, Preston, Malik
Mom: Paris
Dad: Lucas
Wizard: Stephen
Fox: Anna

Stephen's Story

The Girl

One day a grown-up girl was walking in the forest. Then she saw a fox. He was hiding behind the tree. The fox was chasing her until the police came. There was three polices and they caught the fox and all the scary things in the forest. Then they took them to jail. Then they never let them out of jail. And they locked the key on their hand. Then the scary guys put their hand out of one of the holes of the jail and unlocked the door. They got out and went back to the forest and they made a house and then strangers got in the house and they got in the elevator and broke it. Then the strangers were hammering the house to break it. Then they hammered the whole house so hard they broke it. Then all of them jumped off. Before they touched the ground they changed in their attitude and they were being good guys. Then they saw a mom and dad and some police. Then they caught the guys who hadn't changed in their attitude and they put them in jail and locked the door and threw the key away.

The End

Girl: Julia

Fox: Jude
Three police officers: Stephen. Lucas, Conner
Scary things: Aidan, Janna, Malik
Dad: Jared
Mom: Anna
Guys: Preston, Paris

Superhero Stories

Lucas's Story

Batman and the Two Kids

Batman went to the store without his Batman costume on. Then his beeper phone beeped and he went to a rescue. A fire was going on in the forest and two kids were trapped in the fiery forest. And then the children went to a house and a wizard saw them and a fox. Then they put them in the dungeon and they almost cooked them up into a stew. Then Batman's alarm phone beeped and then he went and broke the dungeon open and they all ran out the door. Then two robots came and cut the fox in half and cut the wizard in half.
Batman: Lucas
Two kids: Mika, Julia
Wizard: Stephen
Fox: Jared
Two robots: Conner, Jon

Jude's Story

Spiderman with Venom

Peter Parker was in disguise as Spiderman. Then Poison came in the big parking lot. Then Spiderman swinged in and kicked his face. Then Poison falls down. Then Spiderman jumped on him. Then Poison woke up and kicked Spiderman over the big roof. Then Poison's boots turned red and he turned into Spiderman. (He looks like Spiderman.) Then Poison goes to help someone who's hanging on a big roof and he shoots poison at them. Then they fall off the roof. Then Spiderman comes in to catch them. And then Spiderman tossed the car over at Venom and he goes "whoo." He grabs the window and pushes it back at Spiderman. Spiderman ducks and he thought hard what to do. He webbed a roof and he swinged over on the other side. Then Rhinoman came and pushes through the building. Spiderman makes another web on this side and he swings in and kicks Rhinoman on the back of the head. Then Rhinoman tires to break the web with his horns but Spiderman webs his head and then Venom makes a web and swings into a building then he turns back to black. Poison shoots poison at Spiderman but Spiderman webs the poison. Venom gets webbed and Spiderman pulls Poison back.

Spiderman: Jude
Poison/Venom: Malik
Person being rescued: Aidan
Rhinoman: Jon

Lucas's Story

Batman and Robin

Once upon a time Batman and Robin went to their home and they slide down the Batpole. Then they pushed the button to put their costume on. Then they got in the Batcar and zoomed to the castle. The rescue was at A and B store. There was a fire and the three kids were trapped. Robin and Batman broke down the door and rescued the kids. Then Robin and Batman went back to the Batcave.

Catwoman and Joker and Penguin wanted to kill Batman and Robin. They tried to throw them in the ocean but Batman pushed them into the water. Then Joker and Catwoman and Penguin got eaten by a shark!

Kids: Julia, Jon, Aidan
Batman: Lucas
Robin: Stephen
Catwoman: Mika
Joker: Conner
Penguin: Jude
Shark: Janna

Jude's Story

Spiderman with the Two Bad Guys

Peter Parker was disguised as Spiderman because he heard some trouble on his watch helper. Then he climbs up a big building and the he looked up. Then he saw somebody hanging from a big balloon. And then he webbed the bottom of the big balloon. He climbs up the web then he gets up in the balloon. Then he saves the man who was grabbing on to the bottom so he wouldn't fall off. Then he makes a web all the way down to the building. Then he webs the street. Then the man goes back home.

Then Dr. Octopus came. He grabs Spiderman and then Spiderman webbed the building and then he pulled hisself up. Then Dr. Octopus uses his four tentacles to climb up. Then the Green Goblin comes and gets on his fly board. And then Spiderman webs the bottom of the flyboard and webs the Green Goblin's face. Then the Green Goblin falls down. Then Dr. Octopus climbs down as fast as he can and then he catches Green Goblin. Then he takes the webs off of Green Goblin and the Green Goblin climbs up the building. He climbs up the webs that Spiderman made. Then he knocks Spiderman down. Then Spiderman webs a new building and swings over to it. Dr. Octopus uses his tentacles and Green Goblin uses his flyboard to get to the new building. When they get up they have a big fight and Spiderman knocks Dr. Octopus down off the building. Green Goblin gets knocked off the building, too. Spiderman goes home and changes back to Peter Parker.

Spiderman: Jude
Man: Jon
Dr. Octopus: Lucas
Green Goblin: Jared

Spy Stories

Malik's Story

The Spies

Once there was a spy castle. There were three spies. One spy's name was Malik. One spy's name was Conner and one spy's name was Paris. The three spies went to a bad guy's spy castle. The bad guy spy saw them and the last spy said, "How are we going to get on this creepy bridge is there's hot lava on it?" But then the first spy got a plan. But the bad guy's favorite food was cheese. The first good spy's plan was this: the second spy is going to hold up cheese to the castle and he's gonna say, "Bad guy, you come over here to eat this cheese." When the bad guy was almost at the last step, the other guys threw two ropes and climbed up to the castle. Then they didn't know there was a treasure in there. When they got there they saw the treasure. It was money! They got it and the second spy gave the cheese to the bad guy and then when he got upstairs he saw that the money was gone. Then the bad guy said to hisself, "The good guys tricked me!" Then the bad guy said, "That's okay. I'll get a better treasure and I'll hide it somewhere where nobody will find it! I'll get a fire-breathing dragon so nobody can get in my castle again!"

The End

Three spies: Malik, Conner, Paris

Bad guy: Jared

Conner's Story

The Four Spies

One time there was four spies. The first one was named Conner. The second one was named Malik. The third one was named Jude. And the fourth one was named Preston. They were going to a bad guy's castle. The bad guy, he was making fire. Then the bad guy had a dragon and a wizard and fox guarding him. The spies were making a plan to put fire on the bad guy's head. The bad guy was trying to look like a vampire to scare all of the spies but they weren't scared. Then the spies went to their castle and they got their special weapons. Then they went back to the bad guy's castle. Then they were shooting him with cork guns. Then the spies told the dragon, the wizard, and the fox to be their friends. They said, "Yes."

The End

Spies: Conner, Malik, Jude, Preston

Bad guy: Mika

Wizard: Julia

Fox: Lucas

Dragon: Jared

Preston's Story

The Magical Dragon

Once upon a time there were four spies. They like to eat pizza and their favorite thing to do is spying on the magical dragon. There was a prince who tried to cut the dragon's neck off and to save the princess. The spies are helping the prince kill the dragon. The dragon landed on the floor outside the castle and the prince saved the princess. The dragon went back alive and his head went back on. Then a piece of grass started breaking off the ground and the dragon fell in the hot lava. He had wings so he could fly back up on the other side. He never came back to the castle ever again. The princess got saved from the prince.

The End

Four spies: Jon, Mika, Jude, Conner
Princess: Preston
Prince: Malik
Dragon: Aidan

Jared's Story

The Six Spies

Once there was six good spies. There was Mika, Jared, Conner, Julia, Janna, and Paris. There was one more spy—a bad spy called Jon. Then, the good spies tried to get across the bridge that connected to the bad spy's castle. It had hot lava underneath it. Then they tried to get across, but it was a balance beam. But then, one of the spies, Jared, fell off and was holding on by his fingers and then pulled himself up. Then the spies went back to their castle and thought up a plan. Then they cooked pancakes for the bad guy.

The End

Good spies: Mika, Jared, Conner, Julia, Janna, Paris
Bad spy: Jon

Paris's Story

The Hypnotized Bad Guys

Once upon a time there were three spies. The first one name was Rainbow. The second one name was Lightning. The third one name was Rainbow Dash. The three spies were trying to get the bad guys. They were going to the bad guy castle riding motorcycles. Then Rainbow had a plan. The plan was they would go to the bad guy castle. They went inside the castle and they found some costumes. They put them on and then they went outside and asked the bad guys for some money. Then the bad guys thought they were real kids and some said, "Yes, I'll give you all of the money." Then Rainbow Dash hypnotized them. Then the bad guys never came back again.

That's All!

Rainbow: Julia
Lightning: Malik
Rainbow Dash: Paris
Bad guys: Conner, Jon

Malik's Story

Once there was a spy castle. There were four good spies. The first spy's name was Malik. The second spy's name was Paris. The third spy's name was Julia. The fourth spy's name was Conner. The four spies went to a bad guy's castle. Then the bad guys got a plan. The bad guy knew the first spy was a smart spy. His plan was to kill the first spy. So then, the other spies won't know what to do so he killed him. The bad guy didn't know that there was a potion to make the first spy alive again. Then the other spies knew there was a potion to make the first good spy alive again. They went to hunt for it. The fourth spy found it. Then they came back. When he got better, the bad guy saw them all. He went to the bad guy store and bought a fire-breathing dragon. He made him throw fire at the good guys. The good spies ran back home.

The End

Good spies: Malik, Paris, Julia, Conner
Bad guy: Jon
Dragon: Stephen

Aidan's Story

The Three Spies

Once upon a time there were three spies. Their names were Conner, Aidan, and Stephen. They went to the bad guy's castle. The bad guy's name was Preston. The bad guy went to the bad guy store and bought a fire-breathing dragon. Then the fire-breathing dragon shot fire at one of the spies. And the spy ducked. Then the fire went on the ground and the ground started to shake. Then the three spies went across the bridge that had deep water under it. There were crocodiles under it. They went to their castle, they got their little cork guns, and went to the bad guy's castle. They shot the bad guy and the dragon.

The End

Spies: Aidan, Stephen, Conner

Bad guy: Preston

Dragon: Jon

Appendix C

Sample Transcript of Child Dictation

This sample transcript represents the give and take between storyteller and scribe. Of particular note is the teacher's use of psychologically confirming comments that encourage the child to continue.

GREGORY'S DICTATION TO MS. JOHNSON

J: Stand over here 'cause I want to be close by you. All right Mr. Gregory. Let's put your name—G-r-e-g-o-r-y. This is Gregory's sixth story! You ready? Do you have a good idea for your story? What's it going to be about?
G: A silly wolf.
J: A silly wolf—I can't wait to hear it!
G: And he was flying!
J: He is silly! He had wings?
G: Yeah, he made it out of paper.
J: Oh, I cannot wait to hear this story . . . So, a silly wolf was flying. Is that how you want to start it?
G: [Nods.]
J: [Echoes and writes.] "A silly wolf was flying." Tell me again how he did that.
G: He made his wings out of paper.

J: [Echoes and writes.] "He made his wings out of paper." [Pauses.]

G: He didn't know how to blow houses down because all of them were made out of bricks.

J: Ah, OK. [Echoes and writes.] "He didn't know how to blow houses down because all of them were made out of bricks."

G: He picked on . . . the chicken . . . He, he, he . . . picked on the wolf and he went like, "*Ow*!"

J: He *picked* on him or he *pecked* on him? Which word?

G: Pecked on him.

J: He pecked. The chicken, he pecked? That's a good word. [Echoes and writes.] "He pecked on the wolf and he said . . ." What?

G: He said, "Yowch!"

J: "Yowch!" [Chuckles.] OK . . . So that poor wolf, the poor silly, flying wolf got pecked by a chicken, huh? [Chuckles.] And he said "Yowch!" [Pauses.]

G: A dog came and bit him.

J: He's having a very bad day. [Echoes and writes.] "A dog came and bit him."

G: He said nothing.

J: He said nothing? He was just quiet about that, huh? Do you want me to write, "He said nothing?"

G: [Nods.]

J: [Echoes and writes.]

G: And then a bear came.

J: Oh no, I notice your animals are getting bigger and bigger—first one was little, then a middle-sized animal, now he's gonna get this bear. [Prepares to write.] Did you say a big bear or just a bear?

G: A big bear.

J: "Then a big bear . . ."

G: [Interrupts.] A big, big huge *bear*!

J: [Chuckling at his enthusiasm, echoes and writes.] "A big, huge bear came."

G: Then he knocked him on the head.

J: [Chuckles again, echoes and writes.] "He knocked him on the head." Then what?

G: He stilled.

J: He stilled? You mean he was frozen like that?

G: He is frozen and he can still move.

J: He can still move?
G: Uh-huh. He was frozen and . . .
J: He was knocked on the head and that made him like frozen, like that? [Dramatizes.]
G: Uh-huh. And then someone put water on him and the ice came off him.
J: *Oh!* So he was still—he was frozen. [Writing.] And then what happened? Someone did what?
G: [Unintelligible because of background noise, but clearly it is a different topic. G has moved on.]
J: Wait a minute, let's go back to the frozen part. [Rereads.] "He was still, he was frozen." You said something about someone poured water . . .
G: They poured water on the ice and then it, he, he, the water got off him.
J: [Writing.] "So, they poured water on the ice . . ."
G: Then it got off the wolf.
J: [Echoes and writes.] Can I ask you a question real quick? Who is they? Who poured the water?
G: Jake.
J: Jake. [Laughs.] "Jake poured water on the ice."
G: I want to make a long story!
J: It's getting pretty long! OK, so now your wolf is not frozen anymore, so then what did he do—the flying silly wolf?
G: [Pauses.]
J: He's not frozen any more so he can do whatever he wants.
G: The bear put him on a jelly bean.
J: On a jelly bean? So now I've got a wolf sitting on a jelly bean? Is this true? [Laughs.] OK. [Rereads the last two sentences quickly.] "The wolf got on . . ."
G: The title is "The Wolf"
J: The title is "The Wolf"? That's right, because it's all about a wolf. OK, so the wolf got on . . . What color were the jelly beans?
G: Yellow.
J: OK, can I put that in your story: "The wolf got on the yellow jelly bean"?
G: [Nods.]
J: [Echoes and writes.] Then what happened?

G: He ate it.

J: [Echoes and writes.] Did he like jelly beans?

G: [Nods.]

J: Did you want me to write that? "He liked jelly beans"—or just skip it?

G: [With enthusiasm.]) Write it!

J: [Echoes and writes.] Oh, I wish I had an artist who could draw a picture of a flying wolf who likes jelly beans . . . All right . . . [Rereads last sentence.]

G: Then there was a girl who ate the whole wolf.

J: A girl—like a people girl?

G: [Nods.]

J: [Writes and echoes.] "Then there was a girl . . ." What did she look like?

G: She looked like an Indian 'cause she was brown.

J: Should I put that in? [Echoes and writes.] "Then there was a girl she looked like an Indian . . ." [Interruption from another child saying he found a cocoon. J says, "Good for you!" and then returns to the story.] "She looked like an Indian because she was brown." [Pauses.] An Indian from India or a Native American?

G: From Asia.

J: Should we put "She was from Asia?"

G: [Nods.]

J: [Echoes and writes.] All right. [Rereads.] "She looked like an Indian because she was brown. She was from Asia." Now tell me again what this girl did.

G: She ate the wolf.

J: OK. "She ate the wolf."

G: And then a boy came and a bear. They looked the same!

J: [Distracted by another child.] "And then a boy came . . ."

G: And then a bear.

J: [Echoes and writes.]

G: And they looked the same!

J: The boy and the bear looked just the same? [Echoes and writes.]

G: It's getting closer!

J: Yes, you've about got your whole page here. [Rereads.] "And then a boy came and then a bear. They looked the same." What did they do?

G: They went to a person.

J: Who?

G: They went to an artist.

J: Can I write that? That's a good word. [Echoes and writes.] "They went to an artist." OK. And what did they do when they found the artist?

G: They said hello and then they went back.

J: [Writes with no echo.] What did the artist do?

G: He was painting . . . he was painting a flying wolf that likes jelly beans.

J: "They said hello and then they went back." Should I write what the artist was doing?

G: [Nods.]

J: So how should I say it?

G: The artist was writing a flying wolf that likes jelly beans.

J: [Chuckles.] OK, was he writing or painting?

G Painting.

J: OK. "The artist was painting a flying wolf . . ." We're at the end.

G: We're almost there so we can get a long story.

J: It's long, but you've got to leave me some space because we've got a lot of friends in this story. [Finishes echoing and writing.] ". . . that liked jelly beans."

G: It's almost getting closer.

J: It's very close 'cause we have to have room to write here. Shall I read it to you first, then we'll pick whose gonna be in it?

"The Wolf. A silly wolf was flying. He made his wings out of paper. He didn't know how to blow houses down because all of them were made of brick. The chicken, he pecked on the wolf and he said, 'Yeowch!' The dog came and bit him. He said nothing. Then a big, huge, huge bear came and he knocked"—oh, I skipped a word—"he knocked *him* on the head. He was still. He was frozen. Jaylen poured water on the ice and it got off of him. The wolf got on a yellow jelly bean. He ate it. He liked jelly beans! Then there was a girl. She looked like an Indian because she was brown. She was from Asia. She ate the wolf. Then a boy came and then a bear. They looked the same. They went to an artist and they said hello and then they went back. The artist was painting a flying wolf that liked jelly beans."

That's awesome. So who's gonna be the silly [laughing] flying wolf?

G: Keenan.

J: Of course he is. [Keenan is G's good friend and he had also walked up to the table during the last few sentences of the story.]

G: Sam's gonna be the chicken.

J: I thought Brad was gonna be it, but that's a good pick. Sam needs to be in this story.

Another child: Chicken? Chicken is a funny name.

J: This class loves that word! [J explains to me why the class thinks the word is so funny. Brad had started it. When he first came to prekindergarten he liked to call people "chicken head." He was told not to call people animal names, so then, in order to get the name chicken in he would say something like "chicken pot pie," and the way he says it makes everybody roar with laughter.]

J: All right, we've got a chicken here. Who's gonna be the huge, huge bear?

J: Oh, we skipped somebody. We need a dog. [She speaks just as G answers her previous question: "Arturo."]

J: We need a dog.

G: That's gonna be Ms. C. [the student teacher].

J: Ms. C., she'll do a good job. And you said Arturo will be the bear?

G: Uh-huh.

J: And Jake—who's gonna be Jake? Jake could be his own self.

G: Brad. And Keenan is going to be the chicken.

J: No, you said Jake. Keenan is going to be the flying wolf.

Keenan: I can be the chicken and the flying wolf, too.

J: No, you have to just be one. OK, we need a girl—an Indian girl from Asia.

G: Samara.

J: And we need a boy.

G: That's gonna be Roberta.

J: Roberta is going to be a boy? And I need an artist—is that going to be you? Who's gonna be the artist? [Pauses.] You're not in the story. Do you want to be in it?

G: I want to be the artist.

J: OK, I didn't want you to forget yourself. OK, we're done.

G: Now it's time to clean up.

Gregory's Story

The Wolf

A silly wolf was flying. He made his wings out of paper. He didn't know how to blow houses down because all of them were made of brick. The chicken, he pecked on the wolf and he said, "Yowch!" The dog came and bit him. He said nothing. Then a big, huge, huge bear came and he knocked him on the head. He was still. He was frozen. Jake poured water on the ice and it got off of him. The wolf got on a yellow jelly bean. He ate it. He liked jelly beans! Then there was a girl. She looked like an Indian because she was brown. She was from Asia. She ate the wolf. Then a boy came and then a bear. They looked the same. They went to an artist and they said hello and then they went back. The artist was painting a flying wolf that liked jelly beans.

The End

Appendix D

Becoming a Teacher of Stories

BETWEEN MENTOR AND NOVICE

I began corresponding with Laurie Renfro, a new teacher, in the fall of 2004, after I had demonstrated the storytelling curriculum in her kindergarten classroom. The e-mails below are drawn from that first academic year, an exciting time both for the young teacher and the children in her class. (The children's names, as well as Laurie's, are pseudonyms. The e-mails have been edited lightly to simplify formatting and eliminate minor errors.) I share them to emphasize that the best teacher learning not only requires time and support, it requires a subject worthy of both. I take no credit for Laurie's amazing analytical talents. But I am convinced she found the role she was looking for in the storytelling curriculum.

> 9/17/04
> From: Patsy
> To: Laurie
> Any luck with dramatization?

9/17/04
From: Laurie
To: Patsy
My timing was off on Wed. so I didn't leave enough at the end of the day to do it justice—what I did was just read them *Where the Wild Things Are* and then have them as a whole class be wild things as I read—when the terrible roaring and eye rolling, etc. came up—I'm planning to do it again Monday with different kids being Max etc.—They were very enthusiastic wild things and were irritated at me that I didn't leave enough time to do it correctly! I think I'll shoot for Monday morning to make sure I get it in and leave enough time throughout the week for kids to switch parts, which I can already tell they will want to do. I always forget how small and wiggly they are at the beginning! It is great fun, kindergarten. I feel like I could teach kindergarten my whole life and still have more to learn. I'll let you know how it goes.

9/25/04
From: Laurie
To: Patsy
So, we've done *Wild Things* six times so far and there is no sign of any desire to stop. I need to find some more copies so more of them can look at it during reading time. Ross is the first boy to be on the list to play the mother. Nobody made fun. We've read four versions of Red Riding Hood together now and the kids are really the ones propelling the investigation forward—they ask for it in the morning, they compare the size of the wolf's belly in the different versions we read, they make Grandma's house out of play dough and become wicked wolves on the playground. I want to make some symbolic Red Riding Hood and wolf/granny/hunter garb so they can play in the pretend center. There is so much joy in this kind of teaching—wow.

9/25/04
From: Patsy
To: Laurie
Careful, you're going to make me switch careers all over again. It took dramatization for me to understand that young children's

interest in repeating the dramas revealed not only the way they learn, but what they want to learn about. What do you think is going on here?

Tell me when you're ready to begin dictation.

9/28/04
From: Laurie
To: Patsy
I think they find the repetition and structure of knowing what's coming really satisfying. Comforting. They get to be exuberant and "wild" but there are limits. It feels to me like they are practicing—practicing conflict, practicing triumphing over evil, practicing compassion. I have to think about it a lot more. They are still going strong with *Wild Things* (almost every day!) but we're starting *Three Little Pigs* in reading workshop tomorrow so we might actually head towards doing that one soon. Unless someone who hasn't been Max pipes up. I want to start dictation maybe next week—I am still trying to figure out how to manage a structured and educational choice time. I have no assistant (except for one period a day, usually not during choice time) so it is still pretty labor intensive in terms of management but I'm working on helping them be more independent.

10/1/04
From: Patsy
To: Laurie
I agree with you regarding why the kids love the repetition of the dramas. This is where you need a good background in Jung, or some Chinese philosopher. Also, I wonder if there isn't something additional going on in that the repetition serves the need (or urge) to build cognitive structures that permit the processing of symbols, metaphors, and other abstract linguistic/conceptual knowledge.

Re: dictation. I would love to come and help get it off the ground. If you're just ready to fly, go for it. If you want to wait a week, I'll make a date.

10/3/04
From: Laurie
To: Patsy
I prefer the kind of conversation that springs naturally from natural interest—"Look at his teeth! They are so big!" I should read Jung. I never have. I think you are right that the repetition is building "cognitive structures" that allow for the processing of abstract thought—I have heard often that young children cannot think abstractly, but it seems to me that the stories are a place where they are certainly developing/practicing/engaging in the processing of quite deep and abstract ideas.

10/26/04
From: Laurie
To: Patsy
Thanks so much for launching stories in my room—Peter told one today and they acted it out—so interesting—he was so fascinated by my writing down what he said—he was pausing after each syllable sometimes. I'll write more soon, I've been really busy, just wanted to say thanks again!

10/28/04
From: Laurie
To: Patsy
So. Stories are happening! Thanks again for helping start us off, and for motivating me to try something new. I've taken one dictation each day since Monday and we act it out right after choice time—I love the immediacy of it and so do the storytellers. Most seem to be sticking to real life stories—this must be a result of the writing workshop focus on real life stories. I think it will shake loose of its own accord eventually. (Marisa told a "chapter" in a series of stories she tells at home with her family about an evil being called "Sakemo"—Marisa and her friends lived underground and planned a plan to steal Sakemo's breakfast when he wasn't looking.) Do you recommend telling them outright that they can make a made up story if they seem to be sticking to real life ones? Marshall, who never draws at all (he just sits there during writing workshop unless

I work with him for a long time) told a story today about winning a flag at a baseball game—this seems to be much more where he is at than the writing workshop. I wish I didn't have to ask him to write every day.

I have some questions about what kinds of things to keep an eye out for as I'm taking dictation, too, in terms of how they tell their stories. I am watching to see where they are looking, if they are modifying the speed of their speech, etc. What else?

10/29/04
From: Patsy
To: Laurie
I wouldn't attempt to influence the content except where the kids seem stuck or bored. No doubt fantasy will arrive on its own. ("Sakemo" may have done it already. Marshall can be encouraged to tell more abut the flag, even if he just wants to make up some more.) On the other hand, if you're simply curious, you could attempt to lead them out of personal narrative and simply remind them in group that the dictated stories can be about anything they want (except bathroom stories and those that are too—judgment call—violent).
Things that are true and not true: I think I'd stop short of anything more specific. I want to know what kinds of "non-true" things they think about.

10/29/04
From: Laurie
To: Patsy
Aisha told a story today about a fish whose whole family went on vacation without him and while he was alone he made friends with a good shark and when the bad shark came, the fish and the good shark and the other little fish made a big shark together and chased him away. *Swimmy*-esque. I read *Swimmy* to them yesterday. Interestingly enough, Aisha chose to play the part of the fish's mom who went on vacation—a small part—and wanted Drew (a very calm boy) for the main little fish. Re: storytelling turn taking—I have just been taking kids that ask about stories and checking them off on the

class list—but today both Manuel and Jasmin asked during Aisha's turn if they could tell stories on Monday so I put them down on a list. First Manuel is up and then Jasmin.

10/30/04
From: Patsy
To: Laurie
Re: stories and personal narratives. Enough said. The kids found the loophole.

11/4/04
From: Laurie
To: Patsy
Stories are going really well. They are some of my favorite parts of the day. The kids are getting a real sense of their power, I think. Manuel got to tell his story too—he needed some support sequencing and making sense—it was about going to the toy store to get his Sponge Bob Square Pants lunchbox, and then he fell down the stairs and his dad picked him up, and then he went to pick up his cousin and they were so late. He asks if he can tell a story every day and when it isn't his turn to act in one he is crushed. I show him the lists a lot, and he seems comforted by them.

Elena told a story about a cat named Hobbes who caught a mouse and left half of it on the bathroom floor. When she was at her friend Ariana's house, they saw the mouse in the bathroom and were surprised. The kids laughed at that one a long time. They have been absolutely focused during story acting time. It's lovely.

11/5/04
From: Patsy
To: Laurie
The Manuels of the world are lucky when they land in story classrooms.

11/6/04
From: Laurie
To: Patsy
I am learning so much. There is so much to learn—I feel like I want

to keep teaching K for a long, long time. I am so glad I haven't leapt out of the classroom and into staff development.

I don't feel comfortable with having kids tell stories, for example, about a real kid in the class that might hurt that kid's feelings. But I don't want to squelch their expression, either.

The thing is the more I try to build and enact appropriate curriculum, like stories, in my classroom, the more committed I am to continuing. The kids need these stories, they love them, they are growing in many ways as a result of stories' presence the classroom, and it upsets me to think of stopping them for political reasons. I suppose I don't need to go overboard with broadcasting how great they are, but I am so excited and so many other teachers express interest in them. Each teacher has to lead a staff development session once during the year and Cath (AP) suggested I talk about stories. A video would be useful for that purpose I am sure. I don't want to be caught in the center of a political mess because you know storytelling is not part of our regular curriculum, but I also want to do right by my students and by myself as a developing teacher. I don't know what could happen.

11/6/04
From: Patsy
To: Laurie
Re: stories about real kids. Do you mean the actual narrative says hurtful things or that the simple exclusion of their names is bound to create hurt? Of the first—no way. I'd quit first. Of the second—again, redirect. Manipulate the list so that the unchosen get in there somehow.

Re: stopping stories and being caught in a political mess and doing right by the kids and yourself. Are you really talking about stopping them? I thought your principal said that you could do storytelling, but just not go public with it.

11/8/04
From: Laurie
To: Patsy
It just happened that we were starting a new go-round for picking actors when Emma's story with all those kids came up so each of

them actually was able to be chosen. We looked at the list together and I made sure she understood that she could choose them because they were up for a turn, not just because their names were in the story. In terms of you can't say you can't play, maybe it is not as hard as I think. Maybe I just talk about it with them. Sally next door has a rule that you can't say you can't play unless you want to play by yourself. What do you think of that? Also, I agree, I can definitely redirect stories that seem to be turning into little cool kid stories. I didn't imagine how sad it might make the others. The next day's story, by the way, by Nora, was a lovely little fantasy about getting ice cream twice in one day, once from mom and once from dad. Manuel was chosen for the ice cream man and he was thrilled.

11/13/04
From: Laurie
To: Patsy
Last week Blake told a story about good and bad "I-Robots." He was so excited to tell the story, he was getting up and running around where we were sitting and showing me with his body how the robots were at war. It took a while to make a kind of sense of what he was saying that I could understand—basically he said, "There was I-Robot and he had no mother and father. No, he did, he had one mother and one father." (Blake's home situation is very confused and troubled—he has told me he has more than one mother and father. I have heard from Mary that his actual father may be the boyfriend of one of his older sisters.) "The good red robot's name was Sunny. The bad Blue Robot's name was Sunny too. The good Sunny and the bad Sunny were killing each other." (Then I said no killing—was that wrong?—so he changed it to "play-fighting.") "Then the good Sunny and the bad Sunny got together and they went to get the bad witch. That's it."

Luke and Aaron were playing at the playground after school late one day and they saw a mouse run across the carpet in our classroom. They happened to both be up for storytelling, and they both told the story—different versions. I explained that they wouldn't automatically get to have the other play themselves because of the list—it happened that they both could though. The kids loved this story and could've heard it and acted it many more times. Luke at first wanted to be the mouse in his story, but at the last minute he changed it so that he was himself—he said, "I can make one change on the rug, right? Well I want to be me and I want Manuel to be the mouse instead of the other way."

11/14/04
From: Patsy
To: Laurie
Re: killing. We allow it. Just no touching. No gore. Nothing weird. Re: mouse story. Isn't that terrific? Great. I told you, didn't I, to look for the "class theme." Yours might be running mice. Once we had a class that began every story "Once there was a" (fill in the blank, let's say, for example, Ninja Turtle). "And then he became a *real* Ninja Turtle . . ." and then the intended story would come. It was like the door they had to open first. Very powerful to see it in action.

Re: Blake's story. Sad story. Necessary story. Better story in disguise than in real life, don't you think?

11/29/04
From: Laurie
To: Patsy
Tomorrow would be great for stories. There are a couple I want to show you—very interesting! Daliya's begins, "I went inside a dandelion and there were two monkeys sitting below a ribbon." We'll start choice time at 10. I think James R. is up. (Remember the ultra on-track boy? You took his story first.)

12/2/04
From: Laurie
To: Patsy
So today as Lisa and Claire and Jan and I gathered around the story table with little Marisa and me, Marisa tells *another* version of "Hansel and Gretel" (I haven't read it to them—I think it's playing at the local puppet theater though and maybe that's why they're so

into it) in which, instead of the witch, the villain is the character Sakemo from her last story—but this time, Sakemo is half-man half-woman. (!) There are five kids instead of just H and G. In the end, Sakemo pushes the kids into the oven and they all die. At the end of acting it out, the kids solemnly applaud the five little corpses. Oh boy. The visitors told me they loved seeing stories and it looked like wonderful work to be doing—which is good. I sort of wished for less potentially controversial content, but what can you do. When I chatted with Jan later, she mentioned it but didn't sound horrified, just curious. "Is there a lot of death in the stories?" she asked. Nope, I said. I invited her to read through the storybook so she could get a sense of the variety.

12/2/04
From: Patsy
To: Laurie
Re: controversial content. Always, always on the day of visitors. You can just count on it.

Re: group life in stories. Ah, yes, the group. We must find our place—and better it be a powerful one—in the group.

Re: Killing off the group. Well, I must admit it was kind of dramatic, but I'm more interested in Sakemo. Half-man/half-woman? So powerful s/he can kill the whole group? What is the origin of this character again? Are there other stories with such powerful villains/plot lines (best bet)? I guess we could ask if Marisa's troubled about something, but this is not enough evidence.

Re: Death in the kindergarten. Tolerable, if not necessary. I do think there's some killing off of babyhood (sniff). (Read more Erikson. Read Bettelheim on fairy tales. Heck, watch the news.) Gore, dismemberment, etc. is not acceptable. Marisa has not crossed that line here, though. You'll know when she does (it's a feeling in your stomach). Put down your pen, and say, "You know, what, Marisa? This makes me uncomfortable. It's just too nasty. Make it less scary for me and the kids." She will. You get to say this for the same reason you get to say when the stories get too boring. You know more than they do. Tell James I'll look at my schedule for next week.

12/3/04
From: Laurie
To: Patsy
Marshall's story today when it was just us, was, of course, not at all controversial. A sweet little focused narrative about when it was Mia's birthday in the class and the juice leapt off the counter by itself without being touched and gushed all over and we had to move the green table into the block area and the cleaner guys came to clean it up and the floor was sticky on their shoes.

About Sakemo—s/he's the villain in the stories Marisa tells with her family—she has two very kind and VERY involved parents, she's the apple of their eyes, quite clearly. They seem a little hover-y to me. They read to her a lot, books with pretty sophisticated content—*A Wrinkle in Time*, for example (remember the gigantic brain on the planet Camazotz that controlled everybody's every move?). She likes scary stuff, she says. I personally think, even if a kid has really advanced comprehension skills, why push it with the scary/sophisticated content. What's the rush? Why not save some of those wonderful chapter books for later? I agree about the death—gore is not at all OK, but death is important—they are clearly working things out. I need to read Bettelheim—one of the visitors yesterday mentioned him too. Killing off of babyhood—sad (for us) and necessary, eh? I'll tell James.

12/21/04
From: Laurie
To: Patsy
We have not done stories for two days because of various holiday choice time projects that needed my full attention. Anyway, the kids have been asking nonstop for stories—I'll do them again tomorrow so they don't get out of the groove. I wish I could quit doing writing workshop with them—they are so much more interested in writing when they write signs or cards or notes or lists that have to do with their play. I think they would learn to read and write just fine if stories were the literacy program. But I can't.

It's the stories that captivate them and drive them, it's the stories that they ask for. On days we don't have writing workshop it is rare for a kid to ask about it. Hmmmmm.

12/23/04
From: Laurie
To: Patsy
It was a delicious day in the kindergarten. Andrew's story was about going swimming at the ocean in Jamaica and seeing an electric eel. When he went back to his house, the lights were busted because the eel had shocked everything. Andrew's Mommy called the Light Man, who put the lights back on. Then everyone went to sleep. I'd love to meet/talk/tease things out. I am around the whole time.

1/9/05
From: Laurie
To: Patsy
I have a story question—Mia wanted to tell a story about her birthday party, to which not everyone in the class was invited. I let her tell the story and she chose two other kids to act out the story with her. Kids that happened to actually be at the party. I had the feeling afterwards that I should have said to her something like, "That story might make the kids who didn't get to come feel sad—can you think of another one?" Should I have? Or is that oversensitive.

1/10/05
From: Patsy
To: Laurie
Re: Mia's story I would definitely have had the conversation with her. I'd even think about taking it to the group. Not about birthday stories in particular—though it will be a distracting issue—but about stories that might make others sad. I'd have to see how it was worded to really comment. Ironic—isn't it—that real life can make us sad. Think about the implications of this for "personal narratives."

1/10/05
From: Laurie
To: Patsy
I like the idea of talking to the kids about the too sad issue. It is interesting, sometimes it doesn't occur to me to open up these issues to them—and it's really them I want to hear from. ɪs this too

sad? Why? What can we do about it? Should we make a rule? Yeah, personal narrative . . . I am taking a break for a while—we're reading/making ABC books until the end of the week. Then the little readers come out in readers' workshop and we do list books. Hard to believe it's already January. They are growing so much. They are still absolutely themselves, but they are much steadier on the rug, much more focused during work time.

2/4/05
From: Laurie
To: Patsy
Today Emma told a story about walking into the woods and a storm came up in the night and blew off her coat and her friends' coats. Then she saw a wicked house that had inside a good ghost, skeleton and witch who gave them hot cider and pumpkin pie. They walked home with it and stooped to pick up their coats from the top of the willow tree.

2/5/05
From: Patsy
To: Laurie
What I love about Emma's story is the intrusion of Halloween in February. (Plus "stooped.") I love the way holidays—symbols—are such a sub-text of kids' lives. Jung was right.

2/10/05
From: Laurie
To: Patsy
Daliya and James are both so interesting—it was good to hear what you had to say. Interestingly, I did Daliya's ECLAS [Early Childhood Literacy Assessment System] and she recognizes (out of context) only eight letters and couldn't isolate sounds but could say the names of kids who started with the letters she recognized—M, Marshall etc. James can name almost all, upper and lowercase, and could isolate most sounds. But he has something going on re: print—he doesn't seem to remember the sight words at all, and writes really haltingly in WWorkshop—often not as sure of sounds as he was during ECLAS when he could see the letter, name it, and

then say the sound. Going from word to sound to letter is harder for him. And you saw his absolute lack of interest in the page when you were writing the story. I am not sure what is going on, exactly. Any ideas?

Daliya doesn't much draw representationally—occasionally, a head with arms. She has absolutely no interest in writing workshop—and see how delighted she was by her story?! Until I distracted her with trying to make it make more sense to me, that is.

Little Blake—you remember Blake—told (surprise) not a superhero story today, but a gingerbread story—the gingerbread man stole a carriage from a lady that had three babies and a fox in it, and then he took it back to the lady at her home. She cooked him and he jumped up and ran away to the fox's home, which was in the water. He melted and the fox ate him. When he first started telling, he said, "No girls is gonna be in this story," but then he wanted Marisa, Emma and Jasmin for the babies, and Kia for the lady. Serious Marshall was the fox. Blake was the gingerbread man. He was so happy, he grinned for the next hour. Rare, for him to grin that much.

2/12/05
From: Laurie
To: Patsy
My friend Susan next door is starting stories in her classroom next week. She has her book all set up. Oh, you would have loved seeing Luke's story yesterday—it was called "THE ORGINAL SPEEDRACER." He fills his stories with dialogue. There was a part where the Speedracer song had to be sung—he asked as I was writing it down if the audience could do that part, "Because we're all actors here," and then before acting the story he taught them how to sing it. They were most obliging and when Luke gave them the cue (it was the part where Speedracer jumped into the car) they all went, "Go Speedracer, all around the town," just as he'd taught them. It was a beautiful moment—funny, but also really beautiful—all of them were so intent, so focused, so absolutely absorbed in creating the world of the story—not one child was off task. That almost never happens during other parts of the day. Except when we are having

a discussion about things that matter tremendously to them—like whether or not someone should have to be a bad guy in a game if they don't want to—they all decided emphatically no on that one.

2/13/05
From: Laurie
To: Patsy
I've been working on my list about why stories are so important. Here are some thoughts.

Assessment/Promotion of literacy development

- Children practice making sense
- We support and validate the sense they make in stories
- We notice and support the child's interaction with the dictated text—Does he track? Does he notice letters, spaces, familiar names, sight words, punctuation, left-right motion? Does he slow to match his telling speed to our writing speed?
- We support grammar development as child tells
- Before becoming writers themselves children must have models—they need to see us writing words down often. They are absolutely involved in watching this happen because the stories are their own.
- Children come to understand that writing is for catching meaning on paper.
- Dictation/dramatization helps kids fall in love with storytelling and stories—or rather, they already are in love and we provide space, time, attention (both individual attention while taking dictation and group attention while dramatizing)

Assessment/Promotion of social development

- Stories address issues of fairness; everyone gets a turn on the list both to tell and to act
- Stories provide an opportunity for community building through working things out together (is it too sad to tell a story about a party that not everyone was invited to? Etc.)
- Each child has multiple opportunities to be publicly cherished and celebrated

- Children assert control within the group
- Children see themselves as individuals with individual stories to tell (and direct) and also as members of a group, as audience members and actors. With stories, the idea of individuality and community are not mutually exclusive
- Children tackle/process issues of good/bad, deal with things that frighten them, stories validate this
- Non-threatening forum for children to share their real selves with us/each other

Also—

- Acting the stories fits with their developmental level—out loud, physical
- And the realm of fantasy can enter the room through the structure of storytelling

4/12/05
From: Laurie
To: Patsy
I've been meaning to write to you forever and tell you about James—he's turned some kind of corner, I think. You know how his stories have been, like lists of activities . . . the last one he told was a very relaxed story about his friends from New Jersey (where he moved from last summer and where he will move back to when school is over) and his friends from Brooklyn all having a sleepover play date together. It was very sweet and pretty different from his other pieces. And he was totally engaged by the text as I was writing. He'd slow down and wait for me to catch up, he was breaking words into syllables. Interesting. He's been more relaxed in general lately. It is nice to see. His writing has taken off as well—his reading, not so much, but it seems to be causing him less anxiety. I thought you might be happy to hear it!

All of their stories have evolved so much from the beginning of the year—what a joy this process has been, and is. I've been doing it only four days a week for the past couple of weeks because of choice time stuff I need to be helping with (because all of the helpers in my room have been stationed somewhere else!) and they are so irritated with me on the days we miss.

4/12/05
From: Patsy
To: Laurie
Lost teeth are the beginning of the end. You notice they don't show up in Winnie the Pooh. There is the lamest beginning reader book called *No Tooth, No Quarter.* Almost brilliant in its banality. Of course, the kids ADORE it. Great for kids who can read, but can't read chapter books. Great for everyone who has lost a tooth.

4/16/05
From: Laurie
To: Patsy
I was looking over the year's stories yesterday and I was noticing just how many real-life stories we were getting at the beginning of the year—it really did take a while for them to bust out—now the balance has tipped in the other direction. Do you think that they were influenced by the heavy doses of personal narrative they were getting at the beginning of the year? Is that typical, for classes to start out with more true-life stories?

4/24/05
From: Laurie
To: Patsy
Regarding operationalizing social justice . . . I guess mostly, I just want to be fair. I want to treat students fairly and for them to feel that they are being treated fairly. I want to be able to open issues of justice up for discussion to them—I've thought about this much more this year than I ever have before, thanks to you, actually. For example, we talked about whether or not they think it's fair for one kid to tell another kid what they have to be in a game. The answer was a decisive and unanimous no. I could say more, and will if you like—I will have time to think over this lovely week-long break!

5/21/05
From: Patsy
To: Laurie
Marisa has come so far as a storyteller. There was much sophistication in the way in which she borrowed from her classmates,

incorporated the twin/Siamese idea, and the force that makes everyone nicer at the end. The more I think about it, the more I am impressed. The icing on the cake was the drama, both the audience's full attention, and the investment in the acting. I do wish I had it on tape.

5/24/05
From: Patsy
To: Laurie
I hope you realize how important it was for my students to hear you last night. I'm throwing them a curve with storytelling, since all of their placements or experience is either in workshop schools or ones where invented spelling is the sum total of the writing curriculum. I do feel like I've muddied the waters for you. I really wish you could know the Houston group.

5/24/05
From: Laurie
To: Patsy
It was so fun to meet your students—I feel like we barely touched the surface of the deeper issues. As for my staff meeting, there was, eventually, a lot of interesting thinking through of basic observations of all of our kids on the playground, talking through the kinds of play we see, the kinds of play in dramatic play or in the Duplo center . . . people were wondering how to support superhero-type play within the kind of curriculum we're expected to enforce—I talked about stories and how engaged they are during those times, how important the stories are—easy to fit in! We also talked about how that kind of play is about being on a team, being part of the group—not about being an individual so much. I do feel not at all alone in the way I've been thinking about teaching kindergarten this year—I know the end of the year is hectic, but . . . I wish I could know your Houston group too. And I wish I could see some other, more developmentally appropriate examples of kindergarten. And yes, you HAVE muddied my waters, and I thank you for it!!!! More mud means more suspended sediment which means . . . my metaphor is dwindling . . . more thinking going on, at any rate. A child development/ed class seems important. Good idea.

Notes

INTRODUCTION

1. I do not include here Paley's one-time references to the work of theorist Sara Smilansky and educational philosopher Kieran Egan.

2. I had originally used the phrase "pedagogy of truth" to characterize Paley's work in play, story, and storytelling. I am grateful to an anonymous reader for the University of Chicago Press for suggesting this more accurate description. While all things meaningful are in some way true, and all things true in some way meaningful, "pedagogy of meaning" has far greater range in a discussion of early childhood education.

3. As I discuss in chapter 5, Paley's *In Mrs. Tully's Room: A Childcare Portrait* (2001) features Lillian Tully, an African American teacher and director of a childcare center. While Mrs. Tully's racial identity is clearly a contributing factor in the classroom life Paley discovers over the course of her visits, it is Paley's reexamination of the uses of story in the classroom that takes center stage.

CHAPTER 1

1. Beyond the Puritans' attempts to save their young children from damnation by teaching them to read the Bible, the institutionalization of early childhood education in America began with the infant schools of the 1830s, the earliest version of what we now call day care. Early childhood education formally arrived from Germany in the mid-1800s when Margarethe Schurz, a devotee of Friedrich Fröbel, whose Rousseau-inspired kindergarten movement centered on play, nature,

and tailor-made toy objects, opened the first U.S. kindergarten in Wisconsin. Elizabeth Peabody opened the first kindergarten taught in English in Boston in 1860. Unsurprisingly, the Transcendentalists were ardent supporters of the kindergarten movement. The first public school kindergarten was started in St. Louis in 1873. Chicago had twenty public kindergartens by 1910 (Morgan 2007). While the kindergarten movement ushered in a special response to the unique qualities of the young child's mind, a parallel movement was developing in America that centered more on relieving young children, and ultimately society, of the effects of poverty. The best known of the early intervention programs in America in the first half of the twentieth century were the settlement houses, such as Jane Adams's Hull House in Chicago and the Henry Street Settlement House in New York City. The modern and nationally known iteration of these services is of course Head Start, the federally funded "War on Poverty" program initiated in 1965. Findings on Head Start's efficacy have fluctuated over the years between the impressive and the unimpressive. The (in)famous 1969 Westinghouse Learning Report suggested no lasting effects, but studies since then have supported Head Start's educational value enough to keep it in business. Head Start is currently riding a wave of positive findings of enduring benefits from a study on the Perry Preschool Project, the renowned, but small program in Michigan, with which, curiously, Head Start is often confused by the press (see Kirp 2007, 65). It is worth noting that, in general, early childhood educators remain enthusiastic supporters of Head Start.

2. Related to the appropriateness of formal literacy instruction in the kindergarten and preschool, the age effect is an issue that rarely gets addressed. Taking kindergarten as a set point, how can we entertain national policies on early literacy instruction when the age for kindergarten admission varies from state to state? Whether a child won't be five until December or has been five since July makes an enormous difference in the necessary balance between formal learning and play in the curriculum. To put it more plainly, the presence of four-year-olds on opening day in kindergarten (and three-year-olds in prekindergarten and five-year-olds in first grade) makes for a very different class than one where the youngest child is at least six months older. It happens that nine states admit children who may not turn five until sometime in October, November, or December. The majority of the remaining states have a cutoff date between July 31 and September 1. Indiana has the earliest cutoff date with July 1 (Kauerz and McMaken 2003). Some states allow local municipalities to set the cutoff. Nor does this take into account the increasingly common practice of holding out young children from kindergarten in order for them to be older and thus, the circuitous thinking goes, better able to handle increasing academic and social pressures (see Graue 1995). This has created an even greater age span in the classroom, with many teachers reporting an eighteen-month difference from youngest to oldest. Though Bredekamp and Shepherd's 1989 study of kindergarten cutoff dates found whatever small advantage resulted from holding children out had faded by third grade, what

has not been studied is the impact of the average age on curriculum developers and even teachers' expectations.

3. As this book goes to press, the NAEYC has just released its third edition of *Developmentally Appropriate Practice in Early Childhood Programs* (Copple and Bredekamp 2009). In one of the opening sections, "Key Messages of the Position Statement," the editors reveal the ongoing push me/pull you nature of recommended literacy practices: "Education and quality and outcomes would improve substantially if elementary teachers incorporated the best of preschool's emphases and practices (e.g., attention to the whole child; integrated, meaningful learning; parent engagement) and if preschool teachers made more use of those elementary-grade practices that are valuable for younger children as well (e.g., robust content; attention to learning progressions in curriculum and teaching" (xii). Throughout a revised position statement called "Developmentally Appropriate Practice in Early Childhood Programs Serving Children from Birth through Age 8," the editors stress that the "current context" of early intervention is one in which demands for greater academic achievement and accountability cannot be ignored, even as increased levels of poverty and obstacles to learning that result from unsupported second-language issues threaten young children's school success more than ever. In the section "Applying New Knowledge," the editors focus directly on the need to teach literacy subskills, which they insist can be taught in a developmentally appropriate manner.

4. See the U.S. Department of Education report on the Reading First program: "Reading First Impacts Instruction of Struggling Readers," November 2008 (www.ed.gov/nclb/methods/reading/readingfirst-report.html).

5. By way of contrast, we live in an educational age that undoubtedly will be remembered for its emphasis on testing and accountability. Testing, of course, is characterized by its usefulness in measuring backward, that is, measuring what has already been learned. It will therefore always represent the inverse of what Dewey means by education. If there is no growth and development as a result of the experience, there is no education. This is not an argument against testing or even test preparation. Dewey was not against assessment, only against its substitution for education. "Education," in other words, must be synonymous with "learning."

6. Vygotsky's theory of play focuses on the child of "preschool age," whom he distinguishes from the "very young child" and the "school-age child." The last clearly refers to the period when formal schooling begins. He does not use the term "kindergarten" or "kindergartner." I use the terms "young child," "preschool and kindergarten," and "early childhood" to refer to the period after infancy and before formal schooling. The application of Vygotsky's theory of the role of play in development to Paley's work differs in one respect. This is Paley's consistent use of the metaphor of work to describe young children's play. She notes that both require cooperation, enactment of roles and rules, and shared perspectives. Vygotsky, on the other hand, rejects the comparison, which was common even in his day. He says that while young children's play

is motivated by needs and circumstances, it is not driven by the children's understanding of their motives and needs: "In this respect play differs substantially from work and other forms of activity" (1978, 93).

CHAPTER 2

1. Despite the intellectual theories and traditions that support the role of fantasy play in the preschool and kindergarten, it is important to acknowledge that recent research in the evolutionary foundations and functions of play (see Smith 2007) suggest it may not be the universal medium for learning many theorists, along with Paley, describe it to be. This seems more than logical. If learning is a social phenomenon within a sociocultural context, then fantasy play can only develop to the extent a culture supports it (Gaskins, Haight, and Lancy 2007; Göncü, Jain, and Tuermer 2007). Accordingly, young children from cultures or cultural communities that do not support or value play cannot be considered lacking. This would not apply to American culture in general, though it has critical implications for American children from impoverished or immigrant backgrounds who may be judged lacking in these skills, when in reality their families are not able or do not choose to incorporate fantasy play in child rearing. The relationship of fantasy play to Paley's philosophy of education is interesting in light of Paley's attempts to be culturally sensitive. That said, it would be hard to dispute that an endorsement of Paley's work could be had without a belief that fantasy is a natural response to environments that permit it.

2. In *Boys and Girls: Superheroes in the Doll Corner* (1984), Paley explains that out of the need to serve boys better in the classroom, she substantially increased the time allotted for free play. See chapter 5 for more details. The typical amount of time is about forty-five minutes.

3. Pertinent to our overall discussion, circle time has been renamed "morning meeting" in many schools, hinting at a wider agenda.

4. I develop this argument further in chapter 3 in my discussion of narrative in the storytelling curriculum. Also see Fein, Ardila-Rey, and Groth 2000; Nicolopoulou 1996, 1997a, 1997b.

CHAPTER 3

1. The following is a methodological overview of the storytelling curriculum. It cannot be stated enough, however, that these are suggestions only. This is also true of the more detailed guide methodological in appendix A. All teachers, including Paley, impose their own styles and preferences on the implementation process. Appendices B–D offer sample stories, transcripts, and notes from the field.

2. In *Mrs. Tully's Room: A Childcare Portrait* (2001), Paley suggests ways "to take" stories in a group where the age of the children, time, or classroom dynamics do not permit an individual child's dictation.

3. In the classroom storytelling program run by the School Literacy and Culture Project, many teachers have experimented with taking dictation on

the computer. The overwhelming majority of them come back to paper and pencil. First, a pencil in hand allows teachers to take dictation from anywhere in the room. More important, sitting beside a child as he tells a story creates a far greater sense of intimacy that invariably proves more satisfying and productive than sitting in front of a computer screen.

4. All names in the classroom, including Laurie's, are pseudonyms. The e-mails have been edited lightly to simplify formatting and eliminate minor errors.

5. Pre- and post-test scores were collected on the Expressive Vocabulary Test, the Peabody Picture Vocabulary Test, and Whitehurst's Get Ready to Read. We found significance on both the Peabody Picture Vocabulary Test and Get Ready to Read scores (and hypothesized that the children's English skills hampered their performance on the Expressive Vocabulary Test, which was given in English, according to district requirements).

6. Nicolopoulou's study with Richner (2004) finds that the peer-dependent structure of storytelling and story acting significantly improved the children's narrative skills (as measured on the Expressive Vocabulary Test and Figurine-Based Narrative Task). Also see Fein, Ardila-Rey, and Groth (2000), who correlate children's interest in literacy-related activities with their participation in either the storytelling curriculum or the "author's chair," the place from which children share their stories with the class. Findings suggest children's fantasy play increases in storytelling classrooms, and book-related activities in "author's chair" classrooms. Given fantasy play's role in developing young children's narrative and language skills, it is at minimum an interesting trade-off. Finally, the research on the impact of the storytelling curriculum on young children's literacy development is likely to increase with time. A review of the research on the relationship between three types of "creative drama" and oral language development—thematic improvisation (life themes), story-based improvisation (literature-based), and Paley-style improvisation (child-authored)—finds that only research on the Paley-style version has continued into the new millennium (Mages 2008, 131).

CHAPTER 5

1. There are numerous reports documenting the decreasing number of minority teachers in American public schools over the past several decades (see, e.g., Foster 1997; Grant 1990; Irvine 1990). In 2003, the National Education Association found that approximately 90 percent of teachers in America were white, middle-class females. In 2005, the National Center for Education Information reported that white teachers represented approximately 85 percent of the teaching force, only a percentage point less than the figure estimated by Cochran-Smith (2005), and not expected to drop significantly further. In 1997, children of color made up 76 percent of the students in America's twenty central cities (Anyon 1997). This ratio seems to have changed little, for the National Center for Education Statistics reported in 2008 that 77 percent of students are racial or ethnic minorities in cities with populations greater than

250,000. One clear implication of these statistics is that children of color are very likely to be taught by white teachers.

2. Given the fact that racial differences between children and teachers are often accompanied by class differences, a color-blind approach to race in the classroom effectively eliminates talk about class as well.

3. Writing in the *New York Times*, Samuel G. Freedman (1998) credits Kohl's *36 Children* as a major impetus for the urban school reform movement.

4. See note 1 above.

5. Sheets contends that a focus on white teachers' beliefs and attitudes and not those of teachers and children of color results in "displacing people of color from center stage" in the conversation. She also dismisses what she sees as the prevailing ideology supporting "race consciousness" among white teachers as inadequate to battle racist policies and practices (2000, 16). More important, she insists that white teachers' exploration of their racial identities diverts their attention from a much needed "equity pedagogy" toward such amorphous aims as hope and advocacy. She asks, for example, if Howard's 1999 claim to an "activist and transformationist [w]hite identity" can really result in "skilled teachers who participate competently and responsibly in a reciprocal, complex teaching-learning process with our children" (17). Or, by contrast, does white identity work maintain the status quo by letting white angst stand in for effective teaching? She describes Dilg 1999, Howard 1999, and McIntyre 1997 as exemplars of the white studies movement and echoes Willis and Harris's complaint. In his response to Sheets, Howard acknowledges the validity of her claim that no empirical link has been made between "[w]hite racial identity development and teacher competency" (2000, 22). He insists, though, that the potential benefit to students of color is reason to pursue the issue further. Similarly, Milner believes that racial identity work can help teachers rid themselves of negative stereotypes: "Race reflection can be seen as a way to uncover inconspicuous phenomena; it can be a process to understand hidden values, biases, and beliefs about race that were not to the fore in a teacher's thinking prior" (2003, x).

6. Though emanating from Ladson-Billings' study of effective teachers of black children, culturally responsive pedagogy is recommended for all children.

7. Kwanzaa is the name of a character in a fairy tale Paley makes up and embeds in the book as a story she tells the children. He is a former slave, named for the black family holiday that was created by African American scholar Ron Karenga in 1966.

CHAPTER 6

1. Admittedly, male teachers might have a different view of the doll corner. However, the ratio of female to male kindergarten teachers is so low (98:2) as to make the point almost moot (National Center for Education Statistics 2004). Nor does the presence of male teachers change the standards for kindergarten success, which have been determined by women.

2. Paley only refers to "school work" and fine motor activities. Presumably, this involved literacy subskills as well, such as letter writing, which would have been typical in the mid-1980s.

3. Booth (2002, 27) writes that he learned more from Paley's books about gender differences than from any other resource.

References

Ainsworth, M., M. Blehar, E. Waters, and S. Wall. 1978. *Patterns of attachment*. Hillsdale, NJ: Lawrence Erlbaum.

Anyon, J. 1997. *Ghetto schooling: A political economy of urban educational reform*. New York: Teachers College Press.

Applebee, A. 1978. *The child's concept of story: Ages two to seventeen*. Chicago: University of Chicago Press.

Ashton-Warner, Sylvia. 1963. *Teacher*. New York: Bantam Books.

Au, K. H., J. H. Carroll, and J. A. Scheu. 2001. *Balanced literacy instruction: A teacher's resource book*. 2nd ed. Norwood, MA: Christopher-Gordon.

Balaban, N. 1985. *Starting school: From separation to independence*. New York: Teachers College Press.

Banks, J. A. 1988. *Multiethnic education: Theory and practice*. 2nd ed. Boston: Allyn and Bacon.

———. 1994. *An introduction to multicultural education*. Boston: Allyn and Bacon.

———. 2006. Multicultural education: Characteristics and goals. In *Multicultural education: Issues and perspectives*, ed. J. A. Banks and C. A. Banks, 3–31. New York: John Wiley.

Beatty, B. 1998. From infant schools to Project Head Start: Doing historical research in early childhood education. In *Issues in early childhood education research*, ed. B. Spodek, O. N. Saracho, and A. D. Pellegrini, 1–29. New York: Teachers College Press.

Berk, L. E. 1994. Vygotsky's theory: The importance of make-believe play. *Young Children* 50 (1): 30–39.

Berk, L. E., T. D. Mann, and A. T. Ogan. 2006. Make-believe play: Wellspring for the development of self-regulation. In *Play = learning: How play motivates and enhances children's cognitive and social-emotional growth*, ed. D. G. Singer, R. M. Golinkoff, and K. Hirsh-Pasek, 74–100. New York: Oxford University Press.

Berk, L. E., and A.Winsler. 1995. *Scaffolding children's learning: Vygotsky and early childhood education*. Washington, DC: National Association for the Education of Young Children.

Bernhard, J. K., J. Gonzalez-Mena, H. N. Chang, M. O'Loughlin, C. Eggers-Pierola, G. Fiati, and P. Corson. 1998. Recognizing the centrality of cultural diversity and racial equity: Beginning a discussion and critical reflection on "developmentally appropriate practice." *Canadian Journal of Research in Early Childhood Education* 7 (1): 81–90.

Bettelheim, B. 1975. Some further thoughts on the doll corner. *School Review* 83 (2): 363–68.

Bishop, C. H. 1938. *The Five Chinese Brothers*. New York: Coward-McCann.

Blum, L. 1999. Race, community and moral education: Kohlberg and Spielberg as civic educators. *Journal of Moral Education* 28 (2): 125–43.

Bodrova, E., and D. Leong. 2006. Developing self-regulation: The Vygotskian view. *Academic Exchange Quarterly* 10 (4): 33–38.

———. 2007. *Tools of the mind: The Vygotskian approach to early childhood education*. Englewood Cliffs, NJ: Prentice-Hall.

———. 2008. Developing self-regulation in kindergarten: Can we keep all the crickets in the basket? *Young Children* 63 (2): 56–58.

Boisvert, R. D. 1998. *John Dewey: Rethinking our time*. Albany, NY: SUNY Press.

Booth, D. 2002. *Even hockey players read: Boys, literacy, and learning*. Ontario: Pembroke.

Bowlby, J. 1973. *Attachment and loss*. Vol. 2, *Separation: Anxiety and fear*. New York: Basic Books.

Boykin, A. W. 1992. The triple quandary and the schooling of Afro-American children. In *The school achievement of minority children: New perspectives*, ed. U. Neisser, 59–70. Hillsdale, NJ: Lawrence Erlbaum.

Bransford, J., L. Darling-Hammond, and P. LePage. 2005. Introduction to *Preparing teachers for a changing world: What teachers should learn and be able to do*, ed. L. Darling-Hammond and J. Bransford, 1–39. San Francisco: Jossey-Bass.

Bredekamp, S., and C. Copple. 1986. *Developmentally appropriate practices in early childhood programs*. Washington, DC: National Association for the Education of Young Children.

———. 1997. *Developmentally appropriate practices in early childhood programs*. Rev. ed. Washington, DC: National Association for the Education of Young Children.

Bredekamp, S., and L. Shepard. 1989. How best to protect children from inappropriate school expectations, practices, and policies. *Young Children* 44 (3): 14–24.

Brooks, C. K. 1987. Teachers: Potent learning forces in the learning lives of black children. In *Educating black children: America's challenge*, ed. D. S. Strickland, and E. J. Cooper. Washington, DC: Bureau of Educational Research.

Bruner, J. S. 1960. *The process of education*. Cambridge: Harvard University Press.

———. 1986. *Actual minds, possible worlds*. Cambridge: Harvard University Press.

———. 1991. *Acts of meaning: Four lectures on mind and culture*. Cambridge: Harvard University Press.

Burdell, P., and B. B. Swadener. 1999. Critical personal narrative and autoethnography in education: Reflections on a genre. *Educational Researcher* 28 (6): 21–26.

Calkins, L. 1994. *The art of teaching writing*. New ed. Portsmouth, NH: Heinemann.

———. 2003. *Units of study for primary writing: A yearlong curriculum*. Portsmouth, NH: Heinemann.

Carter, K. 1993. The place of story in the study of teaching and teacher education. *Educational Researcher* 13 (1): 5–12.

Case, R. 1985. *Intellectual development: Birth to adulthood*. New York: Academic Press.

———. 1991. *The mind's staircase: Exploring the conceptual underpinnings of children's thought and knowledge*. Hillsdale, NJ: Lawrence Erlbaum.

Cazden, C. 1992. *Whole language plus: Essays on literacy in the United States and New Zealand*. New York: Teachers College Press.

Cermak, L. S., G. Sagotsky, and C. Moshier. 1972. Development of the ability to encode within the evaluative dimension. *Journal of Experimental Child Psychology* 13:210–19.

Chafel, J. A. 2003. Socially constructing concepts of self and other through play. *International Journal of Early Years Education* 11 (3): 213–22.

Chall, J. 1970. *Learning to read: The great debate*. New York: McGraw-Hill.

Christie, J. F., and K. A. Roskos. 2006. Standards, science, and the role of play in early literacy education. In *Play = learning: How play motivates and enhances children's cognitive and social-emotional growth*, ed. D. G. Singer, R. M. Golinkoff, and K. Hirsh-Pasek, 57–73. Oxford: Oxford University Press.

Clandinin, D. J., and F. M. Connelly. 2000. *Narrative inquiry: Experience and story in qualitative research*. San Francisco: Jossey-Bass.

Clay, M. 1975. *What did I write?* Auckland: Heinemann.

———. 1991. Developmental learning puzzles me. *Australian Journal of Reading* 14 (4): 263–75.

Clift, R. T., and L. R. Albert. 1998. Early learning and continued development for teachers: Teachers as researchers. In *Issues in early childhood educational research*, ed. B. Spodek, O. N. Saracho, and A. D. Pellegrini, 139–55. New York: Teachers College Press.

Cobb, P., and E. Yackel. 1996. Constructivist, emergent, and sociocultural perspectives. *Educational Psychologist* 31 (3/4): 175–90.

Cochran-Smith, M. 2005. The new teacher education: For better or worse? *Educational Researcher* 34 (7): 3–17.

Cochran-Smith, M., and S. Lytle. 1993. *Inside outside: Teacher research and knowledge*. New York: Teachers College Press.

Coie, J. D., and K. A. Dodge. 1983. Continuities and changes in children's social status: A five-year longitudinal study. *Merrill-Palmer Quarterly* 29 (3): 261–81.

Coles, G. 2000. *Misreading reading: The science that hurts children*. Portsmouth, NH: Heinemann.

———. 2003. *Reading the naked truth: Literacy, legislation, and lies*. Portsmouth, NH: Heinemann.

Coles, R. 1989. *The call for stories*. New York: Basic Books.

Connelly, F. M., and D. J. Clandinin. 1990. Stories of experience and narrative inquiry. *Educational Researcher* 19 (5): 2–14.

Cooper, P. M. 1993. *When stories come to school: Telling, writing, and performing stories in the early childhood classroom*. New York: Teachers and Writers Collaborative.

———. 2003. Effective white teachers of black children: Teaching within a community. *Journal of Teacher Education*. 5 (3): 413–27.

———. 2005. Literacy learning and pedagogical purpose in Vivian Paley's "storytelling curriculum." *Journal of Early Childhood Literacy* 5 (3): 229–51.

———. 2009. Children's literature for reading strategy instruction: Innovation or interference? *Language Arts* 86 (3): 178–87.

Cowen, J. E. 2003. *A balanced approach to beginning reading instruction: A synthesis of six major U.S. research studies*. Newark, DE: International Reading Association.

Cooper, P. M., K. Capo, B. Mathes, and L. Grey. 2007. One authentic early literacy practice and three standardized tests: Can a storytelling curriculum measure up? *Journal of Early Childhood Teacher Education* 28 (3): 251–75.

Covaleskie, J. F. 2003. Paley's paradox: Educating for democratic life. *Philosophy of Education Yearbook*, 330–37.

Crosser, S. 1991. Summer birth date children: Kindergarten entrance age and academic achievement. *Journal of Educational Research* 84 (3): 140–46.

Dahlberg, G., P. Moss, and A. R. Pence. 2007. *Beyond quality in early childhood education and care: Languages of evaluation*. London: Routledge-Falmer.

Daniels, H. 2003. *Vygotsky and pedagogy*. London: Routledge-Falmer.

Daniels, H., M. Cole, and J. V. Wertsch, eds. 2007. *The Cambridge companion to Vygotsky*. New York: Cambridge University Press.

De Vise, D. 2007. More work, less play in kindergarten. *Washington Post*, May 23.

Delpit, L. 1994. Seeing color: A review of *White Teacher*. In *Rethinking our classrooms: Teaching for equity and justice*, ed. B. Bigelow, L. Christensen, S. Karp, B. Miner, and B. Peterson, 130–32. Milwaukee: Rethinking Schools.

———. 1995. *Other people's children: Cultural conflict in the classroom*. New York: New Press.

Dempster, F. N. 1988. The spacing effect. *American Psychologist* 43:627–34.

Derman-Sparks, L., and the A.B.C. Task Force. 1989. *Anti-bias curriculum: Tools for empowering young children*. Washington, DC: National Association for the Education of Young Children.

Dewey, J. [1900] 1990. *The school and society: The child and the curriculum*. Chicago: University of Chicago Press.

———. 1904. The relation of theory to practice in education. In *John Dewey on Education*, ed. R. D. Archambault, 313–38. Chicago: University of Chicago Press.

———. [1916] 1966. *Democracy and education*. New York: Macmillan.

———. 1933. *How we think*. Boston: D. C. Heath.

———. 1934. The need for a philosophy of education. In *John Dewey on Education*, ed. R. D. Archambault, 3–14. Chicago: University of Chicago Press.

———. 1938. *Experience and Education*. New York: Collier Macmillan.

———. 1939. Creative democracy—the task before us. In *John Dewey, the later works*, ed. J. A. Baydston, 14:224–30. Carbondale: Southern Illinois University Press.

Dickinson, D. K. 2001a. Putting the pieces together: Impact of pre-school on children's language and literacy development in kindergarten. In *Beginning literacy with language: Young children learning at home and at school*, ed. D. K. Dickinson and P. O. Tabors, 257–87. Baltimore: Paul H. Brookes.

———. 2001b. Large-group and free-play times: Conversational settings supporting language and literacy development. In *Beginning literacy with language: Young children learning at home and at school*, D. K. Dickinson and P. O. Tabors, 223–56. Baltimore: Paul H. Brookes.

———. 2002. Shifting images of developmentally appropriate practice as seen through different lenses. *Educational Researcher* 31 (1): 26–32.

Dickinson, D. K., and K. E. Sprague. 2002. The nature and impact of early childhood care environments on the language and early literacy development of children from low-income families. In *Handbook of early literacy research*, ed. S. B. Neuman and D. K. Dickinson, 2:263–80. New York: Guilford Press.

Dickinson, D. K., and Tabors, P. O., eds. 2001. *Beginning literacy with language: Young children learning at home and at school*. Baltimore: Paul H. Brookes.

Dilg, M. 1999. *Race and culture in the classroom: Teaching and learning through multicultural education*. New York: Teachers College Press.

Dixon-Krauss, L. 1996. *Vygotsky in the classroom: Mediated literacy instruction and assessment*. Upper Saddle River, NJ: Prentice Hall.

Dixson, A. D. 2003. When race matters: Examining race-conscious education policy and practice. *Educational Researcher* 32 (8): 39–43.

Donaldson, M. 1978. *Children's minds*. New York: Norton.

Dyson, A. H. 1994. The ninjas, the X-men, and the ladies: Playing with power and identity in an urban primary school. *The Teachers College Record* 96 (2): 219–39.

———. 1997. *Writing superheroes: Contemporary childhood, popular culture, and classroom literacy*. New York: Teachers College Press.

———. 2002. Writing and children's symbolic repertoires: Development unhinged. In *Handbook of early literacy research*, ed. S. B. Neuman and D. K. Dickinson, 1:126–41. New York: Guilford Press.

Dyson, A. H., and C. Genishi. 1993. Visions of children as language users: Language and language education in early childhood. In *Handbook of research in the education of young children*, ed. B. Spodek, 122–36. New York: Macmillan.

———. 1994. *The need for story: Cultural diversity in classroom and community*. Urbana, IL: National Council of Teachers of English.

Early Childhood Sexuality Education Taskforce. 1998. *Right from the start: Guidelines for sexuality issues, birth to five years*. Available online from SIECUS (Sexuality Information and Education Council of the United States). http://www.siecus.com/pub/RightFromTheStart.pdf (accessed July 18, 2007).

Elkind, D. 1986. Formal education and early childhood education: An essential difference. *Phi Delta Kappan* 71:631–42.

Engel, S. 1995. *The stories children tell: Making sense of the narratives of childhood*. New York: Freeman.

Erikson, E. [1950] 1985. *Childhood and society*. New York: Norton.

Feiman-Nemser, S. 2001. *From preparation to practice: Designing a continuum to strengthen and sustain teaching*. New York: Bank Street College of Education.

Fein, G. 1981. Pretend play: An integrative review. *Child Development* 52 (4): 1095–1118.

Fein, G., A. E. Ardila-Rey, and L. A. Groth. 2000. The narrative connection: Stories and literacy. In *Play and literacy in early childhood*, ed. K. A. Roskos and J. F. Christie, 27–44. Mahwah, NJ: Lawrence Erlbaum.

Forman, E. A., N. Minick, and C. A. Stone, eds. 1996. *Contexts for learning: Sociocultural dynamics in children's development*. 2nd ed. New York: Oxford University Press.

Foster, M. 1997. *Black teachers on teaching*. New York: New Press.

Freedman, S. G. 1998. A century of art on a blackboard canvas. *New York Times*, May 17.

Fromberg, D. P. 2002. *Play and meaning in early childhood education*. Boston: Allyn and Bacon.

Fuller, B. 2007. *Standardized childhood: The political and cultural struggle over early education*. Palo Alto, CA: Stanford University Press.

Gadzikowski, A. 2007. *Story dictation: A guide for early childhood professionals*. St. Paul, MN: Redleaf.

Gaskins, S., W. Haight, and D. F. Lancy. 2007. The cultural construction of play. In *Play and development: Evolutionary, sociocultural, and functional perspectives*, ed. A. Göncü and S. Gaskins, 179–202. Mahwah, NJ: Lawrence Erlbaum.

Gehlbach, R. D. 1986. Children's play and self-education. *Curriculum Inquiry* 16 (2): 203–13.

Gilligan, C. 1982. *In a different voice: Psychological theory and women's development.* Cambridge: Harvard University Press.

Göncü, A. 1993. Development of intersubjectivity in social pretend play. *Human Development* 36:185–98.

Göncü, A., and J. Becker. 2000. The problematic relation between developmental research and educational practice. *Human Development* 43 (4/5): 266–72.

Göncü, A., J. Jain, and U. Tuermer. 2007. Children's play as cultural interpretation. In *Play and development: Evolutionary, sociocultural, and functional perspectives*, ed. A. Göncü and S. Gaskins, 155–78. Mahwah, NJ: Lawrence Erlbaum.

Goodman, J. F. 2000. Moral education in early childhood: The limits of constructivism. *Early Education and Development* 11 (1): 37–54.

Graue, M. E. 1995. *Ready for what? Constructing meanings of readiness for kindergarten.* Albany, NY: SUNY Press.

Graves, D. H. 2003. *Writing: Teachers and children at work.* 20th anniversary ed. Exeter, NH: Heinemann.

Greene, M. 1995. *Releasing the imagination.* San Francisco: Jossey-Bass.

Greenfield, P. M., and R. R. Cocking. 1994. *Cross-cultural roots of minority child development.* Hillsdale, NJ: Lawrence Erlbaum.

Gutek, G. L. 2004. *Philosophical and ideological voices in education.* Boston: Pearson.

Hale, J. E. 1986. *Black children: Their roots, culture, and learning styles.* Baltimore: Johns Hopkins University Press.

Halliday, M. A. K. 1973. *Explorations in the functions of language.* London: Edward Arnold.

Hammerness, K., L. Darling-Hammond, J. Bransford, D. Berliner, M. Cochran-Smith, M. McDonald. 2005. How teachers learn and develop. In *Preparing teachers for a changing world: What teachers should learn and be able to do*, ed. L. Darling-Hammond and J. Bransford, 358–89. San Francisco: Jossey-Bass.

Harrist, A. W., and K. D. Bradley. 2003. "You can't say you can't play": Intervening in the process of social exclusion in the kindergarten classroom. *Early Childhood Research Quarterly* 18 (2): 185.

Hart, B., and T. R. Risley. 1995. *Meaningful differences in everyday experience of young American children.* Baltimore: Paul H. Brookes.

———. 2003. The early catastrophe: The 30 million word gap. *American Educator* 27 (1): 4–9.

Harwayne, S. 2001. *Writing through childhood: Rethinking process and product.* Portsmouth, NH: Heinemann.

Howard, G. 1999. *We can't teach what we don't know: White teachers, multiracial schools.* New York: Teachers College Press.

———. 2000. Reflections on the "white movement" in multicultural education. *Educational Researcher* 29 (9): 21–23.

Irvine, J. J. 1990. *Black students and school failure: Policies, practices, and prescriptions*. Westport, CT: Greenwood.

Irvine, J. J. 2003. *Educating teachers for diversity: Seeing with a cultural eye*. New York: Teachers College Press.

Johnson, J. E., J. F. Christie, and F. Wardle. 2005. *Play, development, and early education*. Upper Saddle River, NJ: Prentice Hall.

Johnson, J. E., J. F. Christie, and T. D. Yawkey. 1999. *Play and early childhood development*. New York: Addison Wesley Longman.

Katch, J. 2001. *Under deadman's skin: Discovering the meaning of children's violent play*. New York: Beacon Press.

———. 2003. *They don't like me: Lessons on bullying and teasing from a preschool classroom*. Boston: Beacon Press.

Katz, L. G. 1993. *Dispositions: Definitions and implications for early childhood practice*. Champaign, IL: ERIC Clearinghouse on Elementary and Early Childhood Education.

Kauerz, K., and J. McMaken. 2003. *Full day kindergarten: An exploratory study of finance and access in the United States*. Denver: Education Commission of the States.

King, J. E. 2005. *Black education: A transformative research and action agenda for the new century*. Mahwah, NJ: Lawrence Erlbaum.

King, N. R. 1990. Book reviews [*Children and play in the Holocaust*, *Bad guys don't have birthdays*, and *The ecological context of children's play*]. *Teachers College Record* 92 (1): 152.

King, S. H. 1993. The limited presence of African-American teachers. *Review of Educational Research* 63 (2): 115–49.

Kirp, D. L. 2007. *The sandbox investment: The preschool movement and kids-first politics*. Cambridge: Harvard University Press.

Kirp, D. L., and J. Wolf. 2007. The imprimatur of science. In *The sandbox investment: The preschool movement and kids-first politics*, by D. L Kirp, 93–135. Cambridge: Harvard University Press.

Kohl, H. 1966. *36 Children*. New York: New American Library.

Kozol, J. 1967. *Death at an early age*. New York: Houghton Mifflin.

LaCorte, J. J., and J. C. McDermott. 2004. Vivian Paley as a model for moral decision-making. *Early Child Development and Care* 174 (6): 505–14.

Ladd, G. W., and C. C. Coleman. 1993. Young children's peer relationships: Forms, features, and functions. In *Handbook of research on the education of young children*, ed. B. Spodek. 57–76. New York: Macmillan.

Ladd, G. W., and J. M. Price. 1987. Predicting children's social and school adjustment following the transition from pre-school to kindergarten. *Child Development* 58 (5): 1168–89.

Ladson-Billings, G. 1994a. *The dreamkeepers: Successful teachers of black children*. San Francisco: Jossey-Bass.

———. 1994b. Who will teach *our* children? Preparing teachers to successfully teach black students. In *Teaching diverse populations*, ed. E. Hollins, J. King, and W. Hayman, 106–29. Albany, NY: SUNY Press.

———. 2000. Fighting for our lives: Preparing teachers to teach African American students. *Journal of Teacher Education* 51 (3): 206–14.

Lake, V. E. 2004. Moral, ethical, and caring education for young children. *Early Child Development and Care* 174 (6): 503–4.

Landsman, J. 2001. *A white teacher talks about race*. Lanham, MD: Rowman and Littlefield.

Laverick, D. M. 2008. Starting school: Welcoming young children and families into early school experiences. *Early Childhood Education Journal* 35 (4): 321–26.

Linn, S. 2006. *The case for make believe: Saving play in a commercialized world*. New York: New Press.

Lionni, L. (1963). *Swimmy*. New York: Dragonfly Books.

———. 1967. *Frederick*. New York: Random House Children's Books.

———. 1975. *Pezzetino*. New York: Knopf.

Lipman, P. 1998. *Race, class, and power in school restructuring*. Albany, NY: SUNY Press.

Long, S. 2005. Review of *A child's work: The importance of fantasy play*. *Journal of Early Childhood Literacy* 5 (3): 312–15.

Mages, W. K. 2008. Does creative drama promote language development in early childhood? A review of the methods and measures employed in the empirical literature. *Review of Educational Research* 78 (1): 124–52.

Manzo, K. K. 2008. Reading first doesn't help pupils "get it." *Education Week* 27 (36): 1–14.

Marx, S. 2004. Regarding whiteness: Exploring and intervening in the effects of white racism in teacher education. *Equity and Excellence in Education* 37 (1): 31–43.

Mason, J. M., and S. Sinha. 1993. Emerging literacy in the early childhood years: Applying a Vygotskian model of learning and development. In *Handbook of research in the education of young children*, ed. B. Spodek, 137–50. New York: Macmillan.

Mayhew, K. C., and A. C. Edwards. 1936. *The Dewey school: The laboratory school of the University of Chicago*. New York: Appleton-Century.

McAllister, G. 2002. Multicultural professional development for African American teachers: The role of process-oriented models. In *In search of wholeness: African American teachers and their culturally specific classroom practices*, ed. J. J. Irvine, 11–32. New York: Palgrave.

McAllister, G., and J. J. Irvine. 2000. Cross cultural competency and multicultural teacher education. *Review of Educational Research* 70 (1): 3–24.

McIntyre, A. 1997. *Making meaning of whiteness: Exploring racial identity with white teachers*. Albany, NY: SUNY Press.

McLane, J. B., and G. D. McNamee. 1990. *Early literacy*. Cambridge: Harvard University Press.

McNamee, G. D. 1992. Vivian Paley's ideas at work in Head Start. *Quarterly Newsletter of the Laboratory of Comparative Human Cognition* 14:68–70

———. 2005. Learning to read and write in an inner city setting: A longitudinal study of community change. In *Vygotsky and education: Instructional implications and applications of sociohistorical psychology*, ed. L. C. Moll, 304–18. Reprint ed. Cambridge: Cambridge University Press.

McNamee, G. D., J. McLane, P. M. Cooper, and S. M. Kerwin. 1985. Cognition and affect in early literacy development. *Early Child Development and Care* 20:229–44.

Milner, H. R. 2003. Reflection, racial competence, and critical pedagogy: How do we prepare pre-service teachers to pose tough questions? *Race, Ethnicity and Education* 6 (2): 193–208.

Mintz, S. 2004. *Huck's raft: A history of American childhood*. Cambridge: Harvard University Press.

Mitchell, R. W., ed. 2002. *Pretending and imagination in animals and children*. Cambridge: Cambridge University Press.

Moll, L. C., ed. 2005. *Vygotsky and education: Instructional implications and applications of sociohistorical psychology*. Reprint ed. Cambridge: Cambridge University Press.

Morgan, H. 2007. *Early childhood education: History, theory, and practice*. New York: Rowman and Littlefield.

Morrison, F. J., E. M. Griffith, and D. M. Alberts. 1997. Nature-nurture in the classroom: Entrance age, school readiness, and learning in children. *Developmental Psychology* 33 (2): 254–62.

Morrow, L. M. 1990. Preparing the classroom environment to promote literacy during play. *Early Childhood Research Quarterly* 5:537–54.

———. 2002. *Literacy development in the early years: Helping children to read and write*. 4th ed. New York: Allyn and Bacon.

———. 2003. Make professional development a priority. *Reading Today* 21 (3): 6–7.

Narahara, M. 1998. Kindergarten entrance age and academic achievement. ED421218. Education Resources Information Center. http://eric.ed.gov/

National Center for Education Information. 2005. *Profile of teachers in the U.S.* Washington, DC.

National Center for Education Statistics. 2004. *Kindergarten teachers: Public and private school teachers of the kindergarten class of 1998–1999*. Washington, DC: U.S. Department of Education.

———. 2008. *Digest of education statistics, 2007*. Washington, DC: U.S. Department of Education.

National Education Association. 2003. *Status of the American public school teacher, 2000–2001*. Washington, DC.

National Reading Panel. 2000. *Teaching children to read: An evidence-based assessment of the scientific literature on reading and its implications for reading instruction*. A report for the National Institute of Child Health and Human Development. http://www.nichd.nih.gov/publications/nrp/smallbook.cfm/.

———. 2003. *Put reading first: The research building blocks for teaching children to read*. NRP Publications and Materials. http://www.nationalreadingpanel.org/Publications/researchread.html/.

Neuman, S. B., C. Copple, and S. Bredekamp. [1998] 2005. *Learning to read and write: Developmentally appropriate practices for young children*. Washington DC: National Association for the Education of Young Children.

Neuman, S. B., and K. Roskos. 2005. Whatever happened to developmentally appropriate practice in early literacy? *Young Children* 60 (4): 22–26.

Newkirk, T. 2002. *Misreading masculinity: Boys, literacy, and popular culture*. Portsmouth, NH: Heinemann.

Nicolopoulou, A. 1993. Play, cognitive development, and the social world: Piaget, Vygotsky, and beyond. *Human Development* 36:1–23.

———. 1996. Narrative development in social context. In *Social interaction, social context, and language: Essays in honor of Susan Ervin-Tripp*, ed. D. I. Slobin, J. Gerhardt, A. Kyratzis, and J. Guo, 369–90. Mahwah, NJ: Lawrence Erlbaum.

———. 1997a. Children and narratives: Toward an interpretive and sociocultural approach. In *Narrative development: Six approaches*, ed. M. Bamberg, 179–215. Mahwah, NJ: Lawrence Erlbaum.

———. 1997b. Worldmaking and identity formation in children's narrative play-acting. In *Sociogenetic perspectives on internalization*, ed. B. D. Cox and C. Lightfoot, 157–87. Mahwah, NJ: Lawrence Erlbaum.

———. 2002. Peer-group culture and narrative development. In *Talking to adults*, ed. S. Blum-Kulka and C. E. Snow, 117–52. Mahwah, NJ: Lawrence Erlbaum.

Nicolopoulou, A., J. McDowell, and C. Brockmeyer. 2006. Narrative play and emergent literacy: Storytelling and story-acting meet journal writing. In *Play = learning: How play motivates and enhances children's cognitive and social-emotional growth*, ed. D. G. Singer, R. M. Golinkoff, and K. Hirsh-Pasek, 124–44. Oxford: Oxford University Press.

Nicolopoulou, A., and E. S. Richner. 2004. "When your powers combine, I am Captain Planet": The developmental significance of individual- and group-authored stories by pre-schoolers. *Discourse Studies* 6 (3): 347–71.

Nicolopoulou, A., B. Scales, and J. Weintraub. 1994. Gender differences and symbolic imagination in the stories of four-year-olds. In *The need for story: Cultural diversity in classroom and community*, ed. A. H. Dyson and C. Genishi, 102–23. Urbana, IL: National Council of Teachers of English.

Nielsen, J., and E. Cooper-Martin. 2002. *Evaluation of the Montgomery County Public Schools assessment program: Kindergarten and grade 1 reading report*. Montgomery County, MD: Montgomery County Public Schools, Office of Shared Accountability.

Noddings, N. 1992. *The challenge to care in schools*. New York: Teachers College Press.

———. 2006. *Critical lessons: What our schools should teach*. New York: Cambridge University Press.

Okshevsky, W. C. 2003. Reconstructing paradoxes of democratic education. From the *Philosophy of Education Yearbook*. PES Publications. http://philosophyofeducation.org/pubs.htm/.

Paley, V. G. [1979] 2000. *White teacher*. Cambridge: Harvard University Press.

———. 1981. *Wally's stories: Conversations in the kindergarten*. Cambridge: Harvard University Press.

———. 1984. *Boys and girls: Superheroes in the doll corner*. Chicago: University of Chicago Press.

———. 1986. *Mollie is three: Growing up in school*. Chicago: University of Chicago Press.

———. 1988. *Bad guys don't have birthdays: Fantasy play at four*. Chicago: University of Chicago Press.

———. 1990. *The boy who would be a helicopter: The uses of storytelling in the classroom*. Cambridge: Harvard University Press.

———. 1992. *You can't say you can't play*. Cambridge: Harvard University Press.

———. 1995. *Kwanzaa and me: A teacher's story*. Cambridge: Harvard University Press.

———. 1997. *The girl with the brown crayon*. Cambridge: Harvard University Press.

———. 1999. *The kindness of children*. Cambridge: Harvard University Press.

———. 2001. *In Mrs. Tully's room: A childcare portrait*. Cambridge: Harvard University Press.

———. 2004. *A child's work: The importance of fantasy play*. Chicago: University of Chicago Press.

———. 2006. The business of intimacy: Hurricanes and howling wolves. *Schools: Studies in Education* 3 (2): 11–15.

Pellegrini, A. D. 1992. Kindergarten children's social cognitive status as a predictor of first grade achievement. *Early Childhood Research Quarterly* 7:564–77.

———. 2005. *Recess: Its role in development and education*. Mahwah, NJ: Lawrence Erlbaum.

Pellegrini, A. D., and B. Boyd. 1993. The role of play in early childhood development and education: Issues in definition and function. In *Handbook of research on the education of young children*, ed. B. Spodek, 105–21). New York: Macmillan.

Pellegrini, A. D., and P. Davis. 1993. Confinement effects on playground and classroom behavior. *British Journal of Educational Psychology* 63:88–95.

Pellegrini, A. D., and L. Galda. 2000. Commentary: Cognitive development, play, and literacy; Issues of definition and developmental function. In *Play and literacy in early childhood*, ed. K. A. Roskos and J. F. Christie, 63–76. Mahwah, NJ: Lawrence Erlbaum.

Pellegrini, A. D., and R. M. Holmes. 2006. The role of recess in primary school. In *Play = learning: How play motivates and enhances children's cognitive and social-emotional growth*, ed. D. G. Singer, R. M. Golinkoff, and K. Hirsh-Pasek, 36–53. Oxford: Oxford University Press.

Pellegrini, A. D., P. D. Huberty, and I. Jones. 1995. The effects of play deprivation on children's recess and classroom behaviors. *American Educational Research Journal* 32:845–64.

Pellegrini, A. D., and P. K. Smith. 1993. School recess: Implications for education and development. *Review of Educational Research* 63 (1): 51–67.

Pipher, M. B. 2001. *Reviving Ophelia: Saving the selves of adolescent girls*. New York: Ballantine Books.

Postman, N. 1996. *The end of education: Redefining the value of school*. New York: Knopf.

Preskill, S. 1998. Narratives of teaching and the quest for the second self. *Journal of Teacher Education* 49 (5): 344–45.

Raider-Roth, M. B., M. K. Albert, I. Bircann-Barkey, E. Gidseg, and T. Murray. 2008. Teaching boys: A relational puzzle. *Teachers College Record* 110 (2): 443–81.

Raines, S., and R. Canady. 1990. *The whole language kindergarten*. New York: Teachers College Press.

Ramsay, J. 2003. Savor the slump. *Education Week* 22 (31): 28.

Raspberry, G. W. 1996. The classroom as living room and laboratory: Appreciating the work of Vivian Gussin Paley. *Curriculum Inquiry* 26 (2): 203–10.

Reifel, S. 2007. Hermeneutic text analysis of play. In *Early childhood qualitative research*, ed. J. Amos Hatch, 25–43. New York: Routledge.

Rescorla, L. 1991. Early academics: Introduction to the debate. In *Early academics: Challenge or pressure?* ed. L. Rescorla, M. Hyson, and K. Hirsh-Pasek, 5–13. San Francisco: Jossey-Bass.

Richner, E. S., and A. G. Nicolopoulou. 2001. The narrative construction of differing conceptions of the person in the development of young children's social understanding. *Early Education and Development* 12 (3): 393–432.

Rosenblatt, L. 1978. *The reader, the text, the poem: The transactional theory of the literary work*. Carbondale, IL: Southern Illinois University Press.

Rosenblatt, L. 1981. On the aesthetic as the basic model of the reading process. In *Theories of reading, learning, and listening*, ed. H. R. Garvin, 17–32. Lewisburg, PA: Bucknell University Press.

Roskos, K. A., and J. F. Christie, eds. 2000. *Play and literacy in early childhood*. Mahwah, NJ: Lawrence Erlbaum.

Rothman, J. 2006. Life lessons: Story acting in kindergarten. *Young Children* 61 (5): 70–76.

Sadker, M., and D. Sadker. 1995. *Failing at fairness: How our schools cheat girls*. New York: Touchstone.

Sadoski, M. 2004. *Conceptual foundations of teaching reading*. New York: Guilford Press.

Sapon-Shevin, M. 1998. Everyone here can play. *Educational Leadership* 56 (1): 42–45.

Sapon-Shevin, M., A. Dobbelaere, C. R. Corrigan, K. Goodman, and M. Mastin. 1998. Promoting inclusive behavior in inclusive classrooms: "You can't say you can't play." In *Making friends: The influences of culture and development*, ed. L. H. Meyer, H. Park, M. Grenot-Scheyer, I. Schwartz, and B. Harry, 105–32. Baltimore: Paul H. Brookes.

Sarason, S. B. 1995. Some reactions to what we have learned. *Phi Delta Kappan* 77:84–85.

Sartwell, C. 1998. *Act like you know: African-American autobiography and white identity*. Chicago: University of Chicago Press.

Sawyer, K. R. 2002. The new anthropology of children, play, and games. *Reviews in Anthropology* 31 (2): 147–64.

Schickendanz, J. A. 1999. *Much more than the ABCs*. Washington, DC: National Association for the Education of Young Children.

Sheets, R. H. 2000. Advancing the field or taking center stage: The white movement in multicultural education. *Educational Researcher* 29 (9): 15–21.

Sidorkin, A. 2000. Toward a pedagogy of relation. *Philosophical Studies in Education* 32:9.

Singer, D. G., R. M. Golinkoff, and K. Hirsh-Pasek, eds. 2006. *Play = learning: How play motivates and enhances children's cognitive and social-emotional growth*. Oxford: Oxford University Press.

Smith, M. L., and L. A. Shepard. 1987. What doesn't work: Explaining policies of retention. *Phi Delta Kappan* 69 (2): 129–34.

Smith, P. K. 2007. Evolutionary foundations and functions of play: An overview. In *Play and development: Evolutionary, sociocultural, and functional perspectives*, ed. A. Göncü and S. Gaskins. New York: Psychology Press.

Snow, C. E. 1991. The theoretical basis for relationships between language and literacy development. *Journal of Research in Childhood Education* 6:5–10.

Snow, C. E., M. S. Burns, and P. Griffin, eds. 1998. *Preventing reading difficulties in young children*. Washington, DC: National Academy Press.

Snow, C. E., and D. K. Dickinson. 1991. Some skills that aren't basic in a new conception of literacy. In *Literate systems and individual lives: Perspectives on literacy and schooling*, ed. A. Purves and T. Jennings, 175–213. Albany, NY: SUNY Press.

Spodek, B. 1985. Early childhood education's past as prologue: Roots of contemporary concerns. *Young Children* 40:3–7.

———, ed. 1993. *Handbook of research on the education of young children*. New York: Macmillan.

Sulzby, E. 1986. Writing and reading: Signs of oral and written language organization in the young child. In *Emergent literacy: Writing and reading*, ed. W. H. Teale and E. Sulzby, 50–89. Norwood, NJ: Ablex.

Tabors, P. O., K. A. Roach, and C. E. Snow. 2003. Home language and literacy environment: Final results. In *Beginning literacy with language: Young children learning at home and at school*, ed. D. K. Dickinson and P. O. Tabors, 111–38. Baltimore: Paul H. Brookes.

Tabors, P. O., C. E. Snow, and D. K. Dickinson. 2003. Homes and schools together: Supporting language and literacy development. In *Beginning literacy with language: Young children learning at home and at school*, ed. D. K. Dickinson and P. O. Tabors, 313–34. Baltimore: Paul H. Brookes.

Taylor, D. 1993. *From the child's point of view*. Portsmouth, NH: Heinemann.

———. 1998. *Family literacy: Young children learning to read and write*. Portsmouth, NH: Heinemann.

Teale, W. H. 1978. Positive environments for learning to read: What studies of early readers tell us. *Language Arts* 55:922–32.

Teale, W. H., and E. Sulzby, eds. 1986. *Emergent literacy: Writing and reading*. Norwood, NJ: Ablex.

Texeira, M. T., and P. M. Christian. 2002. And still they rise: Practical advice for increasing African American enrollments in higher education. *Educational Horizons* 80 (3): 117–24.

Thompson, M. G. 2004. Why are we afraid of our boys? A psychologist looks at solutions. *Children and Libraries* 2 (1): 26–30.

Tobin, J. J., D. Y. H. Wuand D. H. Davidson. 1989. *Preschool in three cultures: Japan, China, and the United States*. New Haven, CT: Yale University Press.

Tracey, D. H., and L. M. Morrow. 2006. *Lenses on reading: An introduction to theories and models*. New York: Guilford Press.

U.S. Congress. 2001. *No Child Left Behind Act*. Public Law 107-110. Washington, DC.

Van Allen, R. 1976. *Language experiences in communication*. New York: Houghton-Mifflin.

Vygotsky, L. S. 1962. *Thought and language*. Cambridge: MIT Press.

———. 1978. *Mind in society: The development of higher psychological process*. Cambridge: Harvard University Press.

Wells, G. 1986. *The meaning makers: Children learning language and using language to learn*. Portsmouth, NH: Heinemann.

Welty, E. 1984. *One writer's beginnings*. Cambridge: Harvard University Press.

Wertsch, J. V. 1991. *Voices of the mind: A sociocultural approach to mediated action*. Cambridge: Harvard University Press.

———. 2005. The voice of rationality in a sociocultural approach to mind. In *Vygotsky and education: Instructional implications and applications of sociohistorical psychology*, ed. L. C. Moll, 111–26. Reprint ed. Cambridge: Cambridge University Press.

Whitehurst, G. J. 2001. Young Einsteins: Much too late. *Education Matters* 1 (2): 9, 16–19.

Williams, L. R., and D. P. Fromberg, eds. 1992. *Encyclopedia of early childhood education*. New York: Garland.

Willis, A., and V. J. Harris. 2000. Political acts: Literacy learning and teaching. *Reading Research Quarterly* 35 (1): 72–88.

———. 2004. Afterword to *Multicultural issues in literacy research and practice*, ed. . A. Willis, G. E. Garcia, R. Barrera, and V. J. Harris, 290–96). Mahwah, NJ: Lawrence Erlbaum.

Wiltz, N.W., and G. G. Fein. 1996. Evolution of a narrative curriculum: The contributions of Vivian Gussin Paley. *Young Children* 51 (3): 61–68.

Wolf, D. P. 1993. There and then, intangible and internal: Narratives in early childhood. In *Handbook of research in the education of young children*, ed. B. Spodek, 42–56. New York: Macmillan.

Xue, Y., and S. J. Meisels. 2004. Early literacy instruction and learning in kindergarten: Evidence from the early childhood longitudinal study—kindergarten class of 1998–1999. *American Education Research Journal* 41 (1): 191–229.

Zigler, E. F., and S. J. Bishop-Josef. 2006. The cognitive child versus the whole child: Lessons from 40 years of Head Start. In *Play = learning: How play motivates and enhances children's cognitive and social-emotional growth*, ed. D. G. Singer, R. M. Golinkoff, and K. Hirsh-Pasek, 15–35. Oxford: Oxford University Press.

Zimpher, N. L., and E. A. Ashburn. 1992. Countering parochialism in teacher candidates. In *Diversity in teacher education: New expectations*, ed. M. Dilworth, 40–62. San Francisco: Jossey-Bass.

Index